Money, Murder, Madness

Money, Murder, Madness

A Critique of the Use and Meaning of Money

Robert R. Fiedler

iUniverse, Inc.
New York Lincoln Shanghai

Money, Murder, Madness
A Critique of the Use and Meaning of Money

iUniverse books may be ordered through booksellers or by contacting:

iUniverse
2021 Pine Lake Road, Suite 100
Lincoln, NE 68512
www.iuniverse.com
1-800-Authors (1-800-288-4677)

ISBN-13: 978-0-595-41500-7 (pbk)
ISBN-13: 978-0-595-85849-1 (ebk)
ISBN-10: 0-595-41500-8 (pbk)
ISBN-10: 0-595-85849-X (ebk)

Printed in the United States of America

This work is dedicated to the many good people that I have known. Special, amongst them is my Family. With a knowledge that, they have treated me very well and that I have had there love and respect, I thank my parents, sister, wife (her good and patient mother) and my children. I also thank my childhood friends, many of which have remained my friends unto this day. Such friendships form an irreplaceable thread of continuity in one's life.

Also I thank the thousands of students, whom it has been my good fortune to know. Though at times some were in disagreement with what I had to say, they were diligent, patient and generous in listening.

Most associations have been important to me in special ways in the becoming of who I am.

I also thank the authors and writers of what was known to them as truthful history. They, together and in part, have provided the information and the incentive for my efforts in this compilation; especially The Several Popes, Douglas Reed, Robert Wilton, Father Denis Fahey, Eustice Mullins, Nesta Webster, Didirae Manifold, Col. Archibald Roberts, USA ret., Michael Jones Ph. D., Jacques Barzun Ph. D., Oswald Spengler, Olivia Marie O'Grady and Antony Sutton, a former colleague. Most are deceased however I have endeavored so that all their experience, insights, wisdom and goodness shall not have been interred in their bones. I have labored to bring their understanding into focus as it bears upon the present.

I thank all the good people of this world, with great respect for whomsoever they may be, for having labored, with positive and decent intent, to build and to create this wonderful Nation, Culture and Civilization.

I thank God, the Creator of all that is seen and unseen for allowing my being.

Finally, I thank the Holy Spirit for providing me with an innate sense of urgency, which has made this exposition possible.

The Illustrations are of my own doing. It is my intention that they might add a bit of humor to what is a rather difficult subject, very complex and one that may not always be within the sphere of interest of the reader. I thank the readers in advance for their courteous and fair-minded understanding of what I have written.

Contents

Preface

Before beginning to read any part of what is written hereunder, it must be understood that this is not a textbook, in the usual sense, concerning money or monetary policy. Rather, what is written is as an attempt to put in context many elements, which do relate to what money is and what money can be expected to accomplish. *Money, at best, is an Objective Means and a Constant, meaning Absolute, Denominator.* Money is an important *functional element* in the everyday life of all human beings, which are dependent upon mutual co-operation. Money, because it is an Objective Means, is what makes widespread commerce, over extended periods of humanly co-operative endeavor possible. *All Nations should, indeed must be vigilant in keeping the control of money under a proper jurisdiction.* Such vigilance, is the primary responsibility of good Government? Thus, money will not become a weapon against the Individual, Nation, Culture or Civilization. We admonish our readers that Nations can and must live in harmony, without which Civilization is doomed. It is urgent that all Nations should eliminate from leadership any individuals not willing to live a peaceful co-existence with others. To foster peace is, not a sign of weakness, rather is decency and wisdom in action.

The Constitution of the United States is, in part, a document, which is intended to make this clear. The control of money, currency and credit was intended to serve all citizens, therefore is placed under the jurisdiction and control of an elected Congress, trusted to guard the best interests of the population, one and all. Such control provides for the well being and happiness of all legally indemnified citizens. The control of money should never have been, nor should it ever be, placed in the hands of private Bankers, as is currently the case.[1] The secret and alien inception of our Federal Reserve System, similar to that of the Bank of England, marks

---

1   Wickliffe, Vennard B., Sr., *The Federal Reserve Hoax, The Age of Deception.* Meador Publishing Co., 324 Newbury Street, Boston 15, MA. Seventh Ed. Pp. 14-70. **The Federal Reserve** was and is a Conspiratorial Fraud, pulled off under the nose of President Wilson, who, as an inept leader of this nation was chosen to run for President with the intention that this monumental fraud be imposed on the Nation. The Federal Reserve serves secret interests, which dominate finance and commerce.

the beginning of the economic destruction of our people and of our nation.[2] The System, was masterminded by *Paul Moritz Warburg an Alien German Banker.* Our money, which is as currency and credit, is largely controlled and dominated by foreign interests, that profit unduly from their greedy imposition on each and every American. Ultimately, it is quite possible that our tremendous wealth and prosperity will be used to implement the destruction of our nation, our Western Culture, Christianity and the Soul of the Western Civilization. Such destruction is the dream and the hope of a number of Alien, interests including Bolshevism, Communism, all forms of Socialism, Fascism, the United Nations, variously connected Conspiracies, Secret Societies and Lucifer, the Anti-Christ.

There are several distinct functions, which money does have and it is wise to understand what they are. Furthermore, it is said that *"time is money"* and this is true in two important ways.

First, _Money provides a store of the value_ of past time expended, as it were, dedicated toward some gainful endeavor. Time *"spent"* is as life given to an occupation or a task of meaningful importance. *Time is "spent" in exchange for that which is useful in the future, namely money.* Time passed is gone forever, nevertheless *lawful money can be held indefinitely,* as bona fide collateral against which other tangibles may be judged. If the value of money cannot be sustained and is eroded by inflation then, such as erodes in value is not lawful money. Inflation robs all that have earned and saved the value of past effort, as is represented by lawful money. Thus, there is an absolute relationship between money and goods, which must remain as a constant. It is the hope of every working person, and this includes most Men and Women in this world, that he/she will have earned sufficient money, *in his/her good time,* to carry him/her through adversity and into old age. This is a very fair expectation of they who have endeavored to provide for a family, a community and a nation. The effort required for the accomplishment of what must be done, needless to say, is the most important of efforts. Many have died in their occupations; thus *"working for a living"* had and does have a certain amount of risk, for which risk adjustments may or may not have been made regarding payments received.

Second, in Time _Money is an objective denominator_ and is able to earn interest, _objectively_ irrespective of ownership. Thus interest rate should remain low, perhaps one percent, so as to not over compensate those that have large holdings of Capital. The earning of interest is problematical since the amount of interest earned, on large accumulations of Capital, can exceed the value of human life, which it is supposed to serve. That is to say, those who have acquired substantial

---

2   **Larson, Martin** Ph D. _The Federal Reserve & Our Manipulated_ Dollar. The Devin-Adair Co., Old Greenwich, CONN, 1975. Chapter 3, Pp. 37-58.

monies, *by whatever means* which may or may not be legal, are able to earn a return as interest. In fact this is what is called usury, especially when the rate is high; for example, high is any increment over one percent. Thieves, Liars and Hypocrites, once they have attained wealth, have the same worldly advantages as those who have gained wealth from honest, prudent and meaningfully productive effort. Those who have very substantial wealth will naturally control the political process to their advantage, as is apparent to any thinking individual.

Importantly, *Money can be and is used as a political weapon.* Money can be stolen, inflated, counterfeited, fractionalized and created from nothing, as merely a book keeping entry. To confuse matters, the process we understand as inflation gives the erroneous impression that one is becoming wealthy. Seemingly everyone has more money than before. However, the purchasing power of money is reduced requiring more money to purchase everything one may need. *The minimum wage is a clever subterfuge.* When the minimum wage is raised all things requiring labor increase in price. Given inflation, the price of all that is for sale is increased proportionately. Euphemistically, a price index is contrived to cover and disguise what is, in fact, grand theft. Cheap labor from Asia compounds our problems, as we fall into a pit of debt and insolvency, which necessarily requires inflation to resuscitate a failing system.

What follows is an attempt to expose and clarify, for the layman, just how and why we have come to our present position of being the greatest debtor nation the world has ever known, even as we have been the wealthiest nation ever to come into existence. Coincidentally, our citizens are deeply indebted and required to pay enormous sums as interest on debt, for the use of our nation's money [debt currency], which in fact could and should be loaned interest free to bona-fide citizens. If truth were known, revolution would be a certainty. If truth were known, monetary reform, including the abolishment of the fraudulent Alien inspired Federal Reserve System would quickly come about. However, individuals are educated in governmentally controlled schools, so as to be kept in ignorance concerning the most important element within a complex political and legal system. Furthermore, the average citizen is distracted by meaningless athletics and contrived theatrics, which numb the mind as vital time is consumed. We are a nation of spectators, watching what is of little or no significance. *Our Money, which should be an objective Denominator, has become as a commodity*, the price of which fluctuates against other currencies in an episode of advances and declines, from which a few Manipulators profit at the expense of all others, that do not understand the system. In fact, the function and understanding of money has been completely corrupted, so as to provide little defense against future need. The most important function, which is as a defense against future need, is what money is supposed to provide. This function has been totally confused with the manipulation for profit by a few that understand the _Game of Finance._ Indeed, it is a very crooked game; rigged with cunning that comes from five thousand years of accumulated understanding, concerning how a few might effectively rob the entire Civilization. Most of what happens, in a political sense, concerns aiding and abetting this monumental fraud.

We place in our reader's mind the following questions. Why has this been allowed to happen? Who is or may be responsible? What must be done to clarify circumstance, so as to encourage/enforce proper and decent action? How can we correct what appears to be an almost impossible and hopeless state of affairs, for our country and for the world? How might decently formulated Law be placed in service of the commonweal? How might we extract our nation from the stranglehold of International finance and criminal theft? And, what might an individual do to guarantee an appropriate change, leading to a more honest and truthful monetary System? The inference of such questioning is awesome indeed.

Keep in mind, the monetary system of any great nation should be of benefit to every citizen. Co-incidentally cooperative methods of _fair and controlled trade_, the _opposite of free trade_, can serve all other nations as well. No monetary system should ever be placed in private hands, as is now the case. The control of money was and is the power of the King, of nobility and the Toadies chosen to directly serve them. Democracy forbids that anyone be allowed to enslave the people that are the rightful beneficiaries of lawful, decently inspired and efficient government. We sense the Civilization, will be captured by Greed, a Cardinal Sin, as is presently in the process of enactment. This is a very critical issue that must be put in proper and fair-minded order soon, or the world will become as one Giant Plantation.

Will you do your part to correct what is wrong or will you buy a banjo?

Introduction

An urgent and disdainful sense of vanity, coupled with a profound sense of greed is what, to a very large extent, drives *a clandestine, vain and contemptuous Elite* toward a position of unassailable power, over the bulk of humanities (now) just about six billion people. For hundreds of millions of good Catholic, Christian people millions of others as well, vanity and greed are considered Cardinal Sins. For centuries it has been known that both *vanity and greed have certain and knowable* consequences, which always result in unnecessary hardship for the mostly good people of this world. *Interestingly, the morally good are often economically compromised by the presumption and conceit of others doggedly determined to gain worldly possessions*.[1] Millions have been killed in wars fought to gain power for the intransigent money-grubbers and they who despise all others not of their kind. The young have not heard mention of *the most influential groups of men* who rule over their government and their existence. The Illuminati, The Council on Foreign Relations, the League of Just Men, The Pilgrim Society, The Round

---

1   **Moral issues**, in principle, are sublimated for expedience. Morality has come to be dominated by economic, political and professional influence, much of which is formulated in secret, combining in an almost hopelessly complex paradigm. To make matters worse, the conjecture, imagination and selfishly vain intent of many psychologists and psychiatrists compound existing personal problems and any consequence arising therefrom. Professional [so-called] counselors have aided in changing the meaning of words and thus have obfuscated understanding, which naturally arises from facing the truth. Truth is what is, has been, and is indemnified by *experience and tradition*, given to correct and proper language. Reality suggests that youth and ignorance are most often, victimized. Practitioners, who make a living offering childishly expedient defense for wrongdoing, encourage sin. Thus, sin encouraged so as to multiply is not considered as sin, rather it becomes a question of *consent and tolerance*, as in "consenting adult" laws, providing legal sanction for what is evil and wrong, pernicious and destructive on individual conscience and human being.

Table, The Bank of the City of London, The International Banking Cartel and The Bilderbergers,[2] have led Civilization to the brink of disaster.

In the judgment of these same good people, which is mostly ignored by the world's leaders[3] (often presumptuous men who have taken over a situation), a Cardinal Sin[4] represents a flagrant violation of and disrespect for others, as well as for the self. Stealing is a Sin, no matter what it is called. Wholesale theft [does] and will deprive millions that do not understand what is actually happening. We call this Politics. A recent example of planning for large-scale theft, with attendant destruction, was [is] the war on Iraq, with the slogan "weapons of mass destruction," which have not yet been found. The present euphemism for political theft is Homeland Security. "And when they were assembled with the elders, and had taken counsel, they *gave large money unto the soldiers.*" (Mark, C. 28. V12.) *Men and mankind have been and are degraded, because of the malignant consequence, which accompanies politically indemnified sin.* War is a **politically indemnified Sin**

---

2   **The Bilderbergers.** The Committee To Restore The Constitution, Bulletins, September 1994 # 392 & September 1975. Colorado Non profit Corporation. P.O. Box 986. Fort Collins, CO 80522. Tel. (970) 484-2575. "That the World Revolution follows an ancient pattern of infiltration, subversion and rebellion is historically irrefutable."
    (Nesta Webster). The Bilderbergers, "just two ranks from the Apex of Secret Government, which rules the World," are part of a complex multi-faceted Conspiracy.

3   **Masonic Orders.** There are innumerable influential members of government, that are affiliated, at some level, with the Masonic Order, notably 33rd Degree Masons of the Scottish Rite, Members of the Royal Arch. All are sworn to an oath of secrecy, which is deemed superior to and above any other oath. Their oath makes all others subordinate including that one regarding the defense and well being of our (their) country, that country which, *presumably* they have been elected or appointed to serve. For a complete, well-researched evaluation and exposure of **who may be a hypocrite** you are able to obtain two professionally presented Videos: *Communist Infiltration of the Catholic Church* and *Freemasonrey's Control of Church and State*, Author, Dr. James Wardner. Both are available, for a very nominal charge, from the Most Holy Family Monastery, 14425 Schneider Road, Fillmore, NY 14735. Tel. 1-800-275-1126.

4   **Cardinal Sins, "The Seven [deadly] Sins": Anger, Envy, Gluttony, Greed, Jealousy, Pride, and Slothfulness.** There are Venal Sins as well, which should be avoided. *Universal Catholicism demands that all manner of sin and any occasion for sin should be avoided.* Who in this world, may we imagine, lives by such ethic? That this considers Sin at this juncture is because *money manipulation, usury and inflation involve sophisticated theft*, by this is meant stealing, *in violation of one of the Ten Commandments.*

as is condescension toward Abortion.[5] (*See Appendix D*) Many are in need that, because of their anxious greed and aggressive pride are unable to acknowledge the need for repentance and an honest existence.

Under all circumstances the function of honest money has a very civilizing and tranquilizing effect. Moreover money provides a means to facilitate and conclude an honest and fair exchange, to the satisfaction of the individuals, who are a party in any given transaction. Money provides a simple, direct and expedient means of accounting, thus to encourage commerce. As such, *the idea of money*

---

5   **War and Abortion** encourage damnable misbehavior, even amongst the *seemingly* good that, in the instance of War, may feel the threat of mortal danger. Helpless infants are imagined to feel nothing. Certainly, **War and Abortion provide the** ultimate pretense for killing another man's child and the **necessary temperament**, which permits [indeed, encourages] all manner of usury, extortion and direct theft, which is justified as being *somehow* honorable. Many men, *engaged in the business of war*, become wealthy and are honored as being the best amongst men. One can appreciate true valor and respect courage in the face of mortal danger, however we *deplore and accuse of Treason* they who promote, by devious means, and who inflame populations toward mortal conflict and/or the killing of their own children. Indeed, wartime propaganda, insidious accusations assumed as truth, has corrupted much of contemporary thinking. Most young men, who may have died a Hero's death, in a contrived political conflict, have little understanding of the phenomenal and pervasive forces, which led them to make the ultimate sacrifice. However, *Secret Societies*, especially those having important political influence, *are not generally* studied in public schools. Nevertheless, the United Nations is rammed into the consciousness of students in all public schools, some private schools as well.

The Conference, in 1911, on Jekyll Island, at which the fate of our nation, possibly Western Civilization, was never mentioned during this author's rather extensive public education. Technology alone cannot and will not compensate for the ignorance, the moral decay and the misunderstanding of the Universal Christian [Catholic] Philosophy, which brought the Western Culture and ultimately Civilization to so high a level of achievement. There may be honor, even a sense of sportsmanship, in a fairly determined conflict, when such conflict is understood for what it is. However, **most politically inspired conflicts are engendered in the minds of cowards, mentally deranged lunatics and clever Orators,** who romanticize and *give curious meaning to what they do not understand.* Populations are confused because the Victor writes the history, even as the Vanquished rests silently in the grave. Heroes may be hung on a Day of Atonement, as was the case after the Nuremberg trials, although few do understand why. A defeated leader, of an enemy, in many instances, may have been a decent man, deserving of some modicum of respect: The name General George Rommel comes to mind. Certainly ignorance and misinformation abound and are responsible for some of *the seasoning in the Stew*, which we understand as present politically and economically dominated Time/Space.

provides a means and has many very positive connotations. *Money manipulation causes dysfunction in the Social Order, which for many causes grave uncertainty, for some it can be fatal.*[6] Initially, this country fought a War of Succession (not exactly a Revolutionary War, as the Russian Revolution, so-called)[7] over the then existing Issue, Taxation without Representation. Was that merely a futile gesture?

To be worthy of the name, money must have certain characteristics, without which it would be unsuitable as money. *First,* money should have *intrinsic value.* It should be valuable because of what it is and the properties it possesses, of and by itself, it should have intrinsic value, meaning *real value.* And, the value of money should remain constant and unchanging, inviolate. "The fiat money now being issued by the Fed is unconstitutional and could become as worthless as the continentals?" (Larson) *Second,* money should be *durable,* of and by itself. It must have tangible properties that are sustainable, indefinitely, for a lifetime or longer, preferably forever. This is why gold has been chosen; being impervious, even acid does not tarnish it.[8] *Third,* money should be *recognizable as money,* for what it is and it should, furthermore, be recognizable in various denominations, so as to expedite commerce. This provides for honesty in each and every transaction.[9] *Fourth,* money should be *functional* without losing its intrinsic value. The

---

6   **Fahey, Dennis, Rev., C. S. Sp.,** *Money Manipulation and the Social Order.* Christian Book Club of America. P. O. Box 900566 Palmdale, CA 93590

7   **Wilton, Robert,** *The Last of the Romanovs, How Tsar Nicholas II and Russia's Imperial Family were Murdered.* Copyright © 1993, the Institute for Historical Review. First British Edition, pub. 1920 in London by T. Butterworth. First U. S. Edition published 1920, in New York by George H. Dorn. French Edition, pub. Paris 1921.

   The Russian Revolution was rather an incidence of Grand Theft, orchestrated by an International Cartel of Thieves, Liars and Hypocrites. Their methods were ruthless and unjust. The consequence of such profound barbarism was to change the financial structure of the Western Civilization. Much has been written, concerning this monumental deceit and unbelievable brutality' nevertheless very little of this tragedy is known or truthfully understood by the general population.

8   **Larson, Martin A.,** *The Federal Reserve and our Manipulated Dollar.*
   The Devin-Adair Co., Old Greenwich, Conn. © 1975 by Martin A. Larson. ISBN # 0-8159-5513-8 (cloth) and 0-8159-5514-6 (paper). The School of Fiat Currency. Pg. 134. And "ART. I, Sec. 10, Par. 1, U. S. Constitution, which declare that no state shall "make any Thing but gold and silver coins a tender in payment of debt…" (Larson, pg. 134) Certainly, there is much confusion and disagreement on this point, such being encouraged by they who, at present, control the money and the government.

9   **Recognition** is an important ingredient as it encourages honesty. In the Middle Ages, it was thought both wise and prudent for a craftsman to work in full view of prospec-

coining of money in different denominations provides for this and for the instant recognition as well as the necessary variable in respect to intrinsic value.[10] *Fifth,* money should be *somewhat scarce* rather than too plentiful, thus providing the incentive to use money wisely. Money, wisely used, helps (to some considerable extent) to ensure that all parties to any given transaction will remain honest thereabout. *Sixth,* money is a manner of *reciprocal for human life and effort*. Money is traded for other things and for human time and effort. *Finally,* ideally, money should be *beautiful,* something one is delighted *to keep and respect as a treasure.* Indeed, *Money should be a real and lasting treasure.*

---

tive customers, assuring that they would "know what they were getting." In an honest transaction, given to the light of holiness, all incidentals are easily and understandably apparent. Within the *fine print,* expressed in words not familiar to the common man, is where anxious greed is hiding. The present trend toward abstract implementation of values gives an *ultimate advantage* to a small minority, that is professionally involved in money transactions and banking. Recently discovered electronic phenomenon provides that billions can be (are) won and lost in cyberspace. In regard to money, cyberspace provides nothing tangible, nothing intrinsic and nothing durable, it is not beautiful or scarce and is not recognizable *for what it is*. Certainly there is an infinite amount of cyberspace, which may *accommodate any notion of value* or lack thereof. A misunderstood *notion of value* is largely what convinces the general population to accept the continued inflation, which is robbing them every day of their life. Central Banks, as presently structured, provide a means whereby the owners of Capital Stock together with those that accommodate day to day complex transactions, are able to take extraordinary advantage of this misunderstanding. Ultimately, the worth of a man will be completely determined by the striking of keys on a computer and will provide for the most vicious of all Tyrannies.

10 **An Intrinsic Factor** is *absolutely necessary* providing a guarantee that one's time, as invested in the acquisition of money, will not be undervalued so as to provide unimaginable wealth for thieves and liars, who accept the notion of a *built-in inflation Index.* Such Index is the means to guarantee confiscating the wealth of the poor and the middle class. In terms of Biology and the human body, the stomach manufactures an *Intrinsic Factor, which is absolutely necessary* for the digestion and assimilation of one's food. Thus the same **Idea,** that being the necessity for continuance and durability, regarding the most important human requirements, spans two critical human concerns for food and for the means to acquire such food. Communism and Socialism, in any form are determined to reduce all but a few to servitude, they are inhuman and deny what is necessary for human life. The **Intrinsic Factors** of Communism are servitude, fear and death. Slaves may live in a building, which they imagine they own, however, taxation and charges for required services, keeps them in a position of servitude, working week to week simply to exist.

The beauty of money originates from two sources. The actual materials, from which the money is coined, may be very beautiful; certainly this is the case with silver as well as gold. Also, each coin might, very well, be a work of art, lovely to behold. Since money should be intrinsically valuable as well as permanent, it makes good sense to give it a recognizably beautiful appearance. This has often been done in the past, very successfully; the $20.00 St. Gaudens and Liberty coins, are a delight to behold.

Paper money may be quite beautiful as well, notwithstanding it should have real and intrinsic value as a *backing*. A mortgage on real property is another form of paper wealth, which has real and meaningful backing, however inflation has driven debt values of real estate to incredible levels.

Although we may treasure money as a reward for our own good works, _we should never worship money_. That which we have should be wisely and generously utilized for the accomplishment of good endeavors. With stable money, we need not hurry in making our decision; rather *prudence should dictate that we act wisely* and unselfishly. _Prudence is a Virtue_. Because moneygrubbers are not so virtuous, being greedy rather than prudent, _the good people in this world have been placed in a very disadvantaged position_. Furthermore, it is unfortunate that the ways of Satan often reward abundantly those who are most dishonest, thus to overburden those who are good. ***The human dilemma has been worsened by various governments, which are too often controlled by vain opportunists, hypocrites and liars.*** Our government is no exception. In fairness, there are some that do well and are decent, however they are not the most effective in plotting the course of a people. It is our hope that circumstances will change and that this might come to an end. Any Nation is hard pressed to find good, decent and honorable men to lead and to administer necessary programs. It is important that Nations remain small in size, autonomous and more familial in nature. Indeed, modern governments are involved in an impossible task; especially having separated politics from universally acknowledged and understood properly formulated Christian Morality, which is an absolute prerequisite to good government. Not all will agree with this, nevertheless, those who do should work more diligently at informing others, without resorting to violence and murder; as in War!

Individuals, who have corrupted most all nations, even as they have stolen vast amounts of wealth, must be stopped in their evil endeavors and they must be stopped now.[11] The primary purpose of any *truthful and honest government* in the twenty-first Century, any century for that matter, should be to stop **Usury**. **Usury** is presently considered "essential" by the greedy, the Vain and the *self-imagined superior* beings, that have taken control of this most vital aspect of human endeavor. Usury compensates for inflation, giving the very wealthy an increment equal to inflation, with an additional perhaps three to four percent as earnings on Capital. That aspect of human existence, which factors time with the store of the value, determined in that same time, appurtenant to productive human effort, must be more fairly considered. Some believe this is happening. They are wrong! *Money must be stable and have an enduring value, not one that goes up and down for the benefit of wealthy speculators.* Money must be and remain as a Standard, unchanging, against which all other things are measured; thus all things would have a truthfully understood money value. *Any truthful Standard IS unchanging, constant and dependable (see footnote 8, above).* In spite of what political racketeers would want one to believe, they who seek an elastic currency, must be fools, morons or charlatans intent on lining their own deep pockets.[12] Imagine what would happen if the number of ounces in a pound, the number of inches in a foot, the number of feet in a mile, the number of quarts in a gallon or the number of eggs in a dozen would change from day to day. The good reader can add more examples of his own. Right now, the can that did carry one pound carries a mere 11.3 or 12.25 ounces, nevertheless it looks just like the can that did contain a pound. Who benefits from this deception?

---

11 **Certainly of interest**, is the fact that presently foreign bankers now (1975) own about 18,000 tons of formerly American gold, which purchased at $35.00 per ounce has yielded hundreds of billions in profit, all tax free. (Larson) One wonders why foreign bankers, with the same objectives as they who robbed the Czar, would want all this gold, a relic from the past? Are they planning in advance for what is certain to occur? Once the currency is inflated beyond reason, as in Germany, the new Standard will be based on Gold, the enduring metal.

12 **Emerging Economies** are especially vulnerable to being plundered by sophisticated Bankers that have a tradition, of *Plundering* those who are *honest and perhaps unaware of their plight*. The English especially have a history of living off the fat of other lands, which truthfully speaking involves a manner of theft, as the consequence of a double standard. Most European nations have been guilty, at one time or another. Admittedly much good was accomplished by colonization however, the thieves were generally given an advantage by the ruling elite. And, generally speaking, there was little respect for the native populations.

I. Money, What is it?

Originally, one might imagine, the *Idea/thought* of using money grew from a concept, which can be defined as one involving a form of reciprocity. Money is an economic reciprocal, as it provides a means of the exchange of one good for another. Thus money must provide (**IS**) that factor, which has a constant value.[1] We are able, because of money, *to save or store past time* for future disposition. *Money is a Call on Future Time!* Money should be assumed as being a constant and dependable store of value. Money, *it was understood*, could function as a reciprocal of any other good. In other words, money was conceived as being *possibly* equal to *time, expended in human effort* and every other *tangible thing*, depending on the various amounts of both money and things. In fact, this is *an Idea born of human genius* in recognition of the advantage gained by fair and lawful trade. Actually, *the Idea is quite simple;* nevertheless the implications are profound. This simple understanding is primary to the development of the human race to the present levels of accomplishment. Unfortunately, the subject of money has been made to appear as being too difficult for the understanding of the common man, beholden to the skewed ideas of self-interested Experts.[2]

A simple, fundamental and basic understanding has been corrupted in man's thinking about money. *Money manipulation, as it is called, is the name given to one person's attempt to somehow cheat the person with whom one is doing business.* Even thieves have a conscience, therefore this type of theft, it was imagined, was a sign of intelligence or a matter of good business practice. Thus stealing might

---

1   **St. Thomas,** "As a measure used for estimating the value of things, money must keep the same value, since the value of all things must be expressed in money, thus exchanges can readily take place and, as a consequence, communications between men are facilitated." *(Comment. in Ethic., Lib. V., Lect. IX)*

2   **Actually, the common man** has a keen understanding of money, however this understanding has been frustrated by sociological and political intervention, destined to enslave an entire Civilization. Communism, Internationalism, Socialism, The United Nations, The Global Village, Free Trade, Capitalism and Wars of destruction are the means, which may be employed in seeking such power.

be excused, or confused with intelligence or superiority. One party, nevertheless, is left with less than is fair, considering the reciprocal values of the money and the things tangible (or goods as they are called), which are involved. However, fairness is always determined in respect to two or more parties, each of which has or has not been treated honestly, each of which does or does not understand the nature of a transaction. We acknowledge that a fair and _honestly known and understood transaction charge_ can be reasonable. However, deceit and theft in any form are reprehensible, thus always objectionable.

A Cardinal Principle: Truth must be known, by all Individuals participating in any money transaction. Presently this is not what is *generally* happening. Money manipulation depends upon the fact that many involved in money transactions do not know the truth, therefore their actions are doomed to engender failure. "So elaborate has the nature of this scandalous proceeding become, surrounded by the confusion deliberately created by some of the most clever and most skillful advocates the world has ever known. Certainly, large-scale money transactions are something of a mystery to ordinary people, most of who can barely add a column of numbers and many of who cannot understand a simple equation. Such as they, hold their heads and confess that they are 'unable to understand finance.' "It is not intended that they should."[3] In fact, much is done to confuse them beyond their ability to understand.

Few would be opposed to the legitimate, quite negligible costs, in the completion of a transaction. However, most honest men are opposed to that, which gives an unfair advantage to one party in any transaction. The term _Moneychanger_ seems always to have had a bad connotation. Most probably, the reason for this is that the _"Changer"_ was seen as taking advantage of the opportunity provided by his _somewhat advantaged_ position. The _"Changer"_ offered a service, however, supplied no tangible good. In fact, the _Moneychanger_ was, in the past, often inclined to "file the coins"; thus we see them as having been fluted, so that this could not happen. Or, the precious metal could have been melted and been combined with base metal, however still retain the *look* of precious metal. A greedy or dishonest King would have been more likely to do this and to reissue new coins bearing a new stamp.[4] The King had the power to enforce acceptance of the newly coined

---

3   **Soddy, Frederick, Professor., MA., LLD., FRS., Nobel** Laureate in Chemistry, 1921; pioneer in the economics of wealth, author of _Wealth, Virtual Wealth and Debt (1926), Money Versus Man (1931), Role of Money (1934),_ etc.

4   **The Idea** that it is possible to cheat in this manner, is an **adulterous** one and has formulated as a pernicious dilemma for the entire human race. Today it is called fractional banking. The **Idea** may be likened to adding water to the wine. The owner of the bottle can take a free glass of wine from every bottle, thereafter add water and

money, with the "veiled assurance" that the new coins were equal in value to what was, in fact, a superior form of money. Pure Gold is most valuable! Our elected leaders "create money" by allowing the printing of more and more near-worthless, worth less, paper, which is [in fact] a debt burden, to be paid by the people with interest added to the original amount. Our money is debt currency issued by a private system, which has importuned our government. Interest is paid annually even as the debt sustains thus guarantees the liability. Presently the debt burden is in the magnitude of seven or eight trillion dollars. No one knows exactly how much! This fraud is indemnified by the wealth and the "Land Holdings" of the nation.

What is worse, we supplied the Soviet Communists, not the Russian Christian people, with our money plates and paper. We provided that Communists were enabled to print our money, equal in value to that earned by American citizens. Billions of such counterfeit currency has found haven in the properties and lands of this and other countries. Communists were given the authority to print our currency [in any amount required].[5] This is a so outrageously treasonous act, that *almost no one would believe this did happen*. At the present time (2006), fictional money is also generated in the process of lending, combined with all manner of derivatives, options and phony obligations, all of which are *a poor money substitute* for sound and stable money.[6] What we have, in fact, may be defined as debt-currency, that is debt become as currency. Jacques Rueff, Finance Minister to Charles De Gaulle, called this the "Monetary Sin of the West."[7] Certainly, the country and the World are more valuable than previously however, whatever value has been created should belong to those who, in fact, are responsible. Instead it is too often stolen, using clever accounting, inflation and *taxation without representation.* Ultimately, the Socialists and One-Worlders intend to place everything in a *"Collectivity"*, which will be monitored by the state. The State will elevate a chosen few, which are imagined to represent the

---

make a profit on the water. Today, we witness the size of the can is constant, whereas the contents is gradually lessened. Habit persists and some believe, as they imagine, eleven, twelve or fourteen ounces *appears to be* a pound. We have seen great progress in the technical development of the human race, especially *concerning the watering of the wine.* Truthful Progress is generally *in spite of politically inspired monetary bungling*, not because of it.

5   **Wickliffe, Vennard B., Sr.,** *The Federal Reserve Hoax.* **Ibid.** Pg. 75 # 8

6   **Fahey, Dennis, Rev.,** *Money Manipulation and the Social Order.* Christian Book Club of America, P. O. Box 900566, Palmdale, CA 93590, first published, 1944.

7   **Mullins, Eustice,** *The World Order, Our Secret Rulers,* (Ezra Pound Institute, Publisher, Staunton, A 24401, Secon Edition, 1992). Chapter IV, Pg. 92.

best of mankind. This is an issue having political, economic, religious, social and moral implications, which have been deliberately confused in reference to syntax, which governs the order and meaning of words.

To continue, Circumstances such as war, death, and unfortunate events, especially war and conflicts, would often place the *"Changer"* in a rather extraordinary position, in which instance he was "better" able to profit. Or the *"Changer"* working within his own community was able to profit [often unreasonably so] from the itinerant, certain to move on. Especially could the *"Changer"* profit from an anxious Prince or, as is currently the situation, from an anxious Political Leader, knowingly or unwittingly, such as Presidents Wilson, Roosevelt[8] or the "Bushes" I, and II,[9] destined to involve the world in armed conflict. The presumption is that the Political Leader is doing what is best for the people, which presumption is generally incorrect notwithstanding many good things do happen, in spite of the monumental blunders of inept leadership. One can interpolate from here, providing all manner of probable scenario. Christ *understood this and for this understanding He was crucified.* Most good men are simply ignored, they are murdered only when it appears absolutely necessary; for example Presidents Lincoln and Kennedy.

Christ is known to have driven the moneychangers from the temple, wherein they plied their trade. In so doing **Christ became the mortal enemy of any man who would cheat another, using money as a means to do so.** Thus, the Catholic Church, Bride of Christ has been under constant assault ever since that day so long ago. We witness a mortal struggle for the Soul of the Western Civilization, other Civilizations as well, with roots in the Church founded by Christ, Son of God. This is not Mythology this is factual. History provides a complete picture of the struggle, which becomes more intense because of modern technology and the electronic transfer of great accumulations of wealth. Christ understood, completely, what was occurring in the process of changing money. One need not blame the

---

8   **Mullins, Eustice, Ibid.,** Chapter IV, Franklin D. Roosevelt, Pg. 90-91

9   **Watch the Bushes!** What has occurred and what is occurring at the present time is very likely a prelude to World War III. No one should be surprised, since the establishment has been moving in this direction for quite some time, encouraged by an insane sense of righteousness, seated in the Philosophy of the Anti-Christ. Few understand the philosophical and theological factors in this equation nevertheless, they do exist and have been carefully weighed and considered, all in view of the monetary consequences. Mayhem occurs at the expense of the Western Christian Culture, what are Catholic (universally good) and the present World Civilization. We depend on the promise of Christ, "I am with you always, even till the end of the World." Who understands exactly what this means?

living for what happened in the past however rather all should attempt to understand truth and the meaning of brotherhood. We abhor that brooding, emanating from an ancient past often does color what occurs in the present. Actually, given the fallen nature of man, it is understood that man is not always reliable.[10] Today, it is likely most will steal, or lie if they are sure of not being caught. Some steal or lie just for fun!

As an added factor, together with the vested interests, which they represent, institutions somehow corrupt events within which men are involved. The politics of leadership and control are often in conflict with legitimate institutional functions. *The tail wags the dog, until such time as the dog is unresponsive and senseless.* Nevertheless, the *institutionalized ideas and programs of fallen man* bear on the nature and quality of the present reality. Institutionalized Undertakings and their consequences, alter the lives of the people (so to speak), that have been influenced. In addition, individuals choose to become involved in Institutionalized

---

10 **The Concept of Original Sin** is Christian, that being particularly Catholic, which sin is removed by a Catholic Baptism. The idea is that the Sins of the Father do rest on the Son, however born of woman, any person can be made free of such sin by means of Catholic Baptism. Many, outside the Catholic Church, do not believe this. Heretics and unbelievers, as well as they who *profess differently* may have trouble with this concept. However, we entreat that all should consider the true meaning of Catholic Baptism. Catholic Baptism relieves the innocent of those sins, which have their consequence in what we [as adults] observe as reality, namely the sins of those that came before now. This is quite simple, direct and certainly fair-minded. One may choose not to believe the truth of this issue, indemnified by history, or may choose to ignore the efficacy of a Codified Tradition. However, then that same man, having exercised his own *God-given* free will, must certainly allow that others may choose to exercise their free will as well as believers, in Catholic Baptism. Certainly, the Catholic Church does encourage that Catholicism has certain requirements, the most important of which are the Sacraments, especially the Eucharist. Even the most adamant Satanists attempt to blaspheme Christ by stealing the Substance of the Eucharist and defiling it in their stupid and assertive gestures. If they do not believe in God, why do they do this? Any philosophy or institution, whether properly or improperly conceived, has rules of conduct. Rules of conduct are what permit, indeed encourage, a manner of being, which will be evident in the development of human progress. The world has made the greatest *real and enduring progress* under the guidance of the Holy Roman, Catholic (universal, from the Greek word) and Apostolic (according to the Apostles' faith or teaching) Church. *To alter, by deception or in any way, what is perfect is to alter the direction of humanity away from what is constructively good, holy and perfect.* The alternatives are what are evil, despicable and *destructively* imperfect.

Entertainment.[11] Thus Consequence, however engendered, may be understood to be as functionally, thereafter institutionally formalized. Then too, men working within any formalized institution, which involves some complex process, are shielded personally as regards the nature of their activity. This understanding is incorporated in the structure of the Corporation, as we understand it, within which entity, personal responsibility and liability are shifted, or given to a legalized legerdemain, thereby placing the responsibility on another, often unknown/unknowing individual.[12] The shifting of responsibility and blame is a very important function, in a contrived economic and political circumstance.[13] This is euphemistically known as *"Shifting the Scene."* Those involved in great financial undertakings, including the taking-over of government responsibilities, are masters at *shifting the scenes*, which is understandable in a milieu, dominated by Hollywood, the Act and the Performance. Even intimate Sex is imagined as a manner of performance. Pornographers seek the ultimate performance of decadence, savagery and lewdness; *all this for a few coins.*

When Christ reprimanded the money changers, He was responding, in favor of Godly wisdom, all-knowing and all-understanding, which is embodied in His timeless and profound teaching as well as in His being as a man. Importantly, He was The Son of God, who knows all. We should not overlook or dismiss this, even if we are skeptical or are an unbeliever.[14] Hundreds of miracles, worldwide, over the course of centuries, attest to the fact that phenomenal, metaphysical and

---

11 **Large scale Events,** such as concerts, athletic contests, spring break and parades, provide a setting wherein individuals, following the dictates of the mob, are *relieved of responsibility for their own actions*, which under such circumstances are always at the lowest level; silly, aggressive, rampant, archaic, presumptuous and noisy. Such behavior is generally condoned, being imagined as Fun! Reasonable forms of pleasure can be honestly enjoyed however the commercially driven imposition on every form of decently conceived human activity is abhorrent. Not without meaning, is the fact, all Revolutions are notable in that individuals follow the hysterical dictates of a mob,

12 **Holders of common stocks** comprise a category of <u>*unknowing individuals,*</u> which simply stated, too often subsidize what amounts to grand theft. Enron is just one example. The fact that some ordinary citizens make a profit within such environment does not justify the fraud, theft and deceit that resides in modern business proctice.

13 **The Pearl Harbor Intrigue and the dismissal of Gen. Douglas Mac Arthur** are two glaring examples.

14 **Unbelievers** need not be condemned by friends and associates, who are very likely very much the same. Since no mortal being has perfect knowledge, it is understandable that many [perhaps most] will have wrongly inspired understanding however, such understanding will not lead to the truth of any issue.

supernatural events can and do occur, thus to indemnify the claims of the one Holy, Catholic (universal) and Apostolic Church.[15]

This Catholic Church, Christ's church, and what is called Catholic effort, is a consequence of universal goodness in action. Sister Theresa presents a conspicuous example of devoted and compassionate understanding, as do the Saints and Martyrs. Are we to imagine that Saints and Martyrs did not live, did not accomplish profound works and have no relationship to Universal Goodness? Saintly effort is most often directed toward reasonable goals, with holy intentions. We say most often because one can imagine, as history does prove, that even seemingly good men are imperfect; some fail to act reliably where others are concerned. *A reliable act is understood to be the universally correct act.*

In the past, good men worked knowingly, assuming the watchful eye of an Omnipotent Presence: God. They were taught, rightfully so, that there existence and purpose should be to love, to know and to serve God. This underscored and made apparent, even to simple people that every individual was responsible to each and every person with whom they might come into contact. The term "one for all and all for one" was perhaps born from this understanding. Each person was taught to be humbly responsible, for all that was freely given by God and each was encouraged in their commitment, to do the very best for others as well as for himself. *We define this as the Christian, Catholic, ethic, or moral imperative.* Christian charity and this <u>*notion of oneness*</u> are understood as an important element in Catholic social teaching and philosophy. Such teaching demands goodness in all things, thus to gain salvation and entrance into eternal life.[16] Catholic endeavor is not a matter of bind obedience rather it is a question of informed participation in the understanding of what is omnipotent, infinite and timeless. The Individual is to humanity as leaves are to a tree or flowers to a species, individually determined nevertheless part of a greater entity.

During the Catholic Mass, the Eucharist (body of Christ) is **given** (one the tongue) to all baptized Roman Catholics, thus the (body of Christ) becomes a part of the recipient. Thereby, each becomes one in being with the Father. This is an eschatological Issue metaphysical, phenomenal and symbolic and a very real act, in Time, extended as repeated since the time of Christ and, as such, is part of

---

15 **Diamond, Michael, Brother,** <u>*End Times Prophecies II, exposing the Agents of the Antichrist*</u>. Video, available from, Most Holy Family Monastery, 14425 Schneider Road, Fillmore, NY 14735. Tel. 1-800-275-1126.

16 **Heaven** is where each single person could become as "one in being with the Father", from whom all good things come. It is difficult to imagine this and impossible to comprehend in total.

an emanating reality.[17] The Eucharist is an extensive Symbol, which becomes a real part of the recipient. It is holy in content and symbolic in Nature. *Whatever one's intimate personal beliefs, the understanding of this universal truth represents an absolutely crucial ideal, without which understanding men are doomed.*

The world does need good people and it is incumbent upon them to teach their children to be good as well. This is best accomplished when the truth is obviated, the whole truth, which as manifest is fundamental to [the] universal reality.[18] Nowhere else is the truth more vital than where is concerned money and the exchange of goods, which is absolutely necessary to every manner and form of human endeavor.[19] This is because a man gives his life for the money he receives in payment for his effort in time. Indeed, all human life depends on obtaining a manner of substance, requisite to health and life itself. *We all know this*, however not everyone accepts the responsibility for such *knowing*, as evil men take advantage, often quite unfairly, of every possible opportunity.

The exchange of a good, for legitimate and intrinsically valuable money, provides an instant manner of accounting, on the spot, for anyone seeking to make some fair manner of exchange. *No third party, or middleman, is required in a debt free money transaction.* Certainly there are many that would attempt to gain more than is fair from any exchange however, one should avoid doing business with them. Seek rather the Farmer in the Dell. We learned from a farmer, a simple, good, hard-working man, actually a very intelligent man as well, a most important truth; such concerning money, trade and commerce. *The farmer believed a good deal must be a good deal for all involved.* When our farmer made a deal, he was more concerned for the other party than he was for himself. His rational was simple. It was important to him that the person, with whom he did business,

---

17   **Reality emanates**, as on a beam of light. We only see light, which is directly reflected, into our eyes; all other light passes by. God is pure light, pure Spirit, all good and is as All. God is the, I AM however, is outside from our human vision. Such as this is a divine mystery, which leaves the obscure scribbling of social philosophers, anarchists, Atheists and the insane writers together with their Masonic Colleagues way behind. What they do not understand is that all time, then-now-then, past present future is [as] but a Single Moment. This can be explained using the most precise and definitive means available to a discreetly objective scientist. *Reality is as an infinite Moment!*

18   **Reality,** inclusive of all, is at once a profound complexity and an unfolding singularity. As individual human beings we see and are aware of an infinitesimally small segment of this infinite phenomenon and this only for a very short time. Which might be considered as an instant, as the light from a firefly.

19   **Fahey, Dennis, Rev., C. S. Sp.,** *Money Manipulation and the Social Order.* The Christian Book Club of America. P. O. Box 900566 Palmdale, CA 93590. Chapter II. Pp. 8-11.

respected him for his honesty. Thereafter that person would trust him, for which trust he was humbly grateful. He believed God was watching and would be proud of a good, decent and honest man. He died a rich man; rich in memories and content in his having been good, beside which he was reasonably wealthy, besides. He explained that he had to live with himself each and every day of his life. He preferred the company of a good man, dependable and trustworthy. There should be millions more like this man and the world would be much improved.[20] The only consolation to the man who has been cheated is in the hope that the cheater will have a conscience and that the cheater may be forgiven. "Father forgive them, they know not what they do." (Christ)

Importantly, the amount of money is not so critical, whereas the stability, quality and value of the money are very critical. With the best of money, given a direct exchange, nothing need be written down, no accounting is really necessary. Therefore each and *every transaction can be inviolate*, not imposed upon by a third party. The imposition of a third party has been the right of Kings, Dictators and presumably legitimate Governments through some manner/means of theft, extortion or a *seemingly fair-minded* taxation. Proper, honestly valued money makes written accounting quite unnecessary; except for the record, so to speak Anyone holding honest money, gold or silver coins not just plated tin, is holding a substance having great intrinsic value, it is durable, recognizable and (hopefully) has a beautiful form as well.

Additionally, title to paid-up property (debt-free, with clear title), is a valuable and intrinsic holding as well, however is subject to tax, often imposed quite unfairly. Communism opposes individual ownership of clear Title to property.[21]

---

20 **The Farmer** was my [the author's] father.

21 **Title to Land** insures, as a legal deed, a degree of independence. Conversely, Communism intends that all individuals will be landless, dependent on a communal handout in one form or another. This, of course, is an absurd notion, however quite appealing to the clever that imagine they can, by selfish and recalcitrant will, control all events. The Communist Rulers, will hold title to the land, however all the while will pretend it belongs to the People. We "the People" however, (which is a euphemism for the Mob, the Commune, the Proletariat or the Population) will have no *specific and legal claim* on even one acre. Furthermore, Communism will make any form of *legitimate inheritance* impossible. This is precisely why the Czar and his family were murdered and why other Monarchs met with a similar fate. It was because they had a *truthfully understood and legally legitimate right of inheritance* to large tracts of land, which lands were confiscated and given to a different, not well understood, form of ownership; communal or governmental ownership. We encourage individual inquiry into such Issues, in asserting that governments are *controlled by opportunistic Interlopers, liars and thieves*, who are also the beneficiaries of the great wealth disbursed

The tax taken from owners of property slowly confiscates as it erodes the owner-interest in that same property. There are innumerable ways of confiscation, in agriculture for example, not generally understood.[22] Money thus taken, under pretense of important need may be utilized in ways, which the owner would never approve. *Thus we have taxation without representation* in many instances, perhaps most, where the federal government is concerned. Who are you? Who are we? Both are very important universal questions. As a matter of fact, "to be or not to be" (someone special) remains today, as in the past, an important question, _the most important question_. This question, amongst all questions, most clearly draws into focus the dilemma of every man, especially where money is concerned. *How any one responds, when money is involved, is very important in determining the very being and soul of every man.* When the spirit is compelled by greed, the soul becomes respondent to that same greed. Man's interaction with his fellow man, when such involves some manner of exchange, is the means whereby our nature and spirit are obviated as determined and the nature and spirit of our civilization as well. Act and being are completely involved, inextricably so, thereafter consequence (as history) remains forever, thus to place in an understandable order what has been enacted as specifically truthful.

Thus "Forever and Ever" (Handel, The Missiah) is most pertinent. This is true because any act has consequence, which tempers and dictates the nature of the future. We note that to be entrusted with free will places one in the most critically important position. Money provides [**the**] means for enacting goodness in this world. *And, the combining of past consequence of all that has happened and is happening, including the trillions of human transactions, in all time, presents man with the greatest phenomenally existential challenge.* Man must seek aid from Divine Inspiration, from God and from the Church founded by Christ: The holy, Roman, apostolic, universal [that is Catholic] Church. Believe this! *There is no other solution.*

---

by governments, under contrived Circumstance. War is the best example of contrived Circumstance, which serves a multitude of illegitimate aims and intentions. It should be understood that any One World Order, as conceived now or ever, will *be a form of Criminal Theft however, in need of competent management,* which management will come from amongst those who created whatever monstrosity becomes of complacent ignorance, dominated by lust and greed.

22 **Twight, Charlotte,** _America's Emerging Facist Economy.,_ Arlington House, Publishers. New Rochelle, NY. ©1975 by C. Twight. ISBN # 0-87000-317-8. Chap. 8, Federal Control, Agriculture. Pp. 184-212.

Farmer. We thought we owned our Land

II. The Perversion of Money

When the value, use, meaning, and function of money are perverted, *whether by deliberate action or inadvertently,* the consequence is the same. The *notion of money certainly has been perverte*d and has lost many of its positive qualities, thus becoming an instrument for the accomplishment of evil doing. In time, evildoing will destroy the individual Soul of the evildoer, ultimately the Culture and the Civilization as well. Presently this is what is happening, to our Civilization, Culture and Faith, all having been pre-empted by powerful alien forces backed by unimaginable wealth, property and influence. We, as a people, are well on our way to accepting this destruction, as we sacrifice our children to abortion, pagan worship, evil mysticism, shameful entertainment, pornography and occult impositions in various forms. Learning has been and is being corrupted by the imposition of nonsense and fantasy, overshadowing truthful history. *Notwithstanding the world is a wonderful place and most people are mostly good* however, most are meagerly informed and have little truthful knowledge, upon which to base positive thinking.

Certainly, a single lie or wrongdoing can corrupt many years of the good and worthwhile accomplishment and effort of thousands of individuals.[1]

---

1   **The bombing of Hiroshima**, at the end of the Second World War is another startling example. For many, this appears to have been a necessary evil however, the entire scenario, involving us in World War II, was one of political intrigue and economic concerns, of which few are aware. It is a curious fact that both Hiroshima and Nagasaki were the most Christian cities in Japan. Coincidentally, the pilot of the plane, the target of which was Hiroshima, was a Catholic, chosen for this particular mission. The pilot assumes himself a hero, justifying murder of thousands by calling on a Fairy Tale, which imagined a million killed in an invasion of Japan. Such destruction and imagined invasion would have been unnecessary had we simply dropped the bomb where the Japanese could have seen the power of this monstrosity. The Japanese were treacherous however, so were we!

Correspondingly in Dresden, the work of genius[2] as exemplified in artifact, architecture[3] and fine art, was accumulated over the course of centuries. Nearly all that was good and beautiful, which resided in the city of Dresden, being symbolic of the Soul of the Western Civilization, was destroyed, Why? This was accomplished by *simple-minded men being duped, thus to imagine that they were rescuing mankind* and the Culture of Western Civilization. In fact, they were encouraging the becoming of a new Dark Age. During preceding centuries Germany, in fact, was at the heart of European and Western Culture, fine art, porcelain, archeology, architecture, music and technology. In England, especially the Bankers and Politicians found this to their disliking. Confusion abounds, to benefit those who foment the confusion. Nevertheless, Germany is still a remarkable nation in spite of all the punishment that has been inflicted upon it.

Money has become, in the past two hundred and fifty years, that means whereby manipulation by just a very few powerful and wealthy individuals and Institutions, with the help of Politicians, Traitors and various surrogate Functionaries control most of the goods and peoples of this world. Working within a complex and profound corporate structure, evil men have little respect and no compassion for the soul of the Man whom they betray.

The Catholic Church, Bride of Christ, has always frowned upon deception, treachery and sin. We, as a people, are admonished by God to treat the least of our brethren with respect, thereby affording them dignity and a sense of well being, when each answers the most important question. In fact, many worthwhile social programs are predicated upon this Catholic understanding, however have been perverted by the socialist thinking and wrongdoing of imperfect human beings, engaging in selfish enterprise. Especially has Free Masonry, perverted and corrupted the meaning and use of money.[4] They, who are Masons, largely control finance Capital. Masons are in directly stated opposition to Christian teaching and philosophy, especially Catholic Christian teaching and Catholic Philosophy. Coincidentally, there are strong and obvious ties between American Higher

---

2   **The bombing of Dresden,** an architectural jewel of Western Civilization, is just one example of the consequence of a malignant and evil-inspired imposition on mankind.

3   **Lonergan, Bernard J. F.** *Method in Theology.* Pub., 1972, Herder and Herder. Winston Press, Inc., 430 Oak Grove, Minneapolis, MN 55403. ISBN: 0-8164-2204-4 Pg. 244.

4   **Dillon, George E., Mgr., DD.** *FreeMasonry Unmasked, as the Secret Power Behind Communism.* With preface to New and Revised Edition by Rev. Dennis Fahey, C. S. SP., B. A., Ph. D., D. D. GSG Associates, P. O. Box 6448, Rancho Palos Verdes, CA 90743.

Education and the corruption, which has become accepted as modern business and political practice, run by men, many who are vain hypocrites and greedy thieves who have no conscience.[5]

Who am I? When treated fairly, every man knows and understands that he is respected. This, in turn, supports the positive feeling that each has for Him as well as for another. It is most important that this be understood, such understanding must be put into practice now, where all forms of exchange and commerce is involved. Why do we tolerate wanton exploitation, usury, theft, extortion and the financial condemnation of so many? Don't we imagine, pretend somehow, that we are enlightened, thus are more aware, properly and truthfully so.[6] Such awareness should provide clearer vision in terms of consequence. _Truthfully, are things better illuminated now, or are we still in a Dark Age?_ The New Age, as it panders to sin, as indemnified by Hollywood, and written in some theatrical and literary publications, portends to be the darkest age of all. It may soon be a felony to discuss the Light of the world; except secretly of course.[7]

Millions of youngsters dressed in black, tattooed, bodies pierced, dancing to the music of madness, parade in the streets, in the schools and in the Clubs, where outrageous and vilified language, manners and customs are encouraged, as

---

5   **Sutton, Antony C.,** _How the Order Controls Education._ Research Publications, Inc., Phoenix, Arizona, 1983© Antony C. Sutton. ISBN # 0-914981-00-5. Pp. 2-3-9-11-15-16-34-37-47-49-53 etc.

6   **The Enlightenment,** so called, has brought much of the world into an extended period of darkness. Philosophy based on corrupt, decadent and overly romantic thinking has driven the Culture and the Civilization to near disaster. Imagined as such, Thinkers of the past three hundred years, have mostly ignored the teaching of Catholic Tradition and, because this is true, we find the world in a state of dissolution, even as technologies should have done much more for the well being of humanity. In response to imperfectly formed mumbling, scribbling by self-possessed lunatics and rhetoric by a poorly informed intelligentsia, we spend our substance on means of efficient killing of the people who might disagree with us. We imagine this as progress. Furthermore as we kill some and prepare to kill others, we imagine we are doing the best for Mankind. Nevertheless "Where ignorance is bliss, is folly to be wise." (Shakespeare) Politically speaking, Shakespeare hit the mark, "right on" so to speak!

7   **Hope does exist** and for millions this is a driving force. We respect and encourage this. However, we suggest there is an eternal reality encompassing all that is. We are wise to recognize this and to consider what is this eternal reality? This is especially important where our effect on others is an issue. When we do this we become closer to an understanding of God and what it means, profoundly so, to simply be good, to be virtuous and to be humble.

practiced by Ignorance, all in search of insensitive and arcane participation. Body parts are displayed and *"dangle"*, as does meat at the butcher shop, whilst Lechers glare at the *"fresh stuff"*, being exhibited. "Immoral" and vile publications have encouraged this to happen, the Internet has brought the most vulgar Vices and improprieties right to the desktop of foul-minded participation. Evil dominates within the Domain, of a corrupt Jurisprudence.[8] This is mentioned, in context with this exposition, because sin and corruption provide such profitable, indeed the most profitable, business.

No one can discuss money, in this environment and overlook the fact that sin pays. Coincidentally, Sin provides a means of transferring the wealth from the young, *susceptible and curious,* to the old, *wrinkled, wizened and decadent,* who promote the desecration of youth, especially do they destroy the meaning of love, all for a few coins.

The youthful and beautiful bodies of a maiden are the object of vilification by stupid lechers, anxious fornicators and perverts of every stripe. To get the picture, one need only view the Internet, or canvas the neighborhood to find innumerable outlets for the most trivial, banal, brutal, disgusting and decadent forms of art [so-called] and literature [so-called].

---

8   **A corrupt Jurisprudence** purposely ignores the moral order, exemplified by Catholic Christianity, as it favors a legal dialectic beyond the comprehension of most in the community. The trial by jury has become as entertainment for the masses, spaced between segments of television advertising. Publicized in the media, events become fictionalized so as to serve a political persuasion. This is especially confusing when, in the minds of citizens truth is combined with fiction, imagination, misinterpretation and the theatrics of an *award winning* presentation. The legal dialectic formulates as what is now defined as *the Rule of Law,* which law is too-often void of that moral imperative so important to the Western Civilization.

III. Corporations

The giant corporations, especially Banks,[1] have, most certainly, done more to pervert the meaning and function of money than has any other single institution known to man. Nevertheless, they are thought to be, in some respects are, a necessary part of a modern economy. The question: Who would want this form of modern Economy? Certainly corporate effort can and does have many advantages, thus to provide amply for man's needs. Who could deny that corporations have provided necessary goods and services and that, in many respects what is done could not be done without _formalized co-operation?_ A Corporation [presumably] is a manner of _formalized co-operation in favor of the Individuals_ that profit from large-scale organizational effort. Rural co-operatives have functioned with success, more or less however, at present, are dependent upon international corporations to market their products.[2] At this moment, such, apparent co-operation is often quite one-sided, in favor of long established international firms, with the ability to obtain large-scale financing, especially important where food, vital resources and government may be a factor in the equation.

We suggest that a somewhat limited corporate effort, when conditioned by the proper moral imperative, could do much to remedy what has become a monster in the market place. We suggest furthermore, there have been laws enacted (from time to time) intended to prohibit monopolization and the becoming of a dominant Cartel. Thus, others have recognized the problem, which is being called to attention just now. There was put in place certain anti-monopoly legislation a century ago by the Trust Buster, Teddy Roosevelt of _"rough-rider"_ fame, who did gain from what was imagined. The size of today's monopoly corporations would

---

1   **Anderson, E. L., Ph. D.** _The Upright Spike I & II._ © 1978, Government Educational Foundation, P. O. Box 1622, Washington, D. C., 20013.g

2   **Morgan, Dan,** _Merchants of Grain, the power and profits of the five giant companies at the center of the world's food supply._ The Viking Press, 625 Madison Avenue, New York, N. Y., 10022. Copyright © by Dan Morgan 1979. ISBN # 0-670-47150-X.

imply such legislation was ignored. Everyone is concerned that all should not become beholden, to the existence of commercial elephants, which given opportunity, crush any opposition. Corporations are thought, somehow, to represent free enterprise and the right of the individual to enjoy great success; become rich and famous, by a home in Palm Beach, as so many entrepreneurs have obviously done. However, beneath the surface, the giant corporation is quite another thing. *Actually many corporate entities work hand and hand with a form of Fascist Government,*[3] *imagined as democracy, to insure that, most all of humanity will sink to a level of menial, existence.* This may be an understanding, which is difficult to imagine, perhaps more difficult to accept however, there is much truth in it. To *Know with certainty*, what is this reality [?] requires a great deal of careful and objective study, much of which has already been completed, recorded and exists in printed form.[4] One must seek the truth, with avid determination, so as to intelligently comprehend what is happening. Furthermore Comprehension requires significantly informed and extended experience, an openly independent mindset and wisdom. Unfortunately, much of the driving force of the Corporation is seated within a young adult population, which lacks both extended experience and wisdom and they have been encouraged to abandon their most important Traditions. Coincidentally the really big money, generally, is made by the "Elders" having the experience and the wisdom gained from "skinning" many cats, or "shearing" many sheep.

The corporate entity is a non-person, however, deprives real persons of much of the opportunity that, without the corporate entity, would be their birthright. As non-person, to the Corporation favors the International Style, in concert with the present mad rush toward One World Government. As such the individual and any indigenous style or interest is overrun by Finance Capital. The nation is becoming quite uniform from coast to coast as the corporate buildings replace what was once truly American. The influences of the conglomerate, with vast resources in wealth and property, pervert as they influence every government in the world.[5] Some recent Scandals have been made public, nevertheless one can be sure that the most influential players cover their trail very well and will never be

---

3   **Twight, Charlotte,** *America's Emerging Facist Economy.* Arlington House, Publishers. New Rochelle, NY. ©1975 by C. Twight. ISBN # 0-87000-317-8. Chapt. 10. America's Accelerating Fascist Economy. Pp. 260-280.

4   46 **Mullins, Eustice,** *The World Order, Our Secret Rulers,* (Ezra Pound Institute, Publisher, Staunton, A 24401, Second Edition, 1992). Chapter V, The Business of America, Pp.101-131.

5   **Perversion** is made manifest by the fact that *hundreds of billions of dollars* have been funneled into private hands as a reward for clever manipulation, involving corporate

exposed, rather they comprise what is a well-respected elite. Corporate influence is a dominant force in public education (so called). Commercial imposition can and does compromise learning, in favor of misunderstood self-interest.[6]Corporations can afford clever and convincing propaganda, assumed as education, thus further a corporate objective. If truth is what we seek by means of education, corporations do not help in finding it. The entertainment industry has been invaded (and captured) by corporate and commercial interests. By means of grants and direct bribes to institutions, corporations serve their own interests in screening knowledge and making certain that they control the mind content of the emerging generation. Corporate directors can depend on the allegiance of thousands of vain faculty members, at all levels that will do anything for money and for attention. Especially Faculty are encouraged who, in their writings and lectures, promote the corporate agenda. The *Dupes are rewarded with fat fees* and mention of their name and their *seemingly important work* (assumed as such, by vain participation), in the mass media and the various *"carefully edited"* professional journals.

Corporate advertising, mixed with a pseudo liberal political imposition dominates the media at all levels. In addition to corrupting education, by means of sublimating truthful enquiry, corporations are incessant with their silly forms of insistence, which is absolutely impossible to avoid. Nowhere is this more obvious than in the Medical Sciences and the treatment of Disease.[7] The brand name, which represents a particular corporate presence, is the icon of our century and will be more so in the next, decorating billboards, walls, magazine covers, even the clothing which we wear on our bodies. Some believe this is the art of the present, a form of modernism, forgetting completely the Soul of the man and of the Civilization as a phenomenally endowed Construct, an entity residing in holiness and in the supernatural presence of the Creator (See #10, Pg. 5). All of the mundane, often silly imagery has sublimated the images of most indigenous cultures as well as those of more advanced and complex origin. Corporation executives have determined that all forms of symbolism and artifact must be simplified and "Disnified" for mass consumption as part of a cleverly conceived form of entertainment. What may have been a holy Icon or of meaningful significance to millions is often placed in "cartoon format" to sell tickets and advance ratings,

---

and political co-operation, which includes incite to war, revenue sharing, corruption of governmental agencies and community redevelopment.

6   **Wormser, Rene A.,** *Foundations, Their Power and Influence,* (Covenant House Books, 1993, PO Box 4690, Sevierville, TN 37864), ISBN 0-925591-28-9.

7   **Privitera, James, MD., and Stang, Alan, MA.,** *Silent Clots, Life's Biggest Killers.* The Catacombs Press, 105 N. Grandview, Covina CA 91723. ISBN # 0-9656313-0-3. Chapters 12 & 13.

determined by individuals that do not comprehend what they see and are certainly conned by the pretense. Corporate nonsense has been, as it continues to be, particularly destructive where Christian imagery is concerned. Cheap junk, the quick turnover and the trend in fashion are dominant elements in mass marketing techniques aimed at the mind of a pubescent. We do acknowledge some beautifully conceived exceptions, however they are exceptions. Unfortunately most of the exceptions are available only to the rich and even they are being conned, thus pay too much for what they receive. All that is Holy has been removed from view in favor of slick merchandising displays, erotic and sensual imagery and plastic forms, destined to quickly become garbage. This is happening whilst millions bemoan the pollution of the planet. *The blockhead, become celebrity, is paid millions* for an endorsement when, through corporate cleverness, *good, hard-working people are paid pennies,* to manufacture and fabricate items, which are designed to disintegrate and to wear out in a calculated time period. Style too is manipulated so as to encourage patronage for that which will be outdated in a few months. Youth are especially vulnerable. Who now speaks of honor?

Corporations control the preponderance of communication and entertainment through advertising revenues, which support preferred endeavor. In this respect, perhaps more than any other, the corporation has polluted both morality and an honest respect for what reality is. Millions live in a make-believe world, created by the incessant imposition of fiction and fantasy on real-life existence. Youth are captivated as never before. As mentioned elsewhere, individuals wear a *costume* (rather than clothing or garments) and rather than live, they *act out their roll* in society. *The profound gesture of procreation has become misnamed as a performance.* All of this bodes ominous for the future as it obviates the preposterous and absolutely malignant nature of the corporate influence on our dying Western Civilization. Our Western Culture is terminally ill, nearly dead, pushed aside by silliness and the imposition of the aggressive salesman and the defiantly obtrusive barbarian. We need only to embalm our heritage, as seems to be happening, before we are buried in history by alien beings, those to whom we have been generous in providing a place of refuge, against what is often a mostly imagined or invented political imposition.

The proliferation of the museum does not add substantially to the viability of our Western Civilization, especially when the establishment is adamant in denying what made it great. The leather bound books, which carry the great literature of the past, symbolize our plight. Beautiful books are often accumulated in sets, perhaps one book each month. Eventually, one will have the whole set and can imagine some manner of knowing has been gained thereby. However, many of the present great Novels (so-called), especially the ones with explicit sexual connotation, while perhaps in some ways interesting, even artfully written are, in fact, part of the problem. Reading them is quite another matter, by many unable to read or to understand what they have read, with golf and the tabloids, television and the VCR. And, of course, with all of our imagined freedom, adult entertainment has captivated or conquered the unsatisfied, prurient, lewdly curious and the simple-minded. Adult ignorance and sin has spilled over and upon the innocence of childhood. "Girlie-men" have encouraged this to happen. Absent fathers too, have abandoned the role of protector for their own children. Many men are promiscuous believing this is some manner of right. Consenting adult laws protect fornication and adultery, perhaps the silliest form of law in the history of the world. Understanding the meaning of Shame and Humility is quite an undertaking for they who spend so much time in mindless motion, stimulated by an imposed, commercially driven urgency. Living in a Christ-like manner is certainly beyond most individual comprehension. Secular Commercialism controlled by an alien-minded corporate elite, ungodly government and the pretense imposed by a watered-down public education, which panders to ignorance and sin, combine in ways difficult to comprehend. Thus, truth, especially concerning the existence of and nature of sin, is too often pushed aside.

Corporations are gaining control of every town and City in this and other nations. Corporations control how and when, why and where money is spent. Urban renewal is a "euphemism" for giving control of property and structures, in the most populated and busy area of every town, to a corporate identity. Concurrently, the flight to the great cities, so called, is away from affordable land, favoring the concentration of populations and vertical integration so glaringly apparent. The compacting of a population in a condominium type dwelling is just one phenomenon attendant to what is happening, whereabouts the substance and the individuality, thus the soul, especially of the small town, are given to anxious greed. Additionally, it is certainly open to question that might own the land beneath the high-rise condominium structures?

In the past fifty years, the corporate Pirates captured the Great-cities. Those same Pirates are now working on the countryside. They have easy "pickens" as the rural folks, known as *"hay seeds"* have remained down on the farm, hoping to be in tune with progress. What has happened has been advertised relentlessly and is interpreted as a form of progress, which it may be for those who direct the orchestration. *Anxious greed is apparent in one's being beholden to the national and international brand names that dominate all commerce.* Unfortunately, most would rather have a name brand item, made on the other side of the planet, rather than one made in the old hometown. And, the kids do not want to wear garments made with loving care by their mother! One can now travel across the entire nation and see the same "in your face" Logos on billboards and freeway signs, ad nausea. Most wear the same denim uniforms, which may change slightly from Season to Season. Consumers, who attempt to keep abreast of the trend, imagine small changes in fashion and color as necessary to enhance a meaninglessly uniform identity.

Whereabouts money is concerned; in many respects the corporation is absolutely the enemy of the individual and the biological family, the soul of any people, any culture, or any civilization.[8] The corporations have changed the meaning of Time: Time, is a consequence of human perception responding to the placement of the earth, in respect to the other bodies in the solar system, especially the sun. Beyond this, Time bears on and causes the being of a psychological self, aware of both past and future. Man is the only animal capable of this manner of awareness, involving individual conscience and free will, which is a gift from the Creator (God, the Father). The ability, to comprehend Time and to remember the Past, manifests as the building of a Tradition.[9] Other animals do not have a Tradition. Tradition is a consequence of recognizing and reiterating, in speech and act, what works best in any limited circumstances, which limitations are a question of when and where.[10] What we deem as genetic transfer, the begetting of children or the giving of one life to another maintains this continuity. Genetic continuity is Familial. Many speak of the Family of Man, however refuse to understand what this means. The child-parent and parent-child relationship should obviate what is being inferred. History, Tradition, or the remembered and recorded past are important as well, providing a reservoir of both information and technique having to do with living and having lived. However, one's individual time is discreet, *absolutely discreet.* This is a phenomenal part of the result of time-space placement, language, genetics and an entire complex of probable and possible elements.[11] *All elements combine, as only God knows why and how.*[12] God, by millions is understood to be all

8   Freeman, Richard and Arthur Ticknor, *Wal-Mart is not a Business, It's an Economic Disease.* Executive Intelligence Review, Nov. 14, 2003. Vol. 30 No. 44. Pp. 4-6.

9   Lukacs, John, *Historical Coinsciousness and the Remembered Past.* Harper & Row, Publishers, New York, Evanston and London. © 1968 by John Lukacs. LC # 67-28809. Pg. 158.

10   Lukacs, John, Ibid. Pg. 110.

11   Lukacs, John, Ibid. Pg. 179.

12   **God is a Spirit**, infinitely perfect, pure light, all knowing, all being and God is everywhere. This definition relates specifically to the meaning of words and is the best way, which we have for defining what is actually beyond most simple comprehension or simple-minded definition. God is not of this world, therefore many have trouble with any definition, nevertheless we must do our best. The Tradition of the Catholic Christian faith, some other faiths as well, holds to this definition or nearly so.

knowing. Thus is provided that each individual is unique, excepting that they are all children of God the Father, Creator of "all that is seen and unseen".[13]

Many individuals have some difficulty understanding reality, concerning the One omnipotent, supernatural or Most Holy Lord, and this in turn constitutes an important part, seemingly the root, of our Civilization in crisis.[14] The Crisis has come about largely because of the sin of greed. Greed has corrupted the meaning and function of Money. Greed compels some, that consider themselves to be superior and who choose to ignore the meaning of a well-formed and good Christian conscience, to act in a manner denigrating to they who are being cheated. Coincidentally, theft and/or corporate greed may be called good business, looking to the bottom line, cooking the books, extortion, clever accounting or some other deviously contrived euphemism.

One's understanding of reality and what is supernatural is directly related to the present World's circumstance. The present can be better understood when one is truthfully encouraged to think independently, in the light of Tradition and is inclined nevertheless to contemplate with independently truthful insight. Pertaining to money, the disposition of wealth and the role of the corporation one is wise to consider some interesting questions. Consider the questions enumerated below. *Let's name them, singularly, and in groups, as being the Dirty Diapers of a falsely imposed "rancid" Modernity.*

1. Was the French Revolution really French? Which groups benefited most from the disjunction caused by mayhem, bedlam, beheading, drowning, turmoil

---

13 **The Apostles Creed:** "We believe in one God, the Father almighty, maker of Heaven and Earth, of all that is seen and unseen..." And, there is more of that which we cannot see than that which we will ever see. Excepting, [**if**] Heaven does exist, individually we might be privileged to view much of what is presently unseen. This is precisely the Call of Heaven. This is a driving Concept; responsible for much of the thinking in this world as it has always been so. Primitive man, with limited technology, nevertheless had the same callings of the Soul. Modern man, more technically adept, has allowed inane rhetoric to destroy, for most of the Western Culture, other Cultures as well, the sensibilities necessary for significant comprehension. This is largely due to the extraordinary impositions of the Corporation in collusion with an illegal and immoral, privately controlled banking system and State-controlled Education. And, Reformations, Heresies, Satanic Mumbling, Purges, Pogroms and Devious Plans have all taken their toll. Then we ask, "For whom [does] the Bell toll?" Do you know whom?

14 **Lukacs, John, Ibid.** Pg. 216-223.

and murder?[15] In what ways did this catastrophe impair the development of Christianity?

2. Was the Russian Revolution really Russian?[16] Who exactly set up the takeover? Who provided the Capital, which made the Russian Revolution possible? How was our good President Woodrow Wilson involved? What about Jacob Schiff, the Financier. How many dissidents were imported from New York under pretense of American citizenship? Who were the beneficiaries from the destruction of Holy Mother Russia? Finally, where is the Imperial Gold? Who did claim the tons of gold, such "relics from the past," which now sells for seven hundred dollars an ounce? Who has claims to the land and the billions, perhaps trillions, in mineral rights and substances that were stolen from the Czar, who was the truthful leader of the Russian People?

3. Who, on what authority, decided the fate of Czar Nicholas of Russia, his wife, children and servants? Were they given a fair and well-publicized trial? (See Appendix A)

4. What was the motivation for such heinous crime? Was there a sinful motivation?

5. Who provided the stolen Capital, interest free, to enrich some of the largest banks in Europe? What about the stolen land and the mineral rights attendant thereto?

6. What has been the roll of Freemasonry in world events during the past 300 years?

7. Who formulated the present United State Monetary system and why was this done? Was such an absurd imposition of any benefit to this nation and its' people?

8. Who owns the Capital Stock in the present *Federal Reserve* System? How might one acquire such ownership?

9. Who determined how our nation's currency should be manipulated? Who did determine this certainly destructive form of monetary policy? Is the good life made better because the currency and the nation is being destroyed?

---

15 **Webster, Nesta,** *World Revolution, the Plot Against Civilization.* Veritas Publishing Company, 7th Ed.., 1994, Cranbrook, Western Australia.

16 **Knupffer, George,** *TheStruggle for World Power, Revolution and Counter-Revolution,* 4th. Edition 1986, ISBN # 0-85172-703-4

10. What must be done to negate the monumentally fraudulent impositions of the past? Might one appeal to the Congress; the Senate; the Supreme Court? Would you know how to do this?

11. How many in government, including Presidents, have been or are presently traitors? Can you name them! Should they be punished? How might one punish who leads the nation in an orgy of spending, mayhem, taxation and subterfuge?

12. Has shopping at the Mall become a new form of Religion? Are you a better person because of the clothes on your back?

When one is better and more truthfully and completely informed concerning the aforementioned questions one should [will] better understand, how and why did present circumstances come to be as they are? Not to forget, corporate influence was felt all along the way.[17] Either we are with Him or we are against Him (Christ). There is no in between.

Countries other than this confused *"Unitized"* States of *"Amerika"* have problems similar to our own and have had such problems for a long time. The problems, which we face, some others as well, are encouraged in the imagination as being a product of what is *propagandized* as progress. "Under the world's present financial system, the money, except for a now trifling proportion, is originally created by the issuance of a loan at interest. *"Bankers, who lend nothing themselves,*

---

17 **Corporate** (kor-per-it), **adj.** [L. *corporatus* pp. Of corporare, to make into a body <*corpus, corporis,* body], **1.** United; combined. **2.** Having the nature, or acting by means of, a corporation; incorporated. **3.** Of a corporation; as *corporate* property. **4.** Shared by all members of a unified group; common; joint: as *corporate* responsibility (Webster). Thus, given the meaning of words and *the kind of action,* which words engender, it is reasonable to assume (imagine at least) that a Corporation is of the same genre as a Commune. Where economics is concerned, the Cartel or Corporation has authority, whereas the socially devised Commune is driven by expectation, beholden to romanticism and eager anxiety. The combining of the giant Corporation, with the business of government (we name this the Industrial Military Complex) provides a subtle means to impose Fascism on an unsuspecting Population, even as this same population enjoys a very indebted form of freedom. Thus the Corporation is the handmaiden of both Communism and Socialism. Where joint-ownership is the rule, it is difficult for a People to determine which part is owned by this abstract "we the people." With titles vested in corporate wealth, the rich usurper is somewhat more certain. Notwithstanding, slogans and the linguistic cliché', combine with misunderstanding to engender hopeless confusion for all but a few. We name the Few, movers and shakers, billionaires who secretly and hypocritically, knowingly or unknowingly implement the process.

in effect make a forced levy in kind on the Nation. Thus is conferred on the borrower the power to purchase a corresponding amount of wealth in the market, which wealth does not belong to them, or those who borrow from them, but to the community. The proceeds of the issue of new money—belong to the Nation in which it is, or is accepted as, legal tender, and not to the issuer. *Herein lies the basic flaw of the existing monetary system.*"[18] Jacques Rueff, Finance Minister to Charles De Gaulle, had similar things to say (*italics are author's interpolation for clarity*). With inflation, money becomes worth less, while as a corollary *what is tangible seems to be* worth much more. Additionally, concerning real estate, location or placement is an important factor in determining value in terms of paper, which functions to attract the interest and investment of more individuals. Much of the present migration of populations is encouraged by this economic-become-social phenomenon.

Hereabouts are imposed some questions. Might it be wise to consider the value of land as being constant, inviolable in relation to a sound, unchanging value of the currency? Or; Should Money and Land have a fixed and unchanging value? What effect might this have on inflation, the migration of people and the general tenor of commerce?

Our educational system does not equip the young to deal truthfully with important Issues or the questions, which might arise from having done so. Political correctness hampers truthful dialogue, in favor of make believe. Most Theory is based on the past and only anticipates (perhaps incorrectly) what will be in the future. Be that as it may, at the present, the young are taught to spend and to incur debt, which is in keeping with the broad path of an only recently imagined reality. However, ultimately indebtedness, at all economic levels, causes individuals to be a slave to the _Money Masters._ Presently (2006) combined debt, in the United States, is considered to be about seven or eight Trillion Dollars. Derivatives are estimated worldwide (2006) in the range of two hundred Trillion Dollars, more or less. As regards money, many perhaps most youth have accepted the role of an indebted, fun seeking, irresponsible and disrespectful moron. This is a serious problem, which may prove our undoing as a nation.

At the present time, the damage being done by corrupt and a too-dominant imposition of the corporate enterprise, is mostly misunderstood, since so many

---

18 **Thompson, Norman A.,** Research Engineer, Inventor or the Norman Thompson Flying Boat, 1914...**and Soddy, Frederick.,** Noble Laureate in Chemistry, 1921. Quotation is taken from a letter (1943) written to His Excellency, Most Reverend William Godfrey, the Apostolic Delegate to Great Britain, to the Anglican Archbishops of Canterbury, York and Wales, and to other Ecclesiastical Dignitaries in Great Britain. Apparently it did little good!

"seemingly apparent good benefits" derive from a co-operative effort. Nevertheless, personal behavior, family dissolution, divorce, illegitimacy, high level crime, the corruption of childhood, the destruction of a wholesome adolescence, the entice-ment into ever deeper debt and the propagation of ever greater conflict are all [in large measure] a consequence of a too aggressive corporate influence. We sug-gest that Government be considered as a Corporation, determined to control the lands, oceans, resources and people of the world. When government influence is combined with economic trickery, is married to what is imagined as happiness and a feeling of well being, few will have the **Reason to undo** what is happening. We arrive at this position knowing most will disagree with our understanding.

The life we have known in the past one hundred years is a "done deal". Our progeny will be more and more subject to forces, which they cannot and will not understand. The Bureaucratic Socialistic System will deny their creativeness, make them more dependent, spy on their personal movements, and make justice a political issue. Finally and most importantly they will not be taught or will they comprehend the difference between good and evil, between right and wrong and they will be denied all mention and comprehension of what is holy, thus to cor-rupt and condemn their Soul.

The Paradigm is complex and the future will be more complex as the Civilization moves through the just beginning twenty-first Century. The Intellect of this nation and of the world is permeated with *thought substance* based on mis-conception, menial judgements, a lack of truthful knowledge, cheap theatrics and the insidious Lie.

Moments

This moment is gone forever: forever and ever **Hallelujah, Hallelujah,**
never to return
As tomorrow becomes yesterday: (**she goes**) tomorrow is just a day away,
time to burn

Time, elusive phenomenally strange is, **always the same:** tic tock, tic tock, when
Robbing tomorrow it gives us only yesterday: **I remember you, the way
you were;** then

Most dwell upon a moment past: (**know what I mean**) the future is thus cast
Knowing no moment can ever last: we must **accept what is past.** Any moment
may be your last:

Before **we do have time to know,** what treasure is held within each moment
Then tomorrow we **begin, anew** (**he goes**) I do, so do you

We make the same mistakes, too high the stakes
Use the same old fakes; grab the same old rakes, bake the same cakes

But God is generous, He will understand, allowing each to play their hand
Thus we have a new tomorrow nevertheless tomorrow we must pay the band.

The Piper plays, marijuana in the shade, for floating this and many days
The Marcher's form a line, its like (**you know**) a Rose Parade, screaming millions
in charade

Millions sit in the gutter, scream, and chortle and clap their hands
Smoke marijuana. Listen to the bands.

The nation watches bouncing balls, men running on the grass,
then the music plays.
The potter turns the plastic clays

Soon Death arrives, all is silent, **somewhere my love,** leaving no time to repent
Life was generous yet Life is always spent. All good and evil came then went

Who knows what evils lurk in the heart of men?
The Shadow knows, but who knows the Shadow?

7-26-2002.

IV. Compound Interest

Another Factor to be considered is compound interest, an idea borne of the mind of a clever man. Compound interest causes wealth [in time] to increase exponentially, with certainty for those who are in possession of any amount of extra money.[1] Money, as explained above, is very useful and could (as it should), serve each sovereign individual equally. By this is inferred that **money is an Objective Denominator.** That is, money should provide the medium of exchange and the store of value required (in time) by those who have given of their service, as in their life's endeavors, or tangible holdings, *knowing* that the same store, meaning value, will be there when needed. Presently one can only *imagine* that such is even possible. **Inflation, the opiate of the middle classes is consuming all value from past endeavor** as it raises prices for the benefit of great accumulations of wealth, maggot-like corporations and speculation in land and real estate. The Cities are as an economic Black Hole, sucking youth and the substance from the broad countryside. Interestingly, many of our cities have become shameless cesspools of violence and crime. Millions, driven to the cities by need are being captured within them. The elderly bar their windows and lock their doors, even as pimps, pornographers and perverts threaten the young. *"My Country 'tis of thee, Sweet Land of Liberty"*...**really?**

1　**Compound Interest** is even more deadly, when augmented by a determinedly planned inflation. Therefore, the really wealthy, in preparation for inflation, acquire various forms of real wealth, such as real estate, farmland, gold, various commodities and fine art, indemnified by history, to cite some few examples. Certain rare coins, historically significant artifacts and the work of artist masters have reached astronomical paper-money values. And, there is always the possibility, for International Finance Capital, to hedge money holdings against a stronger foreign currency. Under a One-World Order, whereabouts just a few control most everything; it will be easy to provide whatever monetary vehicle is necessary to maintain power. This type of legerdemain is euphemistically named "rule of Law" and works to the best interest of they who, in fact, make the law. They who have great wealth own the system and dictate the law.

The idea of interest on money is very problematic.[2] Interest on debt currency, such as the funny money put into circulation by our Federal Reserve Banks, should not be allowed. Ultimately (as is being proven before our very eyes) such interest will consume the nation and all manner of value attained through honestly productive human effort.[3] In fact Socialists, Planners, Marxists and other misguided Bureaucrats do understand this. The Political/military/banking establishment works relentlessly to destroy the Christian inspired Notion that *"All men are somehow deserving of being treated well."*

Our present national debt should obviate what has and is presently happening. Such debt will be paid as it must be paid with money stolen from the people (taxation without representation) in future time. The fact *that prices are relative is a different issue* however, satisfies those who do not understand the nature of economic reality. Assertively is stated, most do not understand this and Public Education offers little, if any, insight. In fact, **Public Education is in competition of being the front-runner in destroying the existing social order.** This is why it is so important for any **[Fascist State]**[4] to control the nation's educational institutions, as well as the nation's money. Such Control should be considered very carefully.[5] **The Fascist State[6] is that state where giant private Enterprise (so-**

---

2   **The compounding of interest** on either excess capital or excess debt can be deadly. Great fortunes are thus destined to increase exponentially, whereas populations are held in servitude paying interest on war debt and often seemingly, unnecessary civic improvements, often born of malfeasance supported by the political hypocrite. The corporate state, with the *assumed power of taxation on income*, is able to contract unimaginably huge deficits, all to the benefit of a privately controlled banking system, partner to private endeavor. Ultimately, the consolidation of the great privately held banking institutions, will lead to total domination of civilization, beholden to a need for a medium of exchange.

3   **Anderson, E. L., Ph. D.** *The Upright Spike I & II.* © 1978, Government Educational Foundation, P. O. Box 1622, Washington, D. C., 20013.g

4   **Twight, Charlotte,** *America's Emerging Facist Economy.,* Arlington House, Publishers. New Rochelle, NY. ©1975 by Charlotte Twight. ISBN # 0-87000-317-8.

5   **Totalitarianism** will Politicize Education, Social Contracts, Common Speech, Habits, Manners, Customs and all forms of Commerce.

6   **Twight, Charlotte,** Ibid. **Fascism is** "a system of government characterized by rigid one-party dictatorship, forcible suppression of the opposition (unions, other, especially leftist parties [? *Author's question*] minority groups, etc.), the retention of private ownership of the means of production under centralized governmental control, belligerent nationalism and racism, glorification of war, etc." First instituted in Italy in 1922. (Webster) Think about this carefully! The United States has *for the effect, a two party system,* both parties being controlled by the same money power. *"Forcible*

called), actually Monopoly Enterprise and the Giant Cartel, uses the power of the State to create and insure that monopoly Capitalism is protected by the Force of Arms, Government and the Law! The *inexorable workings of compounding of interest* during excessively long periods of time, the time of several or many lives, one hundred, two hundred, or three hundred years, places the individual in a determinedly disadvantaged position.[7] This is a profound truth not properly defined in any public school "the shocking story of America today and its silent multi-millionaires (*now billionaires*) who rule, pay little or no taxes and run the country as tightly as any dictatorship."[8]

Public Education provides self-serving instruction or simply ignorant opinions, being extolled as somehow reasonable learning. Youth are buried in meaningless information whilst truthful knowledge is often sadly lacking.[9]

Dictators do whatever they can to prevent truthful enquiry and the in-depth acquisition of pertinent knowledge. It is difficult to find a public school teacher or

---

suppression of the opposition" is orchestrated by the news media, which is mostly controlled by they who benefit most from the system. The Idea of Leftist and Rightist being so very different is an illusion. *Both extremes agree on central control,* abolishment of private property, government control of education, monetary restrictions, wars and revolution, etc., all promoted by incessant pandering to political and monetary ignorance. *Government rules, federal and state,* fill thousands of pages, all of which *impair the exercise of free will,* independent judgement and the use of what is believed to be private property. *Belligerent nationalism* is apparent in our compulsion to make the world over in our own rather confused image, *"seemingly so"* or that of the pretenders leading the charade. *Are we one Nation, under God?* Or are we Dictators attempting to create a world in the image of the International Bankers, all drinking Coca-Cola and eating at McDonald's? And, we do have our share of racism however many of the racists are the "presumably" depressed minorities, many of which have entered our country, both legally and illegally, with the intent to do a make over! Finally, *we have glorified war,* in movies, novels, television and the mind of millions of presumptive youngsters. The Concept that we are a melting pot is ridiculous, we are as polarized as any nation might be, having not one pole however, many.

7   **Corti, Count Egon Caesar,** *The Rise of the House of Rothschild.* © 1928, Cosmopolitan Book Corporation. Introduction to Western Islands Ed., © 1972, Western Islands Pub., Belmont, MA 02178. Pp. 1-26. & 273-338.

8   **Lundberg, Ferdinand,** *The Rich and The Super Rich,* Who really owns America, How do the keep their wealth and power. Introduction to Text.

9   **Gromyko, Nina, Ph. D.** *Pedagogical Exercises in a Russian Classroom.* Fedelio Magazine, Journal of Poetry, Science and Statecraft. Summer 2003. Publisher, the Schiller Institute, Inc., P. O. Box 20244, Washington D. C. 20041-0244. Pp. 73-76.

a college Professor, who understands even a little bit about money and economics, excepting perhaps what is in the required (for control) reading. Especially, they do not understand how our money system has been stolen. [10] They do not understand that our economic fate is in the hands of mostly foreign bankers and wealthy hypocrites, closely related to those same foreign bankers.[11] Interest, which is a consequence of the incessant working of money in time, toward the benefit of some, will at the same time, work toward the financial ruin of almost all others. In his research and writing Antony Sutton (frequently cited in this exposition) has outlined the situation very well. Many authors have done a wonderful job of exposing the fraud that is inherent in giant governments however, their wisdom is not generally found in the classroom. Importantly, as made apparent by Dr. Sutton in his concise, historically pertinent, four volume work on the Order, other books as well, *only a few can be* [or will be] *greatly enriched* whereas billions will become impoverished, or exist as slaves paying interest to their masters.[12] This is happening even as some *seemingly decent* leaders, assumed as such, have the best intentions and may be sincere in their efforts. No one can deny the nature of a Reality that has been carefully and secretly contrived for the benefit of a clever consortium of evil men. Clever men understand this, do you?

True wealth resides in Real Property, land and permanent structures.[13] In Europe there are structures, which are three, four or five hundred years old, they

---

10 **The secret Conference on Jeckyll Island,** has never been discussed in most classrooms, and is correctly understood by very few.

11 **McMaster, R. E.,** *The Reaper, Newsletter*. Who holds controlling stock in the United States Federal Reserve Bank? (1) The **Rothchild Bank** of London, (2) The **Rothchild Bank** of Berlin, (3) **Lazard Brothers** of Paris, (4) **Israel Moses Seif Banks** of Italy, (5) **Warburg Bank** of Hamburg, (6) **Warburg Bank** of Amsterdam, (7) **Lehman Brothers** of New York, (8) **Kuhn Loeb** Bank of New York, (9) **Goldman Sachs** of New York, (10) **Chase Manhatten** Bank of New York. "The Staggering wealth of this *international banking cartell is illegally and unconstitutionally extracted from the American people.*"

12 **Sutton, Antony, Ph. D.,** Four volumes. I. *An Introduction to The Order* II. *The Secret Cult of The Order* III. *How the Order Creates War and Revolution, and* IV. *How the Order Controls Education.*

13 **Admittedly,** unimaginable amounts of wealth do reside, *seemingly so*, in the stocks of great Corporations however, much of *this wealth is notional rather than real.* Large holdings, insurance companies, pension funds and civic entities provide some sense of stability and there is [seemingly] a great deal of prosperity, which is perhaps the calm before the storm. And, individually many do profit in the near term from their involvement in such speculations. Nevertheless, the true value of most stocks is fractional, may be only one tenth of a cent or less: at a time when

are often beautiful and still suitable for use. In the United States, construction rewards the builder, not necessarily the community. Contemporary building methods, compared to past achievements do not result in permanent structures, excepting some commercial buildings may last two centuries. The majority of our buildings are of recent origin. Our cities have been decimated by a population of seemingly **reckless individuals who destroy what others have created, especially so concerning the use of land.** What renewal is accomplished benefits speculators, contractors, and mortgage bankers as it furthers the take-over of the nation by a corrupt, albeit seemingly altruistic government.

The Western notion of a fancy front, with nothing on three sides, rather like a set for a movie, or a play, or *the performance*, is evident in our sprawling suburbs. Homes have reached heretofore-unimaginable prices, measured in debt currency, and the misunderstood *compounding of debt values,* denominated in funny money, increases the liabilities of those that claim ownership. In fact, when money values increase there is a compounding effect on what must be paid in both interest and taxes. Coincidentally, the Condominium surge will place individuals in spaces, cubits defined with meets and bounds, above the land without certain claim to ownership of the land. One wonders; in one hundred years, when such *condominium structures* are in need of replacement, what form of legerdemain will be imposed to solve this tricky question? Certainly money will provide a means, for a price.

Neighborhoods, which in the past, provided a comfortable and secure place of residence, have been destroyed to accommodate [great] freeways, whereupon speeding automobiles create noxious and offensive fumes. In many areas within the city, the noise is intolerable. In all instances, any attempt to add or to improve what does exist results in greater congestion and all must be paid for. Great amounts of notional money are a necessity, to continue the monumental blunder. And, the compounding of interest continues in relentless pursuit of the workingman's earnings. One wonders what Boston will do to rejuvenate their monstrosities when renovation becomes necessary?

The Marxist and Socialists dream is of all humanity being in debt to a State controlled Bank.[14] Central Banks have been established for the express purpose

---

a dollar is worth perhaps (?) two cents, based on the values in 1900. We do have more creature comforts, for which we may have paid a too high price!

14   **Manifold, Didirae,** *Karl Marx, a Prophet of Our Times.* G. S. G. & Associates, Publishers. P. O. Box 6448, Eastview Station, Rancho Palos Verdes, CA 90734. ISBN# 0-945001-00-2. "In every Communist Country, a small clique at the top has everything". Pg 88. "Communist States everywhere have been set up with Monopoly Capitalist funds." Pg. 96.

of consolidation, leading ultimately to the *complete control of the Nations and lands* of this world. Actually there is no reason for a central Bank. *Banks are better servants of the people when they are numerous and decentralized, meaning localized,* independent and not tethered to an abstract notion of a means of control. Technology has not done the common man a favor, when in fact every penny he earns can be traced for a lifetime. *Electric Money, is the ultimate set-up?* Lives and personalities are thereby reduced to a bar chart or a square full of indistinguishable dots. We speak of privacy, even as government is gaining complete knowledge of every man, woman and child in this nation (others as well). *All that is required is the insertion of a computer chip at birth and big Brother has "got'cha".* Some foreign governments already have dossiers on our people, those who might do what is found objectionable to their alien interest. They are called thought-police. In this nation, free speech does protect the pornographer and the writers of fiction. Truthfully, free speech for Christians and those who are critical of the system, which promotes every form of excessive, perverse and disruptive behavior, is limited by an ideology formulated from intolerant ignorance. Wisdom is something else.

With interest free money, provided by the American nation and controlled by the Congress, as was intended by the Constitution, the Sovereign individual, that being the lawful citizen, would be granted better opportunity for acquiring a fair share in the prosperity that is inherent in the wealth of this nation. The only expense would involve paying for the transaction, which would be quite minimal. Uniform pricing is not necessary! Businessmen know that they can buy cheap (in Asia) and sell dear (in America) and they make a killing in the process. *We name this exploitation.* It should be made impossible for a multi-national conglomerate to profit, more than is reasonable, from each and every transaction. And our population should be encouraged by aggressive advertising to buy American-made products and to do much more for themselves. If this would happen, many of our problems would be solved.

If Norway and Denmark and Switzerland can exist, as nations, some of the most prosperous and desirable places on this earth, so can the United States of America. This was the situation in the past and can be reconstructed for the future benefit of our citizens' children and the posterity of this nation and the Christian Culture. Who are those that would have other plans for our nation and for our people? By what authority can some aliens, outside the mainstream of Nation, Culture and Civilization, impose their limited, myopic, self-centered vision on all of humanity?

Truthfully, Intelligence resides whereabouts any group resides and is most effectual in dealing with problems, which are well understood and close, at hand. This suggests that the best and most truthful intelligence is not included in the equation defining modern economically driven Politics. And, always keep in mind Money talks and can buy almost any Man that walks and can muffle or reduce to silence all forms of disagreement.

"Mind, thought and memory reside in, and, are recorder in the atomic nuclei, at many virtual state levels, in many hyper dimensions. Everything "mental" can be directly interfaced with and engineered. That is to say, the mind can be loaded up or down. Communications can exist, within, hyper-space. Ideas and some-how contrived interpretations can be directly loaded into the human mind, much as is done in a computer" (Col. T. Bearden). What might be the political and economic possibilities of such manipulations? How one might process such phe-nomenal input is difficult to imagine. However, we know that politics and greed will combine to deny the voice of a decently reasoned Catholic Christianity from influencing the system, which is in place. Furthermore, we also know that thought may be directed by good or evil intention. In terms of philosophy and ontology the common forms of political thought are abysmal. Politics seems driven by the moment, for the benefit of those that intend to capture the nation and the world and is generally both malicious and unwise.

Who knows those knows.

V. Responsibility and Liability

Beside the workings of corporate finance over long periods of time, the corporation shields opportunistic men and women from personal liabilities and protects slight of hand, which evidences something other than the truth. This is suddenly quite apparent! Numbers are supposed to be objective and accurate calculations are possible, however, there are many tricks.[1] Once again, such tricks enable a few to plunder many, legally, dependably, and over long periods of time, thus providing millions for those who play the game well.[2] There are many that play the game well. Much about this is made clear, in the writings of Douglas Reed,[3] Eustice Mullins[4] Anthony Sutton[5] George Knupffer[6] Ferdinand Lunberg, Nesta Webster,

---

1   Spengler, Oswald, *The Decline of the West, Vol. II, Perspective of World History.* Pg. 490. "The decisive event, however, was the invention—"contemporary"—with that of the classical coin about 650—of double entry bookkeeping by Fra Luca-Picioli in 1494. Goethe calls this, "one of the finest discoveries of the human intellect...to be ranked with Columbus and Copernicus."

2   Lundberg, *The Rich and the Super Rich. Who rally owns America? How do they keep their wealth and power? Bantam Edition, June 1969. Pp. 252-254, 263-267, 272-291, 429, 452, 476-77, 760.* Admittedly, the numbers would be much larger at present, because the swindles, subterfuge, theft and the deceitful and treacherous practices have continued this past thirty five years, since this edition was published.

3   Reed, Douglas, *The Controversy of Zion,* Veritas Pub. Co, P. O. Box 20, Bullsbrook, WA, 6084 Australia. The work is a treasure of knowledge, information and understanding.

4   Mullins, Eustice, *The World Order, Our Secret Rulers,* (Ezra Pound Institute, Publisher, Staunton, A 24401, Second Edition, 1992)

5   Sutton, Antony, *The Secret Cult of the Order.* Research Pub., P. O. Box 39850, Phoenix, AZ©1984, Antony Sutton. ISBN # 0-914981-09-9

6   Knupffer, George, *The Struggle for World Power, Revolution and Counter-Revolution,* 4th. Edition 1986, ISBN # 0-85172-703-43 Economic Roots of Power. Pp. 28-36. "Taxes are levied, not so much to pay for public services as in order to sustain the

Olivia O'Grady and many others, cited within this exposition however; they are not widely read. Their writing is quite intimidating for the Establishment, *certainly too truthful for the eyes of the public school student*. Nevertheless, their work should be made available to every young person, as required reading; thus the young might better understand the meaning of words, especially when they relate to economics. For example, "Double-entry book-keeping rests on the basic principle, logically carried out, of comprehending all phenomena purely as quantities."[7] According to *Spengler "Double entry book-keeping is a pure Analysis of the space of values, referred to a co-ordinate system, of which the origin is the "Firm."* [8] Unfortunately, understanding at this level is beyond most that call themselves educators. Of itself, the understanding of the word Firm has interesting implications on what has been and what is considered Commerce. In respect to Information Theory and present day implementation of Commerce, the Skeptic may inquire regarding the Firm. What is it? This was hinted at in a Nobel prizewinning insight by economist Ronald ASE, in "The Nature of the Firm," published in *Economica* in 1937.[9]

The Modern railroad, with freight containers, and the millions of semi-trailers, in concert with container shipments from overseas, changes the nature of time/

---

political, economic and social system of the money-lenders....."Capitalism" is **not** the system of private property and free enterprise...Finance Capitalism actually created Soviet Communism....money in circulation is created out of nothing, by book entry....all State and Private Business is controlled by finance through debts...the escape from slavery is only possible by rejecting all materialism whether of the Capitalist or the Socialist kind." (inside front cover)

7   **Sombart,** *Der modern, Kapitalismus*. II, p.119.

8   **Firm** (furm), **adj.** [ME. & Ofr. *ferme* < *L.* firmus], **1.** Not yielding easily under pressure; solid; hard. **2.** Not moved or shaken easily; fixed; stable. **3.** Continued steadily; remaining the same: as, *a firm* pressure. **4.** Unchanging; resolute; constant: as, *a firm* faith. **5.** Showing determination; positive: as, *a firm* command. **6.** legally or formally concluded; definite; final: as, *a firm* contract, *a firm* order. **7.** In *commerce,* not rising or falling considerably; steady: said of prices, etc. **v.t. & v.i. 1.** To make or become *firm.* **2.** [*Archaic*], to establish, confirm.

9   "**The question arises,** is it possible to study the forces which determine the size of the firm. A firm expands until costs of organizing another transaction become equal to the costs of carrying out that same transaction, by exchanging on an open market. *Costs increase with an increase in the spatial distribution of the transactions organized* (within that same space), so *efficiency will tend to decrease as the firm gets larger.* Inventions, which tend to bring factors of production neared together, *by lessening spatial distribution, tend to increase the size of the firm.* Changes like telephones and telegraph, which tend to reduce the cost of organizing spatially, will intend to increase the size

space relationships regarding international commerce, aimed at distribution in North America and Europe. Asia, at present, is in quite a different position. With this in mind, it becomes reasonable to assume that most could understand time/ space functions in regard to, for example, what they are wearing as clothing. This explains why, in America, Tailors, Jewelers, Shoemakers, Artists and most crafts- men have become middlemen rather than producers. Admittedly, it is difficult to determine if this is good or evil, in reference to future time.

Coincidentally, to make certain learning, therefore understanding/meaning (of) is tightly controlled, we have the corporate dominated textbook industry, printing millions of copies of texts, mostly picture-books, which often function to distract the youth of our country from truthful and useful information. The publishing giants print textbooks for mass consumption, whereas many great books enjoy very small circulation (*see footnotes below*). The public school system, somewhat corporate in nature (pertaining to thought structures and idiom), is all too quick to accept the *newly published and presumably vital works* provided by the giant publishers. *Public education encourages the distribution of texts, which are timely in place of what may be somewhat obsolete, having been distributed by the same giant publishers a year or two ago.* The Teacher, presumed expert, is not given much authority rather <u>*State Bureaucrats determine what shall be peddled or "piddled"*</u> as learning. Few know who are the State Bureaucrats? Why are they in such position? The Owners of property are held as victims of extortion, forced to pay too much for, what are deemed, important books, which are outdated, before the ink is dry, thus worthless in money, within a year or two.[10] Such are the benefits of an intru- sive and monopolistic public school system.

---

of the firm. *All changes, which improve managerial Techniques, will tend to increase the size of the firm.* Most Inventions will change the cost of organizing and of using price mechanisms. Whether the Invention makes the firm larger or smaller will depend on the *relative effect* of these two sets of expenses." (Author's interpolation from; J. D. Davidson, Vantage Point, Vol. 2, No. 12, December 2003)

10 **The Pretense,** driven by vain Educators, which makes them appear as diligent and worthy of their often excessive salaries, is that there is so much new knowledge. In fact, excepting in rare instances, this is patently false. More books, written with the same intent and covering what is known already, do not add substantially to new knowledge, rather they may broaden the interpretation and/or applicability of what is known. There is known to be a core of Knowledge and Understanding necessary for reading, writing and arithmetic, other subjects as well. Most important is the understanding of words, without which information becomes as incidental. Serious Students can push the frontiers of "significant knowledge' on their own when, they have acquired the intellectual competence to do so. *Common sense dictates, truthful knowledge should be useful year after year.*

The publishers, teachers, unknown experts and the government, working with extorted funds, together comprise a consortium, which is robbing those who pay. Those who pay, one can imagine, might be considered blinded by their own ineptitude and condescension to a confusingly conceived fraud. The wise amongst them are considered reactionary, old fashioned, intolerant, illiberal or worse, politically naive. Flatly stated, the most influential of what is done, *presumably educational,* is done for profit, tendered to manipulations imagined as somehow educational. The level of moral integrity, literacy, habits, behavioral patterns, and the commonly vulgar speech, should obviate the Truth. In fact, <u>*Public Education has failed to do, what those who pay the bills imagine*</u>. However, it does very well what was intended namely to distract youth from serious learning during their formative years.

In the realm of children's toys, the corporations searching for profits, with all their made in a foreign country junk, are outstandingly irresponsible, in respect to the damage they have done to this nation, and are certain to do in every nation where they operate. Consider, <u>*toys are pus*</u>! Our youth are exploited, so as to line the pockets of unknown middleman. **The days before and just after Christmas, a most holy day, have been divisively reformed into a buying orgy of personal gratification.** The Little Drummer Boy and Tiny Tim, as manipulated for profit, have replaced Jesus. In addition to <u>*milking the children*</u>, the middleman exploits hundreds of thousands of captured, dependent workers, who have become part of an all-pervasive and destructive World Economy. All is done in the Spirit of Christian charity, or so it may seem. **The World Economy thrives on the manufacture and distribution of that, much of which is plastic junk, "cheap and shoddy."** destined for the garage sale, ultimately the Dumpster and the garbage can. Summoned by an elusive prosperity, millions of rural inhabitants have moved to overcrowded cities, where they live in poverty and squalor. This monstrosity, applauded by bankers and opportunists, cheats nearly everyone, including those involved in the production of worthless, ugly and monstrous toys, which are peddled at Christmas time, a most holy day.

To continue, the birthday of the Son of God has become a buying orgy, led by the corporate execs who use this most Holy Day and Season to fill every house in the country with stuff, much of which is ugly, insensitive, sensational, plastic junk. The latest is "Shrek." This same plastic junk carries the logos of all the great names in children's toys and panders to every silly or pretentious idea ever conceived; **all for the good of the dear little ones, bewildered by the obnoxious pretense,** which substitutes for the birthday of the Son of God. Furthermore, if these same toys were really positively influential, instead of what they are, our children wouldn't have become the threat to the civilization, culture and to their very own families.[11] Why are so many adults and the elderly afraid to walk down a street at night? Why can we not face the reality of what truthfully is the problem? Why do we not move, individually, toward appropriate solutions? We need no government help; a state of goodness, ultimately grace, is a personal achievement. Conditioned as most are, they have not the will, nor the inclination, to do anything meaningfully constructive. Adults are ill equipped to face the problems, or are perhaps unable to set and to exemplify the necessary standards for their own children. Known and decent standards, defined by a universally Catholic Christian moral tradition, are necessary for any sustained improvement. Rather, *adults have adopted all the childish and silly mannerisms of a pubescent.* Individually, *uncounted adults, so-called, are a part of the problem.* One might elaborate even further however, by this time our good reader certainly has the picture. What shall one do? This may seem a difficult question but; it is not an impossible situation; yet! As a people, we should rethink our actions. What are we doing?

In the past, we have heard of the trust busters and anti-monopoly legislation, however, so far we have heard only words. We note many mergers occur as the giants are consolidating, reforming, and consuming all the little players.[12]

---

11 **The dress, demeanor, and attitude** of many present-day adolescents should be enough to convince even the dullest amongst us, that something is wrong. Why the sullen pride, arrogance and vicious animosity of so many youngsters?

12 **K Mart and Sears** have plans for consolidation, recently announced, so as to compete with Wal-Mart, which has become as a sociological Disease. Low prices, can only be gotten by cheapening the product and/or paying low wages. What we have is a combination of both. Admittedly, *some technological progress is apparent* along with the plastic handles that fall off and the tremendous number of meaningless choices. This presents a dilemma, whereabouts inflation, created by government, appeals to ignorance and greed, thus raising the price of all land and property while, at the same time, encouraging those who import more and more from other places, especially Asia. When we purchase from abroad we deny our own skilled and unskilled labor the opportunity for gainful employment. They whom we patronize in other nations, especially Asia, become wealthy, move to our country and buy land and property that our citizens cannot afford. These 'immigrants", many of whom are illegal, double up in dwellings and account for much of the overcrowding in our cities. *Interestingly, illegal labor will reconstruct what our own citizens abandon as they flee to the suburbs.* Citizens flee from what the system has accomplished namely blight, overcrowding, crime, noise, ugly outdoor signs and the near complete ruination of our once congenial neighborhoods and our *"once great Cities"*. As we fill the nation with foreign speaking illegal aliens, that have various political, social, economic and political understanding, serious conflict is near at hand! Coincidentally, simple-minded women have murdered forty million of their own children. We pretend to have empathy that two thousand and six years ago Herod was looking for Jesus?

Occasionally there is a spin-off, probably for tax considerations. Greedy, vain men who control things are not going to relinquish their control. Keep in mind, at present control is applied in very subtle and ingenious ways, even as all seems well. Indeed, much is very well. People have more *Stuff* than ever before. Nevertheless, the **Usurpers** will seek greater control in the future, of both the lands and the means of production. *Control resides in having Title to Real (not imagined) Wealth.* **Usurpers** will attempt to control transportation, communication, and the postal service. **Usurpers** will gain more complete control of all food processing and the garment industries together with a top to bottom system, from the ground to the table, and from the sheep to the sweater on one's back. The **Usurpers** have named this ultimate *"business plan"* as being an Integrated Corporation. In concert with the State, the giant Corporations comprise a nearly unassailable obstacle.[13] Correspondingly, Greed and Vanity are Cardinal Sins. Furthermore, greed is insatiable. The vain man is blind to the needs of his brother. We are admonished by Christ to be humble of heart and to be meek and fair in our dealings with each other. The nature of the corporation, in too many respects, is antithetical to the best advice we have been given. We ignore such advice at our own peril.

Pope John Paul II did often speak of a Culture of Death. *However, even the Pope seems confused, concerning what it means to be Pope.* In any event, the Pope is not given much attention by mass media. *What the Popes have championed, respective of morality, finds little acceptance in a world, which is often militantly anti-Catholic.* Beside, at the present time, the same dark forces that hope to control Mankind are using the Pope, who appears almost as a caricature. Pope John Paul II's brand of Ecumenism is what they who hate Catholicism encourage, with great effectiveness. What heretofore was the responsibility of the Church and a Morally Christian Imperative has been pushed from the stage, replaced by the Rock Concert, the situation Drama and Commentators in pinstripe suits. And, of course, the sluttish woman is a distraction for millions of men, including some *"Great Men"* that pretend to lead this nation".

Individually, however, we do have some small amount of freedom. However, our freedoms are eroded day by day. For millions there is no freedom at all. For millions, there has never been or will there ever be any opportunity excepting one, carefully put in place, by an unknown beneficiary. The status of being a beneficiary is a completely phenomenal consequence of history and the ways in which men have taken *economic advantage* of others, without assuming a fair-minded

---

13 The Feudal State, *American Serfs Labor for Directors of The Federal Corporation.* Bulletin, The Committee To Restore The Constitution, November 1992 # 370. Colorado Non-profit Corporation. P. O. Box 986. Fort Collins, CO 80522. Tel. (970) 484-2575.

liability. In the present circumstance we witness individual vanity, coupled with greed, working to gain wealth, to corrupt government and to control the land and the production of each nation.[14] Much of our reality, including what is and is not possible, is determined by a messianic persuasion, with a countenance alien to Christianity,[15] especially antagonistic toward Catholicism however, it is not prudent to speak of this. There is a *need for prudence,* made necessary because of a *deceitful and treacherous political and intellectual atmosphere*, which is difficult to understand and near impossible to change.

Once again, a corporation is a non-person person, a contrived form of legality, providing a shield against liability. This does provide a means of encouraging investment, however for what purpose may be questionable. In any event, the Corporation is a means for legal maneuvering and is a discreetly complex construct, whereby a few are able to manipulate circumstance to favor the manipulators.[16] Admittedly, common men do benefit from corporate production, however *the benefits as exist can be gotten in other ways.* Regarding Things, especially children's toys, perhaps fewer things, however of greater beauty is what the world needs. "He is most content, who is satisfied with least."(Socrates)

As a first step toward a solution, the individual, wherever possible, may opt to avoid any entity, which involves some manner of corporate structure. This could be difficult, however, is not totally impossible and gives a point of departure. ***Monopolies of all kinds should be denied individual patronage. Insurance companies, banks, franchises of every kind, networks, brand names, logo bearing products and any designer line should be avoided like the plague.*** This would open countless new opportunities for truthfully individual, more locally inspired participation, which can be more responsive and proficient in what will be accomplished. Remember

---

14 **Tugwell, Rexford G.,** *The Emerging Constitution.* Reprint, Bulletin, The Committee To Restore The Constitution, June 1991 # 352 & Aug. 2003 # 501. Colorado Nonprofit Corporation. P. O. Box 986. Fort Collins, CO 80522. Tel. (970) 484-2575.

15 **Beaty, John Col., USA.** *Iron Curtain Over America.* Chapter II, pp. 15-43. ©1951, 25th. Printing.

16 **Incorporations** are most profitable for those who initiate a new offering. Millions are made on I P O's, Initial public offerings, which are known to just a few. Dealers that cooperate do well on commissions and fees. Excepting for a few, mostly Specialists, those who buy on rising prices will most likely lose money as prices fall, encouraging them to sell at the wrong time. Long-term holdings go up and down. Under ideal circumstance, common stocks appear to do well for Investors. This may or may not be true, probably isn't. Charts used to sell the client are based on the past and disclaimers announce there is no guarantee for the future. Certainly, the greatest profits are made by Specialists, who manipulate, on a daily basis and by a lucky few.

the *5-cent cup of coffee* in the local restaurant. It is replaced by the **Logo-brand for a mere $2.25 to $5.00 per cup!** Th-th-th-that's all Folks! How often do we now enjoy penny candy? In 1950 fine leather shoes, made in America could be purchased for Just $9.95 to $19.95 the pair. They are now in the $200.00 to $450.00 price range, per pair, the same type of Shoe however a decidedly different type of money. We do understand that times change and it can be imagined that many things are relative. The poor remain with us and there are many more millionaires, even some billionaires, attesting to the fact that the really big money is easier to steal.

As hundreds or thousands of new competitors are brought on line we are hopeful that the giants, like rotten fruit, will fall. The giants will fall because there are not a sufficient number of hypocrites in this world to hold them up, once the money begins to vanish and, no one prefers rotten fruit. The financial liabilities seated in the over-priced urban real estate, which combine with silly government rules and regulations will kill most of the bloated "Biggies". Even now, the giants are moving production to other parts of the world, notably China and India. We see honest, efficient and energetic adversaries emerging in All of Asia. We imagine, as China develops they will require less and less from us who will be even more dependent on them. Think of it? We note that honestly structured co-operative, localized manufacturing banking and variously, functioning mutual companies could be the bright lights on the horizon.

Most importantly, as mentioned elsewhere, one should do whatever one can for themselves and for those close to them, mother, father, and siblings. *The encouragement of the biological family, formed in holiness, is primary* and is *absolutely necessary.* The biological family was once a proud, prosperous, capable and formidable force in the history of this nation and the world and is what is now most desperately needed. Familial love, unselfishness, a forgiving and patient mutual understanding, backed up by productive enterprise, will demolish the giant maggots that feed on the residuals of a decaying civilization. That maggot is the monopoly-corporation, the cartel which sucks the individual dry as it corrupts all the peoples of the world by means of the slick pub, easy credit, the national brand and all of the opium of commercial seduction, which appeals to ignorance and a false sense of well-being.

Families should protect their children from all manner of adultery and from all forms of personal and commercial whore. The pimp and the pornographer are always searching for youth, which they can and do corrupt, bringing them to Satan's clime. And *The marketplace of today, the great whore amongst whores, is a seducer of the young.* In spite of all the wonderful efforts of millions, corporate undertakings have reduced life to a game of who has the most of what is mostly unnecessary. As this is happening, families are destroyed by monumental impositions, which they do not understand and cannot escape.

We have attempted, to apply democratized thinking, in the realm of education, where such thinking is most inappropriate and is leading to disaster? We witness college graduates that cannot write a meaningful paragraph. We also know some young "ladies" work their way through the university as strippers and pole dancers. Regretfully, television gives us tainted episodes of Easter Break, during which time, it is inferred, our young scholars engage in orgiastic behaviors, including all forms of sensual excess. The assumption is that all youth can benefit from illicit sex combined with "higher education," so, we have encouraged even the dullest amongst our youth to attempt such study, for which they are simply not qualified. Administrators, Educators and over-paid Professors determined to increase enrollments, pat themselves on the back as they imagine being successful at what most amongst them refuse to understand.

Our children will suffer, as Educators, that have little or no comprehension of what is important, devise and administer the programs that students are obliged to pursue. Athletics and simple forms of job training are not the same as serious study, which prepares one to think objectively and to know truthfully. This is especially so in state run institutions where party politics and the flawed study of economics are determined as primary. Coincidentally, the faith of Western Civilization is importuned because of the politically contrived separation of Church and State. One cannot abandon the philosophy and the Intellect upon which the Civilization and Culture have been built and expect to not meet with disaster. Our Institutions are staffed with many Zealots that corrupt learning with a Marxist bias. Most youth are not trained in critically thoughtful contemplation and imagine that every endeavor must be fun. We will pay a high price for the strange delusions that Educators harbor regarding what it means to learn and to know. The fact is with all our technologies, we are not able to keep our cities from being destroyed or our country safe from invasion, even as we imagine we are protecting the world.

Biological Family.

Goodness.

VI. Money and Being

Being one's self is closely related to goods, to what one does, to what one has and to how one might have gained or acquired whatever that something is. Objects and things, as well as various manners, style and attitudes attendant thereto, are important elements pertaining to one's being. Almost everyone can be somehow understood, in respect to the objectivity, which surrounds one's being. This objectivity is a consequence of both chance and direct involvement. Both culture and civilization afford opportunity for chance occurrence. One's position and language related to immediate surroundings, nation and culture are important existential determinants. One should also consider that the passer-by (the stranger), whom one may meet only momentarily, may (or does) have a significant effect on what does follow. *It is not uncommon for individuals to be profoundly impressed by what may appear to be a chance or meaningless encounter.*[1] Furthermore, every individually motivated act thereafter could be (or is) somehow slanted in reference to what, at first may have seemed insignificant. Individual personal encounters are unique, as they are evocative, often in ways difficult to understand. The Existential forces of Reality are difficult to comprehend. This is especially critical whereabouts is concerned parent/child relationships. It is very well known that a youngster becoming an adult may ignore the counsel of a parent, whereas the counsel of a stranger can be profoundly influential. This is true especially when the stranger appeals to that which, the youngster may desire or that which will make the youngster feel grown up. Especially, Pimps and Charlatans pander to youthful insecurity, anxiety, ignorance and childish aspiration. All children aspire to be adults and to be independent; however, they are not always wise in beliefs concerning adulthood.

Education, as the disseminator of information, learning and knowing ultimately the attainment of wisdom, should define and encourage the best forms

---

1   **Life is a continuum,** the incidents within which most often unfold with unpredictable consequence. The most obvious example of this is marriage, which defines who shall inherit your place in a future unknown.

of human participation in light of the most eminent, meaningfully inspired and structured Traditional Values. Any Tradition places in evidence *"the good the bad and the ugly."* Chance encounters may alter belief, change attitudes and alter the direction of an ideal and they should be taken very seriously. This is especially true in heavily populated cities, with populations diverse in background and ideals. Indeed, many marriages are between strangers become intimate. This is an effective and profound form of assimilation/integration and is responsible for the burgeoning nature of what is "simply" defined as race.[2]

The *politically inspired mythology* which accompanies the idea of a pluralistic society, or what we call multi-culture, is in direct conflict with what most every individual would desire on their own. Certainly any form of institutionalized encouragement has economics as a primary motivation, perhaps the only motivation. Everyone wants to be somebody special. Each hopes to be important and the only way this can happen is for each to be distinguished in some obvious manner. All athletic events, the theatre, the army and any specific family or group offer an opportunity to become someone special. One's possessions and how one may have acquired them are outward signs of distinctiveness.

Ultimately, individuals will group around distinguishing characteristics, which, within a single group, are importantly commonplace. Shared beliefs and aspirations offer a common denominator, which may set one group apart from another. All great religions are a product of this phenomenon. Among other things, the Ghetto or the Barrio, are outward signs of continuity and compatibility. Politicians attempt to deny this. Opposing armies are a manifestation of opposing consensus as well. Teams, debate societies, clubs and gangs are all manifestations of this phenomenon, obviating the fact that *people are eager to be distinguished, however, do require the support of others of their kind.* In so doing, distinction is given credibility as it may place one in a higher category, within a group. Money, more or less, at all levels, is an important factor in the equation.

---

2   **Racial continuity** is an important factor in the continuum, as it defines the individual relative to appearance, genetic potential, propensities and various unimaginable possibilities.

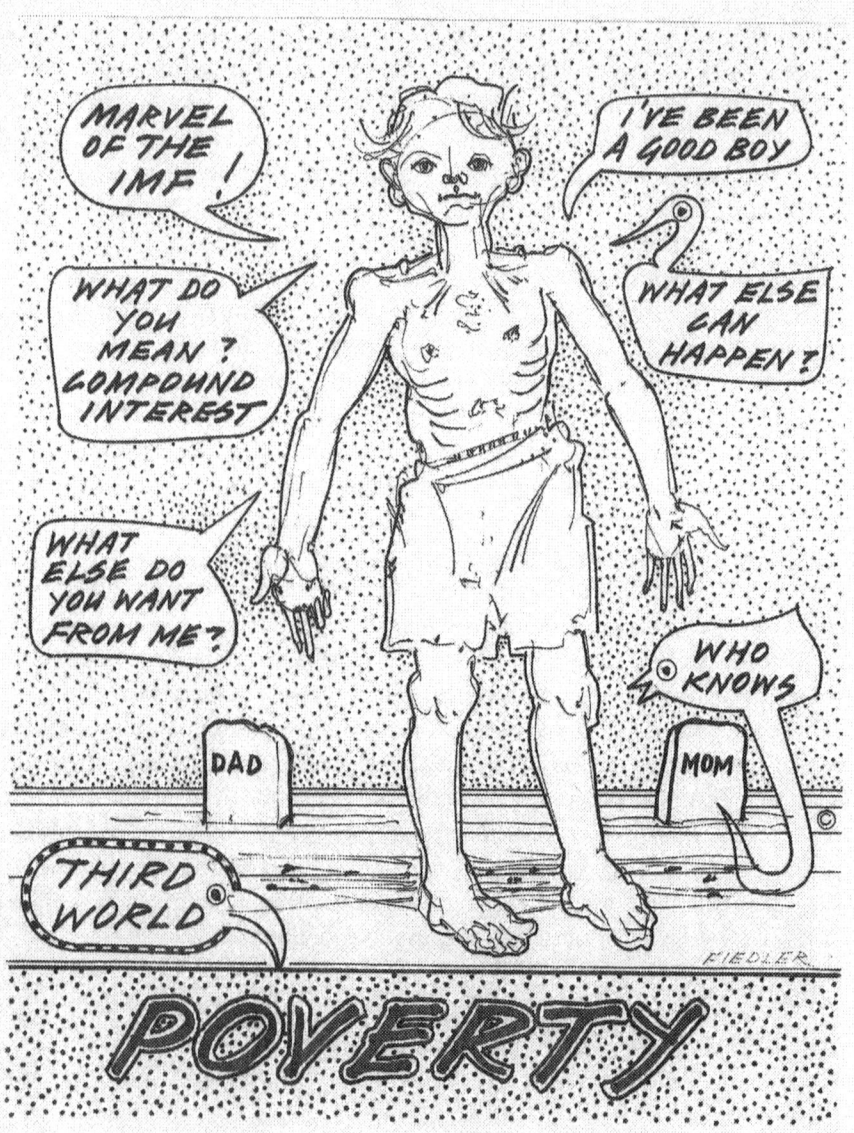

Poverty

Child of the 90's

VII. Social Structure, Language and the Family

Of great significance, is that there are so many individuals in the world that they must, in order to find the obvious support which they do require, form smaller groups.[1] The smallest group interestingly is the couple (two) and is that entity upon which all others depend. *The couple, truthful lovers mated for life, is what provides the setting for the most profound and rewarding manner of intimacy.*[2] "When the one that you love is in love with you, that's the greatest blessing by far." And still "you won't know how lucky you are." A carefully and exclusive shared intimacy provides what is necessary for a feeling of sustained well being, which is named Contentment. One may attain a tranquil sense of well being in

---

1   **Common Sense**, indemnifies the fact that a One World Order is a vain and an impossible dream.

2   **Lovers**, truthfully considered, given the physiological nature of the sexes, *must be a man and a woman.* Physical intimacy is the basis for procreation, which is a necessary function, for the human race to survive. This is not a political or economic issue, a matter of rights or privileges and should not be addressed as such. The issue, as defined by Catholic Christianity, concerns primarily and essentially, procreation and sexual compatibility. Procreation stems from a profoundly distinct, mutually compatible biological-physiological make-up. This is evident in what we term simply as a difference in sexual make-up. Differences, simply defined, involve body structure, hormonal signals, physical strength and make-up and positioning of anatomy, all for the purpose of insuring continuity of the species. A sense of family and of belonging one to another, unique in complexities, has given rise to the various required disciplines expected from each participant. *Social characteristics are secondary* and involve elements, which concern cultural differences and civilization. The confluence of such elements has grown to become very complex. The number of people, on this earth, and how they have evolved to govern themselves makes the totality insurmountably complex for most. Love is the most stabilizing factor in this complex universally acknowledged totality.

knowing they will not be deserted; even, "unto death do us part," as in a sustained and exclusive conjugal friendship, that is marriage, Christian (eternally committed) forever! *The greatest compliment, which could be given to any individual is to give one's life, moment by moment, day by day, year by year and to love, honor and obey, till death shall part two beings.*

It is true of every sustained marriage, every army, and every significant group and of street gangs as well, all being affected by whether or not one individual can trust the other party in the agreement, the husband, the wife, the soldier, the cleric, or the gang member. Unfortunately, not everyone is able or willing to accept the same common understandings or the responsibilities, which are part of any form of intimate or close relationship, most especially spousal love. Spousal love involves the complete Being, emotionally as well as physically, all placed in parallel time, two beings following the same time space format. Of great significance is that, **within any human group, they are most respected who are (in fact) most trusted in reference to the secrets and intimacies, which are somehow shared.** All this is quite complex, however, not beyond understanding and, by this, is meant the understanding of most individuals involved in our present time-space construct. What is imagined/perceived as misunderstanding is very likely a consequence of a vain imposition, that is opportunism in action?

Language and the comprehension attendant thereto are also important factors, which hold individuals and nations together. Intelligence, comprehension and complexity of thought, as well as aspirations and various set goals, pertaining to *what is understood by the meaning of words,* is an important factor in any personal or intimate human relationship. Indeed, most industries, which deal in various products whereabouts some manner of style is a selling feature, are primary examples of the function of such understanding. All manner of fashion advertising depends upon the meaning of words. Actually, what has been heretofore phenomenal has become commonplace in this respect. Marketing managers are expected to make *profitable decisions* whereabouts is concerned the meaning of words as it affects sales totals and the bottom line.

Historically, style and form have been a matter of location, materials available and the development of rather simple hand processes. In the past, people were more localized and were not often likely to meet others from far away places. *Money functions well, in such circumstance, when what is being accomplished is fully understood by the participants of each and every transaction.* In the past, there were fewer things and/or objects to attract one's attention. In any event, what did attract one's attention was, most likely, useful and had evolved over an extended period of time, often in a local atmosphere. Thus the value of something was better understood in reference to why one would want it. Heretofore, the design of an implement was a process of becoming under the pressure of "truthful" need. Often, what was *embodied in an object* was a matter of real importance, possessing <u>*an inherent and known value and symbolism.*</u> Only recently have so many things been "consciously" *designed for the market*; so to speak.

Who might buy garments, or anything designed by Ralph Lifshitz. Contrarily Ralph Lauren is a rather pleasant sounding name, even noble. Importantly, because of the nature of mass-production, designers today may receive, or expect to receive large profits from their efforts. By profit is meant money and the things which money will buy. Brand names, limited editions and designer labels are examples of the exploitation of anxious millions, seeking some form of identity, for the benefit of a <u>*well-placed few.*</u> Great estates are, most likely, the Place where dwell the Few. Co-incidentally, the few are well positioned in the great cities and do contribute a bit however, they do benefit disproportionately from the system, which they exploit. Whereas our ancestors were very ingenious in developing their various implements (some of this is still apparent in a few products and objects), presently "designers" are rather very clever. However:

Clever is not goodness, nor is clever wise.
Certainly, clever is more often evil in disguise

One may or may not believe this, never the less, it should be considered. For millions it represents the truth. Importantly, various problems surface when we determine, by clever means, to hide the truth. This can be imagined, in many instances, as being a form of adultery. "Oh, what a terrible web we weave, when first we practice to deceive." (Shakespeare) Interestingly, regarding marketing, in general, many aliens change their names so as to conform to the names of a targeted population. This is a form of deception, providing a cover up [seemingly harmless], that has been successfully employed for several centuries. Genealogies are interesting, from this standpoint, since race, religion and place of origin are all part of a complex equation. Names can be deceiving; nevertheless racial and familial types are more certainly revealing of origin and complex tribal, racial and religious thinking.

Everyone's fortunes will vary. One day may be a bit better than others, even though all days are good somehow. *To simply live and be healthy is to be provided with the most important fundamental, as well as profound, good.* One's life is given in exchange for money. This is a profound manner of exchange and is precisely why integrity is so important regarding the value of the money. Importantly, integrity is a functional influence, primary and fundamental. This notion is especially well defined in respect to biology and the reproductive process. It is also obvious in that "as we sow, so shall we reap." It can be no other way. On the best days we succeed and accumulate beyond our needs. Any intelligent man would wish to retain some of what has been gained in good fortune, such against possible or certain adversity. However, we should not be greedy in our accumulation of treasure, nor should we want what is truthfully the possession of another. We may not "covet our neighbor's goods." Also, there is the concept of "noblesse oblige," when one imagines to be noble one is admonished to act that way. Truthfully founded, charity and generosity require a degree of nobility, even holiness, seated in one's character. Unfortunately, in a political sense, the word nobility has been maligned, especially in the scribbling of the Socialists, Pretenders, hypocritical Masons, Revolutionaries, Secret Societies and other malcontents. False words, spoken, or written by vain malcontents, schemers, or self-adoring romantics, combine with the musings and imaginations of the writers of fiction. Works of fiction, which are mostly misunderstood by a barely literate Population may be considered to have caused most of the world's problems.[3]

Nevertheless, Money should provide an ideal means to store what has been gained, until future need demands of one what has been stored. In an abstract sense, *money is an ideal containment for the value of one's past efforts, as a jug is to water taken previously from a well.* Most generally, what we value, as money is a product, traded for our being and for our doing, [somehow] and can or will equal our needs. All personal income and acquisitions happen in one's good time. *Ideally money, earned in past time, would be equal to the value demanded of a future need.* Thus each is equipped to provide for one's self. Inflation denies this fundamental need of the elderly; namely that the money accumulated by whatever means should not be devalued so as to support a corrupt and deceitful system.[4] Socialists, vain Politicians, puffed-up Demagogues, evil Tyrants and the somehow mentally confused Utopians all despise that one can provide for the self what is needed. Organizers hope to "convince" a group or population, thus are better able to control them, for personal gain.

---

3   In this respect, we consider *Fiction is a form of Propaganda,* the purpose of which is to alter truth, or create or arouse suspicion, obscure reality, defame an individual or group, gain acceptance of a [Lie] or encourage a form of aggressive or illegal action. Fictionalized history, as portrayed in multi-million dollar spectacles confuses all who are not truthfully informed. Most people cannot possible be well informed on many subjects and [at best] *think or imagine from a very limited understanding.*

4   **Inflation** is nothing more than theft. Having used one's energy, youth and vital life in exchange for lawful money, which ideally is a store of value, it is a profound Tragedy that governments choose to rob the elderly of what they have saved. Furthermore to deny that this is being done is a despicable hypocrisy.

The Catholic Church has always taught that every individual being is made in the image of *God the Father* and must be treated with dignity and respect, including the opportunity for gainful participation in human existence. Presently there is much misunderstanding concerning what is meant by gainful participation. Socialism, which is overtly compulsive, bureaucratic and dictatorial, forces full employment with no decent or lasting humanly sensitive solution. There are many deliberate attempts, on the part of some within and outside from the church, to confuse and divide one being from another. Our time, in history, is marked by insatiable greed and as has happen in the past, this will provide for our own undoing. For any good man, this is a most unfortunate situation since we do have, more than ever, the ability to help one and all. However, *when powerfully organized groups insist on having the most of everything, one can be certain that millions will continue to starve.* We do not recommend Socialism or Government intervention, rather we suggest honesty, integrity and adherence to Catholic Christian Virtue.

Presently, much of the Third World, so-called, is in an absolutely degraded position and will remain so. Free trade robs millions for the profiteering of unknown middlemen, providing some part of the tremendous wealth of the usurper, many of whom are hopelessly warped by a stultified insensitivity and complete disregard for their fellow man. The truth of the matter is absolutely beyond the comprehension of most everyone who has been "educated" (spelled indoctrinated) in our government controlled schools.

The way known to have worked in the past, is a truthfully inspired return to a belief in God, together with a fostering of a universal, understanding of brotherhood, meaning a Catholic, sensitivity and understanding. Is this even possible? Is it likely? Given present circumstance, wherein leaders are so easily corrupted and so inclined to avoid knowing the truth, it is unlikely that any meaningful changes will occur in the near future.

In any event, tomorrow will be the consequence of, what happens today!

(Arthur Schopenhauer, German Philosopher)
"All truth passes through three stages:
First it is ridiculed, Second it is violently opposed, and
Third it is accepted as self-evident."

VIII. One World Government

A monetary system, to be honest, demands that _responsibility and liability must be understood as being intimately related_, in any and all transactions. Economics has become an adversarial endeavor, we hear speak of economic warfare. As in any conflict, if one is to suffer or be killed it is only fair that they know who is perpetrating an injustice and why they have been victimized. If this notion/understanding were implemented we would have far fewer Victims. Indeed, very few citizens of the United States realize that the Capital Stock in their "privately controlled money system" hypocritically named the Federal Reserve System, is held mostly by foreign banks. Where New York banks are Participants, they have strong ties to foreign interest, thus forming an international Consortium. Consider that, _in large measure, the start up Capital for many Secret Adventures may be imagined to have originated with the money and treasures stolen from Czar Nicholas and from the Russian people. The Czar and his family were butchered,_ in the basement of the _building to which they had been taken for protection._[1] (_See Appendix B._)

Recent political dialogue has centered, to a very large extent, on the discussion of a One-World Government. This government, as proposed, will guarantee, for the foreseeable future, at least, that just a few individuals will be given to near-unimaginable luxury at the expense of most everyone else; especially those least able to defend themselves, the humble and the poor. This is simply unjust and is not right.

Douglas Reed and Eustice Mullins have documented the positions of some of the most wealthy, powerful and influential persons in the world. Without concern for others, they will certainly pass that same power and the wealth, which they control, into the hands of those whom they select, their family and others just like they are. Before any such positive endeavor, we do commend and respect all that will do truthful and just works. However, most will maintain their secret hold, by

---

1   Wilton, Robert, Ibid., _The Last of the Romanoffs_. Pg. 89.

means of a Central Bank; controlling that which, rightfully, in a Republic[2] like the United States of America, should be controlled by the people through their "elected" officials; such officials, presumably, being accountable to the sovereign individual. We assert that the sovereign being is every man and woman made in the image of One Omnipotent God, personified in the Son, Christ, and given to the working of the Holy Spirit, in time, everywhere and "especially" now.

"Seek and yea shall find; ask and it shall be given." The world has more than enough for all people. Money is simply that invention, by means of which, *men are able to trade fairly,* one with another. *One's feeling and acts, tempered thereby, are largely motivated by whether or not one has been treated fairly.* The term "rage" has, in recent memory, been used rather indiscriminately, however, one can certainly understand the rage men must be compelled to feel when they are cheated mercilessly, with little or no compassion and absolutely no respect for whom they are. The rage we witness in some Islamic nations is a product of frustration and a feeling of despair, for which America must accept some considerable responsibility. Additionally, young men *imagine they are Heroes,* when they sacrifice themselves in defense of a common cause. We assert that killing is wrong,

---

2   **Wardner, James, Ph. D.,** <u>*Communist Infiltration of the Catholic Church*</u>. Video. Produced by Most Holy Family Monastery. 4425 Schneider Road, Fillmore, New York. **The United States is actually a Masonic Republic,** which, in many higher spheres of influence, is especially adamant toward Catholicism. No one wants this to be made obvious by open and free discussion; nevertheless this is what is our Reality. However, we do consider ourselves to be a Christian Democracy, with justice and freedom for all, with just a few exceptions. Furthermore, all religions are to be considered *somehow* equal, which is, at best, an absurdity. And, the separation of a true and eternal Church (that one supporting the major intellectual thrust of the past twenty centuries), from the State (which should ensure the common good), causes all legality to be tainted. In effect, to a large extent, the Supreme Court (so-called) is a farce and a charade. This is true because what is lawful in a civil or criminal issue does have moral and ethical dimensions. Laws are hopelessly bound by conventions, which run counter to both truth and common sense. However, philosophers are few. And, in our State dominated Educational Institutions, excepting in rare instances, Catholic Christian Philosophy is not given much attention, excepting to be ridiculed, in respect to the more *progressive, dogmatically liberal, demonic, arcane and politically correct* dominant philosophies (so-called). The Philosophy of Saint Thomas, singularly concise in reference to right and wrong, precise in language and meaning, demanding of serious thought and not given to fashion or politically motivated nonsense, is avoided like leprosy. Eternity and forever are eliminated from consideration, excepting as depicted in make-believe entertainment, even though eternity is inclusive of all time. And, Sin is never mentioned, thus cannot be contemplated!

nevertheless it is wise to attempt to understand the cause for any such behavior. (*See Appendix C*)

Any intelligent individual can view the peoples of the world and immediately know that people are wonderfully diverse. Their personal identity is ethnic, or familial. They are distinct in their physical and biological make up, also in language, habits, manners and customs, to name the most obvious. As individuals they have traditions and preferences, which have been developed and acquired by their ancestors over long periods of time. Also, peoples are habituated to various climates and geographic conditions by virtue of their having been "born" to them. In a word they are indigenous; they belong where they are. Presently there are remaining about three hundred million [absolutely] indigenous or native peoples throughout the world. In addition, there are related groups, numbering in the hundreds of millions, which have grown (somehow) from various indigenous groups and tend toward one or another manner of being. Obviously an Eskimo is quite different than a Berber, in reference to wherefrom and whereto, however they are for "whom the bell tolls." However, what can an Eskimo do in Los Angeles or New York and still remain an Eskimo? Work at McDonalds?

One could imagine especially if one is a "planner" beholden to some particular philosophy, that all individuals might want to be the same. This of course is not true. Witness that, in the recent past ethnicity has become a major concern of many (perhaps most) of the minorities that live in the barrio, the ghetto or in cluster groups, which constitute today's complex populations. Importantly, every individual has a sense of and longing for home, there are few exceptions. Popular culture is riddled with the notion of going home, returning to a very special place and finding your roots, "I'll be home for Christmas" and (of course) there are millions who try to trace their ancestors. All this is telling us something. People are proud of whom they are, of whom they have been and shall be, witness the interest in education, learning and knowing, especially when considering the connotation of being (somehow) good or special. Some are proud of their blond hair, others of their blackness, others of their olive skin and the world does have room for all people. This understanding can be the catalyst for encouraging people to love and respect others. Or, distinctions can be manipulated so as to create animosities between ethnic groups. Right now we witness the promulgation of hatred toward Islam, antagonism between the people of Africa and subterfuge involving the migration of millions of aliens.

Because of the intervention of hypocrites that encourage the antagonisms, knowingly or unknowingly, all such animosities are not truthfully understood. Because of this one group is chosen or assumes to be the policemen, serving the establishment, in keeping control of other distinctly ethnic populations. All this transpires with little understanding of why. Why? *Familial animosity has been made apparent in Great Literature.* Or, circumstance can be contrived so as to become a tragic Reality

One world government will be totalitarian: as such, it must be so. It can be no other way. Millions will be forced to do what they do not want to do because someone, alien to them, imagines it is what they should be doing. A better solution would be partitioning and learning to tolerate difference. Everyone does not want to drive a new car. In the desert a camel might be just fine; it has been so for centuries. Animal rights activists should be more aware that many people, in the past, had great respect for animals. In the past, shared accommodations were quite ordinary and the animals helped with the work. This is especially notable in European Farmhouses of the past, also in Asia of the present and in igloos and various forms of the tent. Civilized people (so-called) might find this intolerable. With a few exceptions, dogs and cats, birds and reptiles are generally chosen as pets.

A *"People"* as for example *"we, the People"*, should be allowed to choose their own way, to develop meaningfully from where they are or, if they so choose, not at all.[3] What is the meaning of Democracy? We have been told and we believe, that the right for the individual to exercise their "God-given" free will is, generally speaking, what is the meaning of Democracy. Understandably, free will is not unbridled license. *Democracy implies that a people as well should have the freedom to continue as they have been, if they do so choose.* And emerging people should be allowed to settle their own differences, without the intervention of conflict engendered by they that pretend to help. To supply modern war materials to those, that cannot read an intelligent sentence is despicable and should be stopped. Change should, will and does emanate from Tradition, one way or another. Positive change for all people is based on understanding what works best in any pertinent *known and understood* situation.

The problem facing the world is seated in the supposition that advanced nations should exploit those less advanced, sooner rather than later. This introduces *a*

---

3   **Future time is infinite**, therefore it is not necessary to rush to the future. Such *"rushing"* generally speaking, benefits those who do not live within the community being imposed upon. This is an intricate and complicated issue, which begs for a fair-minded and decent understanding. Where a complex, advanced industrial society imposes upon an anciently conceived and established status quo, conversation and mere words are not able to make the necessary connections. Nevertheless, one can know there are economic benefits that will accrue to the stronger participant. Therefore a consensus, which demands mutual understanding, is not and cannot be easily reached. It may very well be impossible to reach peaceful consensus however, Time does provide for the necessary inputs as is apparent from the role of thoughtful, holy and truthfully meted contemplation.

profound-existential dilemma, when considering the nature of global endeavor. Different powers require different levels of subsistence however, the stronger power very likely will determine most of the consequences, this is the meaning of what is Imperial, even though a weaker power may be correct in their suppositions and opposition. And, it is possible, given peculiar circumstances, that the weaker may even have the best-structured *"thought form."* Indigenous people may decide to change in ways different from what is expected by the force in power. They may prefer their own terms, rather than respond (perhaps militantly) to the will of another. Nevertheless the Imperial force has the power and (presumably) better-suited means. Any aggressor imagines or presumes to be better able to guarantee "life, liberty and the pursuit of happiness." This is presumptuous and is a form of **Romanticized Socialism, which may be considered as "a species of Idolatry**, in which the State is the Godhead." (But, what does this mean?)[4] Or, they guarantee the annihilation of the weaker power from achieving their own gains. Selfish thinking, based on imperfect knowledge, has profound implications, which should not and cannot be easily ignored.

Our own native populations believe, perhaps somewhat correctly, that white Europeans cheated them, which for some may have been true. The wound is still open! What is considered by some, as progress, given a different point of view could be understood as exploitation. "What the neo-idealists have been tackling are the conditions in which history appears in our minds. This is a very important issue....But, here I am dealing with a simpler question: not how history is "made" by the historian but how the events of history are "made" by their participants. In other words, not how the "past" is spun out of our minds *post facto* but how the past is made by people into their own "present."[5] Here we face a complex paradigm involving the "Will to Power" as an **Idea,** which has been pondered, by many writers of distinction. However, most writing is bias and is formed from deliberate intent or *the will to power* of the writer.[6]

Mostly, whatever is done is done for money, the medium of exchange, and store of value, as insurance against future need. Much of what is deemed Socialism is just silly however, is imagined to be profound, even necessary. Marxist doctrine

4   **Wheeler, Richard S.,** *Pagans in the Pulpit.* Arlington House, New Rochelle, N. Y., © Richard Wheeler 1974. ISBN # 0-87000-264-3. Pg. 133.

5   **Lukacs, John,** *Historical Consciousness, or the rmembered past.* Harper Row, Publishers. New York, Evanston, and London. © 1978 by John Lukacs. LC # 67-28809. Pg. 153.

6   **A feeling of superiority,** accompanied with an overtly expressed will to power, derives directly from the personality of the individual. Thereafter others may and do learn to help in whatever aggressive endeavor may be formulated.

and Socialism generally has been taught with the certainty that water is wet or that ice is cold (Marx, Hitler, Freud, Nietsche, Marquis de Saade, Mao). Professors are found to be jumping up and down, over ideas that have been and are silly, dumb, retrogressive, vainly inspired and destructive, socially and politically. Nevertheless, to state an opinion has some merit, by this means we begin to understand what thinking is all about. One world government will leave most people totally dis-enfranchised for the benefit of a few who will lead. Men who lead us toward Totalitarianism will encourage that such *progress* is a certainty and these very same men are in control of much of the world's governance. They equate their bar-ren and half-witted ideas as defining and leading to the ultimate and necessary consequence of social evolution. We are not certain just what is meant by such *revolutionary imaginations* in this regard. We are certain that most such *miscreants* haven't a clue regarding the meaning of Holiness and fair participation. And, it is difficult for them to honestly understand the meaning of their tenacious, destruc-tive and presumptuous utterances.

Revolutionaries assume history will have a happy ending because of their vain participation. Many such Revolutionaries have fallen as Victims to the bullet and to the knife in the hands of those, of there own kind that harbor a similar form of madness. Such, if they survive and become leaders will work, whenever possible, toward the accumulation of greater wealth for themselves and the usurpation of ever more power. What the world fails to understand is that such "Revolutionaries" that appear from time to time work for those who, obviously or very secretly, con-trol them. The *vain fools are chosen to play a part* that the real social planners have chosen for them. If the real social planners succeed, humanity's testicles will be under an iron boot. Woe to the man when Satan steps down![7]

---

7   **Manifold, Deirdre,** *Karl Marx, a Prophet of our Times.* G. S. G. & Associates, Publishers. P. O. Box 6448, East View Station, Rancho Palos Verdes, CA 90734. ISBN # 0-945001-00-2, Pp. 11 & 13.

Beat it farmer, we're taking over

IX. Money, Property and Personality

Money is related to and may be *the reciprocal of property,* that is real property, as land and structures thereon. There are various Titles that determine ownership of land. There is a Color of Title, most common however, is not a clear title. Until you obtain the "Land Patent" and bring the "Allodial Title" *forward in your name,* you are merely making payments on "public property" as opposed to "private property." The King does not pay taxes. Are you the King in your home? It is understood, by some that your home belongs to the government. *This is a subject that the reader should most certainly investigate.*

Property rights are of the most valuable rights. It is important, therefore that, within an economy, trades involving money and things are fair trades. Each element in the trade must have a known and real value. Inflation coupled with depressions make the value of something difficult to determine and we are reminded that things are relative. (?).

What exactly is meant by this is difficult to determine. The thing or item has a tangible value, which may include a functional factor. Money too must have a tangible value, however is of no use other than as a medium of exchange. One can imagine that ideally money is a store equal to a thing, which is of use. *The imposition of bogus wealth, given a real denomination, is destroying the system and cannot be tolerated forever* (Lindon LaRouche). The Catholic position, documented over nearly two thousand years, is that money and property rights are second only to life itself. The value and quality of one's life, both as regards the individual as well as those related to him (child, wife, mother, father, friend), is directly influenced by a man's possessions (money is a possession), and is a means of survival, from one's own efforts; all in this world.

This principal is very easy to understand. The question for many however, is not a question of understanding, but rather is centered on a **Will to Power** and becomes as a Religion.[1] Those most affluent, generally speaking are not willing to give up their position. Notwithstanding, some are generous, often for personal reasons however, they do make token commitments. Certainly, there are some very decent, reliable and trustworthy amongst the wealthy, however it does appear they are a minority. Much, perhaps most philanthropy, has an element of self-interest, which is vanity. And, those receiving billions from the system, which they do exploit, can afford to give a few million away.

The best way for anyone to begin, of course, is to not steal from another. One of the Ten commandments from God is that "Thou shall not covet your neighbor's goods". And, "Thou shall not covet thy neighbor's goods, or his cattle, or his wife". Nevertheless, many individuals presently find themselves in a position of being privileged thieves. Certainly, those guilty would not admit this. Many more would not will to understand. Most who are conspicuously wealthy believe, probably erroneously, that they are somehow smarter than the rest of humanity. Are they? Perhaps yes, perhaps no! Those who inherit are not necessarily more intelligent, they are certainly privileged and have many advantages that a poor man would never have: they have problems as well. For many that become truly wealthy it is as a consequence of phenomenal opportunity within their understanding, especially so in reference to trading paper assets, which can be traded for tangibles. Often they benefit from privileged information and a bit of subterfuge.

Honesty must be encouraged, in the home and in the community. And, there should be some reward for honest behavior. If everyone were honest, all would be rewarded, immeasurably. Jurisprudence and the laws, which derive therefrom, should be more mindful of truth and the effects of dishonest behavior on our Culture and our Civilization. Ours is a perfect example, declining as it is, with little resistance from the law. Police departments, as presently functioning, are presumed to be an obvious defense against lawlessness. They must do what they do because the civilization and culture are under a constant attack from the wrong Ideologies, which too often represent the interests of evil over goodness. Individual behavior is influenced by too many bad examples, made conspicuous by mass media programming.

---

1   **Ultimately** Socialism, Communism, Utilitarianism and Futurism evolve to being religious in nature. All assume a form of religious nature, have a church, have some manner of vestment, chant slogans, preside over legal inquisitions, engage in ritual and presume to be especially concerned for the welfare of the Community. As such they seek converts and may, by legal means and intimidation force conversions. Their hope is inclusive of all the living, seeking to control every situation, from any moment forward.

Goodness stands silently and wins no prize
By most abhorred, goodness is its own reward.
Why is this so?

Many notable individuals, though well meaning and occupying positions of importance, remain silent as malfeasance and corruption are encouraged. And, the average person is easily deceived by false promise of some imagined advantage, often at considerable expense for the individual life made less because of it.[2] This includes all manner of propaganda deemed appropriate during war.

One can imagine that soldiers, *presumed to be an enemy,* have parents and sweethearts, wives, and children and *that they too will be missed when killed for no good reason!* Confusing any issue is the chatter of reporters heard on the airways and, of course, cleverly written editorials, which omit much (if not all) of the truth. Such *acceptable news* is delivered by *well appearing Pimps,* some that make millions for their efforts. They become celebrities for reading what they have been given to read. News stories, not incidentally, are considered by some as the absolute truth, by others as a form of intellectually questionable entertainment and diversion. The whole truth, especially concerning political and monetary issues, will almost never emerge from the newsroom and certainly never be given to mass distribution.

The beneficiaries of deceit, notably those in government, however, those in banking, media, and production as well, are able to gain control of extraordinary numbers of properties for their own use and that of their family and friends.[3] This is exacerbated by the great corporations (great in size, however, not fine in manner nor truthful as regards their devious scams), which exist as a legal entity that protects theft by means of the law. The *rule of Law* does not guarantee that all laws will be morally good and decently conceived, especially when *the Law, in many*

---

2   **We wonder** how many of those, who knowingly are standing by in silence, do so because they have been intimidated or threatened, thus they are *encouraged* to not "spill the beans"? Furthermore, we wonder, how many, who represent the people, have taken a secret oath, which might prevent them from doing what the population expects should be done. In plain words: how many of our elected officials are Traitors? Several very important ones come to mind including Presidents Wilson, Roosevelt, Truman, Nixon, Clinton and the Bushes. We accuse them of such because not one of them has made a move to abolish the Federal Reserve System or has any one of them done anything to defend our nation against a take-over by an imposing, illegally conceived and presumptuous United Nations. The United Nations represent the moneyed interests of this world that aspires to control all, even as they hope to steal from most all of humanity that which is a birthright.

3   **Lundberg, Ferdinand, Ibid.,** Chapter VIII, Pp. 327-387.

instances, may be (in fact is) structured (contrived) by clever thieves, importuned liars and vain hypocrites. The ownership of farmland, apartment complexes and office space is certainly very lopsided here and elsewhere. Where ownership is in the hands of a common man it is most often mortgaged (to the hilt) to cover current expenses and places a call upon future income. Recently individuals have been encouraged to refinance their homes so as to have more funny money to spend for that which is made on another continent. We give our wealth to others as we acquire much of what we do not need. How smart is this?

What is imagined as a legitimate form of property rights, is driven by the wrong social philosophy. Where the multitude is concerned, in terms of the Catholic ethic, giving control to an unknown interest is wrong, to be sure. We admit intelligence and ambition must be considered and that some will out per-form others, in the acquisition of properties. Nevertheless, common sense dictates that we reconsider what we are doing and try to better deal with this exasperating dilemma.

Of special concern are corporations, which control the communications indus-tries, television, radio, movies, newspapers, and magazines. They also control the minds and thoughts of populations. Very often, such as exists is in a manner of a monopoly or cartel, this especially true where money and finance are concerned.[4] Much has been written about this and it is not our intention to deal with any extensive arguments. It is important to understand, however, that what is being promoted in the mass media (as it is called) is to the financial benefit of they whom most do not know. *The purveyors of news urgently communicated for effect encroach upon the mind content of our civilization.* A steady and relentless stream of information, most very carefully screened and controlled, is aimed at all seg-ments of our population. This is a form of brain washing! Furthermore, as enter-tainment and amusement, *many perverse and unwholesome ideas are being projected upon the population,* many of whom are barely literate and understand very little of what is happening to them. They are being *indoctrinated* to accept that which is being planned for them even as they are being *desensitized with entertainment, the noise of a mob, the false excitement of the athletic spectacle and the blatant display of perverse obscenity, imagined as somehow humorous.* Sin is protected by corrupt law, emboldened with pretense, and given new and different names, so as to encourage acceptance.

Tragically, many of the top earners in our nation are comedians, pop-culture idols, sluttish women, bad actors, athletes and various celebrities who, generally speaking, cannot be considered wise. Some, they admit, are driven by Satan and *enamoured* by evil, *possessed* by demons and *beholden* to darkness. They are

---

4 **McMasters,** *The Reaper, Newsletter*

arrogantly boastful, often informing the rest of us of the millions they lavish on their own properties. Architectural Digest, the magazine, provides a random selection of opulence and excessive living that would embarrass a Sultan. No cost is spared, in decorating the bedroom for a whore! Often the "movers and shakers" boast of having little or no education and (as practitioners) they are not inclined toward significant learning. Often their manners and dress are vulgar and pretentious and many are boastful showoffs besides. There may be some exceptions; however, one might have difficulty in locating them.[5]

Ignorance has a too prominent place in the scheme of things. Because Sin sells, this has become an emotionally charged economic issue as well as one involving *merely* intellect. The Idea behind what we have as money is part of the Intellect, having grown in time as Tradition. The symbols vary from place to place and from time to time, however the Idea remains as fundamental to the exchange of goods and services. *Wisdom, gained from experience and certain knowledge, has been eclipsed by well financed ignorance.* Lust and Greed are very profitable, curiously they are not only sins practiced of ignorance. Intelligent men, even some *seemingly wise men* are corrupted by sins of the flesh, especially the flesh of youthful vitality.

The pornography industry flourishes as a gigantic commercial enterprise, even as it corrupts the participants in a sordid and humiliating affair. Sodomy is considered as a right, protected by law. Pornography is as a giant rotting rat, stinking up the entire Civilization.[6] Grown men, are taught by savages and fall victim to

---

5   **When self-acclaimed fornicators** are paid millions for just about nothing, this does have some impact on what money is and who has it and, of course, why? Thus, in such circumstances, money is made cheap. Then, who will work for it? The _Good Man's Way to Riches_ is not appealing to a thief, a braggart or someone on welfare. Work, in the past, provided for an honest means of acquiring property, even as it added to a feeling of well being. Why work when playing games, jumping up and down, screaming with serious amplification, displaying one's tits and ass, together with the rotten joke and the use of foul-mouthed innuendo pays so well? Any vain and sensuous idiot can succeed at a task requiring an idiot, unfortunately such as is being promoted for profit does influence all others.

6   **Pornography** refers to what is sluttish and profane and should be considered truthfully for what it really is. **The slut** is simple-minded and aggressive in the display of body parts, which normally are decently and discreetly clothed. **The Reprobate** is reprehensible, not particularly adult, inclined toward voyeurism and enjoys corrupting others, especially young women inclined toward promiscuity. **The young women** are enticed with money, imagined necessary so as to enhance their (often-imagined) personal beauty. Once entrapped, the young woman is quite unable to defend her person and falls victim, to **mindless and erotically vain gestures of savagely ignorant**

a sinful and disgusting anxiety, centered on the body of a young and beautiful woman, especially are they interested in the crotch and mouth. Sucking and performing has replaced what was romantic love and devotion between a good man and a good woman, mother and wife. Anxious viewers of pornography are corrupted as well, who are expended however remain unsatisfied.

If one could remove all the blatant sin, which is the hallmark of the pornographer, the pimp, the vile opportunist and the perverted idiot the economy would certainly suffer. We pose a question. What *kind* of economy do we prefer, one that supports those who are good, decent, kind, moral and giving or one that supports those who are evil, sluttish, indecent, immoral and are thieves, especially considering that they deprive the young of an innocent and uncorrupted childhood? Also they have near completely destroyed the mystique of womanhood and have encouraged woman to assist them in destroying the family, the community, the culture and the civilization. Individually, we make our own choices and will be responsible for any consequence.

> *Silly man, with itching gonads,*
> *Stupid, banal glee, your prick a stick*
> *Sing to your mother, in concert with a flea*

---

and vainly perverted manhood. Admittedly, a beautiful woman is a delight to behold however, there are known limitations concerning the display of what is simply perverse and obscene and no decent woman would wish to be so considered. There are also limitations concerning how one is to be abused for the pleasure of an idiot, a fool and a moron. Pathologies do surface, under the rhetoric of freedom of choice, which are difficult to understand nevertheless, as such (a form of mental illness) they should not be encouraged. To encourage what is a perversion has no social value and, when given to mass communication, lewd magazines and the Internet, such vice will ultimately corrupt millions. If some individuals enjoy viewing and becoming involved in what is indecent, vulgar, vain and anti-social, this should be considered for what it is. And individuals so inclined should be shamed, avoided if possible. They, who are lewd and perverse, should act out their perverted fantasies, with like-minded individuals, without corrupting others. Such behavior should not be legally sanctioned or allowed to corrupt the mind and soul of an entire Civilization. We admit, in such instances, where aggressive behavior patterns dominate, "curiosity **will kill** the cat."

Consenting Adults

Pugh left her

X. Property Rights & Inflation

To repeat, property rights are of primary significance. Property, as it is, should be more fairly shared. Since, some are more capable than others it is necessary to be truthful and not take advantage of one, that is not well-schooled in business. To cheat someone may seem clever however, is never wise and is certainly unfair. Those who are clever, well financed and/or simply greedy must not take unfair advantage of those, who are less adept. *We must consider and respect all others.* The "least of our brothers" actually require the most of virtuous men. Admittedly, there are millions of good and decent people. It is they who are exploited by a few others with less character that have a fanatical need to be superior. At times, government intervention attempts to address this need, however, without much personal sensitivity and with too little regard for the individual, victimized by the Bureaucracy. _Important governmentally sponsored Social Programs_ addressing property rights are, more often than not, carefully structured and can be manipulated to the advantage of the well-placed and clever few. Sound and honest money and the use thereof, would go a long way toward making fairness, which is now only an ideal, into a very real possibility. By this means, *good men could more reasonably benefit from the fruits of their labors.* To be great, a nation must correct injustice, criminal theft and government sponsored sin of all kinds. Admittedly, first we must define sin in absolute terms, which in some instances would be easy, whereas in other instances might be quite difficult.

In the modern world, and especially in the United States of America (a free nation, we are told), one is given to believe they have "title" to what they have acquired by means of personal effort. However, too often, there are many conditions, which are arbitrarily imposed on such title, for political and economic reasons. One of the most onerous conditions, which has been already considered, is that billions are extorted from citizens, as taxes on their homes and businesses, to pay for public education, which millions do not need or want and from which they cannot or will not derive much positive benefit.[1] We concede there are some areas, given a dedicated and intelligently informed teacher, where truthful learning does occur.[2] Such can be observed mostly in the lower grades or in classes the subject matter of which is reasonably objective, Mathematics and the Sciences.[3]In most instances it is difficult to determine whether what children are learning is a product of schooling or other influences such as television, family circumstances and the child's curiosity' which motivates how children spend their own free time.

Certainly, regarding ownership, there are some conditions fairly imposed; for example, the asset must be paid for within a designated time period. Title cedes a form of ownership and the owner, as such, should be given to all of the benefits, which derive therefrom. In many instances, because of the deflation/inflation syndrome, this is not the case. The inflation/deflation syndrome obfuscates the meaning and value of ownership, placing too much emphasis on the efficacy of time and fluctuating money values. To repeat, this often makes it impossible to determine the "truthful" value of ownership. Unfortunately, a depreciating currency, factored against the cost of a home, makes it appear as though all, that own a home, are becoming wealthy, which is certainly not the case. Some things are improving however, this is in spite of all the illegal, secret, greed—inspired and clever manipulation.

---

1   **Blumenfeld, Samuel. L.,** *Is Public Education Necessary?* Brilliant Revisionist History, Fortune Magazine. Public Education is a cleverly formed attempt to indoctrinate a reticent population, causing them to submit to a brutal attack on their psyche and, ultimately, corrupt their soul. Public Education is in competition with making believe, as propagated in Hollywood and on the Television Stations, as all attempts to please and attract the attention of the children. Without any question, advertising and foul-mouthed drama do more to *teach the little ones* than any other force on the planet. Thus, we need better attend to the requirements of the mind, in the acquisition of truthful and productive knowledge, which includes education in matters of economic importance.

2   **Youth does learn** something within a fraudulently structured educational system however; this is because there are many wonderful teachers within the system, who function well in spite of serious limitations. Nevertheless, privately sponsored and more honestly structured programs are what are needed. To some extent this does exist at the present time. **And,** there should be much less emphasis placed on athletics, which should be set apart from serious learning. Athletic activities should be extra curricular, separated from formal education, for fun and genuinely motivated sport.

3   **Our magnificent Technologies** obviate this for all to see. How we apply what we have brings other subject matter to our attention, especially concerning issues involving politics, morality, psychology and the social sciences.

When speculation becomes the dominating influence, upsetting the under-stood and reasonable value of various commodities and real property, which is exactly what has happened, it is impossible to make intelligent choices. Commerce has become a dog eat dog situation. The recent inflation, in the United States, is a prime example of what speculation can do to a once powerful, stable economy. Certainly Argentina, other countries as well, have had a more devastating experi-ence than the United States however, we will get to the same position, sooner or later.[4] For millions, the price of a house has risen to levels, which make it (almost) impossible, given the salaries earned by most citizens, to save the necessary down payment.[5] Furthermore, the payments are beyond the reach of large segments of the population.[6] This translates into the need for each household to have two, rather than one income. The absence of a mother in the home has caused an entire

---

4   Davidson, James, _Vantage Point, Newsletter._ July 2003 Issue. Pp. 3-5.

5   **Single family homes** in California, which were built for perhaps six to eight thousand dollars, in the late forties are currently selling in the half-million dollar range. There are many factors involved however, the deliberate government program to depreciate our currency tops the list.

6   **Low interest rates,** function to drive prices up, as families assume twice the liability, with about the same monthly payment. Few occupy a dwelling for a long enough period to pay for the asset. Inflation gives them cash, which in turn is invested against a greater liability. The automobile is especially prone to depreciation thus, an infla-tionary incremental gain will be consumed, by a depreciating automobile. In the long term, inflation will do little good [_economically_] for the average working man and his family. Certainly, for most families, more money is lost to the depreciating auto-mobile than to any other asset. In fact, with careful and prudent management, what is lost by youth, in the purchase and depreciation of a new automobile, if invested wisely, would guarantee a substantial nest egg at retirement. However, the young are impatient and imagine they derive an enhanced self-image from an automobile. But they have fun, _remaining poor, perpetually in debt to an unknown other_. Consequently, what seemed necessary in youth places one in debt for life.

Ultimately the banks _gather all the mortgage liabilities placed against real estate_ into giant holding companies. Thus, most individual families support a liability without ever having clear Title to, or income from, the property. Families are encouraged to move frequently, so as to improve upon their social standing, however this notion denies tradition and has resulted in creating a population of nomads. Furthermore, during the first seven years, very little is paid on the principal sum of a thirty-year mortgage. Interestingly, those who sell real estate encourage moving to a new resi-dence every seven years. The traditional understanding of a home, that being a per-manent place, to be improved as circumstance allows, has given way to _a series of adventures_ in real estate speculation. This favors developers and sales persons even as it destroys the sense of contentment that was found in a permanent, lasting and

generation of children to be without the required maternal love and guidance, when it is most needed. Much of gang violence and other children's problems can be directly traced to this cause. Inflation encourages speculation and causes a too high value being placed on housing, the place "to be or not to be". Also, all values are warped by the *notional value* of the building. In fact this value (so-called) does not exist as imagined by most homeowners. All value is *"somewhat"* relative and, while most do not understand what is happening, most all will suffer. The paradigm is given to greater complexity when housing values become as collateral, to pay for depreciating Chattels and consumer goods, which in short order may become near worthless. Or, moneys so acquired are expended to finance questionable speculation. Such speculation pays for commissions and charges, which make others rich, even as the principle may be lost in a transaction.

The right to legal and secure ownership of what is truthfully one's own is, more and more, being threatened by inept and devious politicians, eager and deceitful professional Businessmen and by appointed bureaucrats. All this, seemingly happening by chance has been cleverly orchestrated, devised and carefully imposed upon an inattentive and distracted population.

The Catholic point of view asserts that, <u>free men should have proper "title" and an inviolate ownership of what is truthfully theirs;</u> that which their person has caused to become, by means of their own and known effort. *(See Chapter IX, paragraph 1)* Simple; isn't it? "…For St. Thomas money is meant to be the servant of Politics and Economics." The act of manipulating money or exchange-medium should not have been allowed to fall uncontrolled into the hands of private individuals, as they will be tempted to work for instability of price levels, in view of their own gain. *A fortiori,* **the rulers of the State must see to it that the manipulators of money do not get control of the government."**[7] We have not heeded this advice!

---

meaningful place to be; namely home. And, be it ever so humble, there is no place like home.

7   **Fahey, Dennis, Rev., C. S. Sp.,** <u>*Money Manipulation and the Social Order.*</u> Christian Book Club of America. P. O. Box 900566 Palmdale, CA 93590. Pg. 12.

XI. Money, Culture, Civilization

Beyond economics and the discussion of money as a commodity and as a means to facilitate and enhance the exchange of goods and services, there are greater questions, regarding Language, Fine Art, Music, Architecture and generally, Culture and Civilization. As evil and sin violate the practice of fairness, in the exchange of goods, any individual, a victim of such affected transaction will be despoiled, both in their property and perhaps, more importantly, in their humanness. They may become angry, defensive and possibly destitute.[1] This describes the present state of uncounted millions of beings, all over the world. Such beings, when armed and given any hope, what so ever, will form the chanting mob that will pull all that is noble into the furnace of ignorant and vitriolic revolution. One need only to read Nesta Webster's book on the French Revolution and/or World Revolution to

---

1   **Such human Anger,** is *imagined to be caused* by Religion. Religion, especially the universally Christian Catholic Religion has been accused of being the cause of much conflict. The Church militant does fight for what is right, for what is good for all human beings, paying special attention to what is important, in the light of eternity. The Church continues to feed, to clothe and to care for the children of all nations, unselfishly and devotedly. The Church did *crusade* to defend Christianity against they who would have annihilated all Catholics, to the man. And, there are those who would do that at this moment, if such were possible. If the Church had not defended the Culture, who might have done so? Most in the West would not and could not have enjoyed the prosperity and freedom, which has emanated therefrom. And, the *Inquisition* has been misunderstood, editorialized by the enemies of Christ. There are good reasons why one might react when the threat to one's being is a mortal threat. Shall Catholics be accused of brutality for having fought to defend what we believe, against those that would slay us for our beliefs? Movie productions can be masterful examples of confusion, deliberately engendered, where sensitive issues are involved. Furthermore, all gruesome events have been given to romanticism and story telling, so as to sell books and tickets. Just check out the newsstand, the theatre and the shops featuring the Occult. *In fact, most conflict is caused by political turmoil, generated to gain economic advantage, for they who devise the manner of conflict whilst presuming another is to blame.*

be given a reasonable understanding of what has happened and may, most prob-ably will, happen again.[2] Human nature is what it is, because of one or another motivation and because some hope to dominate their fellow man, wary of such domination.

The intent, together with the objective, toward which any act is perpetrated, as well as for what purpose materials are used, is of vital importance to why anyone does anything at all. What is considered a work of art or culture is no exception. Indeed, such entities embody the very unique and special sensitivities of individu-als. An active response, or reaction, to what is, may be simply an attempt to carry forward in time a cultural heritage. Any significant work of Art or Architecture reaches toward the future as an embodiment, which inveighs in future time upon other individual sensitivities. *The unborn, in a near or distant future, will be beneficiaries or victims of what is done in present time.* In all instances, what is, is a product of and consequence of some individual being. We acknowledge [imag-ine or presume] we are made in the image of God the Father, Omnipotent, All-knowing. Also we acknowledge that Lucifer has followers of his own, fallen and in danger of eternal damnation. The struggle between good and evil is a struggle between Christ and Lucifer, between God and Satan. Individually we accept or reject one Idea/notion/belief, about what is. How and why an Idea is implanted within one's mind has great effect on what one will and will not do and is precisely why a decently Christian education is so critical.[3] This must be understood if mankind is to improve upon what, at present, bodes ominous for millions.

When one is confused in respect to intent and/or is not certain of a desired objective, any activity will become to appear as a waste of time and effort. Furthermore, it is also a waste of the materials involved, which have been expended

---

2   **Webster, Nesta,** *World Revolution, the Plot Against Civilization.* Veritas Publishing Company, 7th Ed.., 1994, Cranbrook, Western Australia 6321.

3   **Separation of Church and State** has done much to destroy the continuity and struc-ture, of our once Christian Nation, Culture and Western Civilization. An alien inten-tion has superceded much of the good that was being accomplished. *The **idea** of a melting Pot will be the undoing of what had been accomplished over the course of two hundred years.* Equilibrium will be found only where there exists a reasonably under-stood sense of belonging to one group or another. As soon as there becomes large-scale differences there is a natural tendency to become fragmented and to polarize. This has happened in the past and will happen in the future. Habits manners and customs, including religious customs, are the glue that will hold a people together, without which there is certain to be conflict, as we see presently between Islam and a faction of Christianity motivated by an alien money power determined to rule the world. Similar religious convictions create a sense of oneness within the social body, hence the Ghetto, Commune, Compound, Family, Tribe and Nation.

unreasonably.[4] Many are engaged in what is a vain pretense or are confusedly involved in some manner of self-administered therapy, which includes the assuaging of Vanity, by means of the acquisition of things. The situation is obscured by the fact that so many amongst us are doing the same meaningless things uncertain in their intent, confused as to objectives (why) and obviously wasteful in their consumption. Many amongst our numbers have lost completely, or nearly so, all manner of common sense. *Common sense works in concert with an accumulation of the Intellect, carried forward in time as Tradition.*[5]

Consider when accolades are given to silliness and ignorance, those who seek to become wise, are ignored in their effort. We imagine, among other things, that some amongst us are lucky, rewarded obviously, far in excess of what might be appropriate. All of this is a manner of improper or inappropriate motivation for others whilst it corrupts the understanding of nearly everyone. And, of course, it devalues the work of those who struggle just to live. *The path is short between stupid admiration and soul-felt envy.*

Vanity, or self-centeredness, is one of the qualities which education encourages when it panders to the importance of ignorant subjectivity. At the same time, objective learning (which should be stressed) is, in many instances, omitted and may even be set up for ridicule. Objectivity may be labeled as dogmatic, inflexible or old-fashioned. Concerning the meaning of money and value, this is a near fatal tragedy.

---

4   **Much, perhaps most in some cases,** of what we pretend is educational is defined by what is here stated, a waste of time, effort and materials. This is true because secret motives influence what are *named behavioral modification, Values clarification and outcome based education.* Unknown others benefit from the promotion of collective ignorance and the confusion generated by meaningless information. This author bears witness to the fact that in a University, one faculty member eager to teach *her course*, declared that "it must be taught now; next year the information will be worthless". And there does exist treason, hypocrisy and the lie!

5   **Tradition** is an enigmatic accumulation, peculiar to time/space and placement, having familial and historic continuity. Implements, materials, methods and modes of existence are specific to the time/space placement phenomenon, as is the level of language, which imposes limitations on what can and will be communicated. Language and the meaning of words are what are most important to serious study. Writing is what has made possible the development of Tradition beyond story-telling and verbally communicated mythology. Written history conveys opinion seated in reality, with evidence of the writer's imposition, attitude and understanding, which may or may not be correct, and is what obviates the essential aspects of one's peculiar existence as part of a greater tradition.

Interestingly, what one may be seeking or pretending to seek is directly related to whom one is and to what ideology one is committed. This is precisely how practitioners beholden to their master extend thoughts in time. Great traditions in philosophy, architecture, painting and other plastic and thought forms share in the _phenomenal nature of humanly structured extension: **there are no exceptions.**_ Every individual is beholden to a part of what has been accomplished before their brief personal existence.[6] It can be no other way. The past represents what has been truthfully accomplished. Count on this, **Reality will accommodate what is wise, stupid, honest or deceitful, with certain consequences to follow.** History contains all that has been and is, broadened as it is articulated and intensified day by day.

Civilization, culture, nations, tribes and families become, as they do, because they may or perhaps may not, share common interests as well as objectives. And, all use materials and resources, wisely or foolishly, in the process. That which is somehow a profound symbol of their being (in a particularized sense) remains as a sign of their having existed and their having become somehow special. Archeologists attempt to understand from what is left for observation. We may call the physical remains art, certainly we consider the best as such. Some groups build wonderful churches filled with all the delights of an intelligent sensitive being, others are wanton to destroy, rape, and pillage or to amuse themselves endlessly with various forms of titillation, not the least important of which is fornication and voyeurism. *History is full of examples of the vanquished being pillaged and raped by the proud and vain Victor.* A beautiful work of art, together with a comprehensively written Literature and Philosophy, will form as a high and noble Civilization. The cravings of a Savage and the psychology of a mob provide an interesting contrast. We understand what has been as the unfolding of events, which we study as history. Great Russian or European Art is the work of great and positively fruitful human intelligence, imagination and sustained abilities. Those who would tear this down are of a very different nature.[7]

---

6   **The nature of tradition** is and can be altered by the exclusion or alteration of prime symbols. Modernism tends to simplify and thus to destroy significant meaning. Catholicism and Christianity are being eclipsed by what is meaningless, primitive, banal, decorative or mundane.

7   **Wilton, Robert,** _The Last of the Romanoffs, How Czar Nicholas II and Russia's Imperial Family were Murdered._ Copyright © 1993. The Institute for Historical Review. ISBN # 0-9394-1. First British Edition, pub. 1920 in London by T. Butterworth. First U. S. Edition published 1920, in New York by George H. Dorn. French Edition, pub. Paris 1921. Russian language Edition, pub. Berlin 1923. Chapter II. Pp. 22-29.

Within a complex civilization there will be confusion, which will distract from common instinct and corrupt the workings of the mind. Unless one is able to understand the relationship between cause and consequence, past errors will be repeated and intensified because of an inappropriate use of Technology. War is a glaring example of misused technology.

What is called "common sense", perhaps not so common at the present time, 2006, is that sense, which has been tested over time by and within the workings of reality. *Reality, as it unfolds, provides the conclusive and ultimate source of information for conscious being.* Importantly, not to be overlooked, millions of individuals have considered human being as being, in some manner, a reflection of Supernatural Being; that is a being made in the image of God, the Father. Presently, many (perhaps most) individuals disparage the idea of God the Father, or they have an unreasoned idea of what this means? Nevertheless, God (as is imagined by Catholicism), is the Progenitor of the Universe, "of all that is seen and unseen". Man has most Problems with what is not seen.[8] Many have been taught and encouraged, by those who wish to "*direct*" them toward opposing beliefs, to deny the Trinity, God the Father, Christ the Son of God and the Holy Spirit. *The Directors are individuals that imagine they are the center of all. Such is personal vanity or self-centeredness carried to the extreme.* Such vanity is, in large measure, the consequence of a complete misunderstanding of what is meant by equality. Men and women are only equal in the eyes of an Omnipotent God which, interestingly, many (perhaps most) of the assertively equal do not accept; even as a Possibility. The assertion of equality in the eyes of an Omnipotent Being is a Catholic concept, being so because it is universally applicable, all-inclusive and is neither vain nor presumptuous. Christ, Son of God, to understand and respect what is true, admonishes us. We are admonished to love one another, even as He has loved us, each and all. This is a very important point to consider.

Without love for one another, coupled with actions and works, which obviate our nature and understanding of Reality, we, as individuals, will never succeed. Never! The consequence of man's failures are too numerous to list, however, should be obvious to any sane man, and any sane man should take heed. Avoid all manner and form of sinful activity, <u>*especially the Cardinal Sins*</u> and various forms of war, which exemplifies the ultimate disrespect for "the Creator of All that is seen and unseen". In a sociological sense especially lust and illicit sexual

---

8   **What is Unseen** gives rise to the imagination. Religion and Philosophy are confused, in the minds of millions, by the scribbling of men, who possess only imperfect Knowledge however, they do influence others. This confusion can be addressed as it is obviated in light of Tradition, which affords an historical and reasonably accurate approach to learning and knowing.

misconduct, are the origins of almost all-serious personal and social problems. *The Bastard Child is spawned by an unwillingness of the father and mother to love one another, truthfully and eternally.* The disrespect that men and women have for each other *formulates as an economically destructive burden on the community of good men.*[9] Some *merely use others* for pleasure without reservation, irresponsibly in respect to what may become as a consequence of a profound physical union: another child, a human being with body and soul. Not to forget, we assert that man's noble and decent achievements must be held in high regard. Such achievements must be viewed with admiration, appreciated for being the best possible of what men have done.

Our American Culture of the twentieth century, which is in some ways, no doubt, positively brilliant is, *at present* the most pervasive force on the Planet. Nevertheless, we have done more, in many ways, to dull healthy common instinct and to corrupt the natural and decent functions of the human mind than any other force of destiny known to man. All this in spite of the fact that there have been many wonderfully good, decent and productive human accomplishments, which are a benefit to millions. And, *America has been and is a wonderful place to live, however not all agree on why this is so.* We are a blessed nation and should be mindful of such blessings, which have profound economic and social consequence, which millions have enjoyed in abundance.

However, *what exists in fact, at the present time, in many respects, is a monumental hypocrisy;* from top to bottom; from the boardroom to the bedroom, from kindergarten to the grave. Our nation is in many ways an exemplification of a shallow, showy, venal, and corrupt pretense on a monumental scale, in spite of the good intentions of distracted millions. To list the manner and form of distraction, which we have encouraged and, which is made possible by the scale and confusion of our too large cities would fill a volume. Actually this has been done.[10] It is not intended to elaborate on this just now, that such has been done in numerous other places.

There are many reasons for this having happened, some of which we are certain, others unknown that will remain unknown. There is the boastful prattling of experts, specialists, men of particular expertise, men with just the politically correct understanding, men who say what a fool wishes to hear, men who have

---

9   **Abandoned and abused Children,** many born out of wedlock, are a consequence of sinful excess. Men who defend sinfully destructive notions and activities find the truth very difficult to accept. Indeed, many who do wrong deny adamantly that what they do is wrong and consenting adult laws place a corrupt legality on their side.

10   **Pius X, Pope** *The Encyclical Quanta Cura and the Syllabus of Errors.* Issued in 1864. Reprinted by the Remnant, 2539 Morrison Avenue, St. Paul, MN 55117.

corrupted common sense with much useless learning and men with little under-standing of what words mean. This same cadre, as listed above, is busy working, in their own narrow self-interested ways, toward unknown goals for secretly held reasons. Therefore, the goals and reasons of this, often self-anointed Phalanx are not well understood by millions within the general population, which does not and perhaps could not understand anyway. Nevertheless, these same millions are the uncounted victims of the pillaging and subsequent degeneration of Western Civilization and Western Culture.[11]

As the civilization collapses, the young are given (more and more) to suffer-ing, the consequence of adult ignorance and sinful behavior. To repeat, *too many adults are easily proven ignorant and sinful.* What is worse, *the ignorant and dis-respectful are being encouraged in both their ignorance and their sinful ways, by corrupt associations and a divisive legality.* Especially youth are ignorant of the consequences of their behavior since consequence exists after the fact. One must live long, thus to know much. Having lived it is too late to change what is past nevertheless consequence emanates from Acts, inexorably, no matter what are good intentions, before or after the fact. The consequence of misconduct will remain in spite of later feelings of guilt or penitence. Feeling remorse will never change the consequence from what has happened in the past. This should be known and understood by all. St. Thomas did obviate and define this for all, how-ever, truth must be shared; indeed, encouraged. This is what education should do, teach the truth (in spite of any greedy self-interest). Importantly, our educa-tional systems must include obviating the merits as well as the flaws in Western Catholic Christian Civilization and Culture. Certainly this can be done for other great Religions as well. *Serious and truthful study of comparative religion is wel-comed as long as political bias does not dominate the dialogue.* There are studies in Comparative Religion, however in matters of religion, the instruction is often bias in favor of the instructor. This is not all bad, being one manner of conversion, as long as the truth of the intent is made obvious. Religion is that subject, the objec-tive discussion of which is, for most, difficult to maintain.

Uniformly, good and decent behavior, as should be evident in a mature parent, presents the model for the development of the young into dependable, decent adults. Poor and unruly behavior will do just the opposite. Common sense tells us all about this when we observe what has happened in the past in various places, such observations having been given to the literature by innumerable profound men, the most important of which was the Son of God. From the Son of God, to our place in time we have been given the Popes (as Vicars of Christ) who, generally speaking, provide guidance and continuity in learning and knowing.

---

11   **Jones, Michel, PhD.,** *Degenerate moderns*

All this under the watchful attention of dedicated men who make certain of the details and provide succinct and truthful dialogue as it relates to what is happening; in fact, in reality, day by day. Unfortunately, heretics have worked their evil doings into the fabric of that which is Holy and the consequence surrounds us.[12] Noteworthy, *a heretic is one who is not trustworthy* and, when one lies in the face of grave consequence, that one is especially sinful. Heresy, probably most often, has an aegis in vanity or personal conceit, that is, *the heretic presumes to know* better than the true believer. Vanity is a cardinal sin. Nevertheless, in the case of the teachings of Christ, the Son of God, who might "presume" to know better. If one defers to common sense, the greatest depository of such common sense is found in the nearly two thousand years of careful Catholic scholarship.[13] Nothing else, in this world, is equal to this. Regarding money and economy, the Catholic ethic is unequalled in respect to applied morality, concerning vital economic issues.[14] And the Catholic Church distinguishes critically between what belongs to Caesar and what belongs to God! The Knowledge and understanding embodied therein are available to anyone who wishes to inquire. With a degree of humility, we submit that some other great religions attempt to follow what is truth and encourage goodness as well.[15]

---

12 **Anti-Popes** have also held the Chair of Peter. Some have done great damage to the Catholic Church as has happened in the recent past. Nevertheless, *the sinful or negligent behavior of men does not, in any way, change the nature and mission of the Catholic Church.* The Catholic Church has powerful enemies working assiduously to destroy all that has been accomplished in the name of the Lord. Ultimately, they will fail in their endeavor however, not until they have rendered great damage to the soul of the Western Civilization, including the millions that are being deceived.

13 **Other World Religions** may make the same claim, which claim we attempt to understand. Who is right? The Catholic Faith, founded by Christ is our choice. We are humbly and patiently committed, encouraging that *others should make fair and reasonable* comparison, without preconceptions, malice or prejudice. We accept that Free will allows each individual to accept this or not. We caution that, when one ignores the one holy, Catholic and Apostolic Faith, that one is placed amidst the "slings and arrows of outrageous fortune" and also may suffer the consequences of eternal damnation. This is a theological issue, dealing with eschatology, which is beyond the scope of our exposition.

14 **Fahey, Dennis, Rev. CS, Sp.** *Money Manipulation and the Social Order.* Christian Book Club of America. P. O. Box 900566 Palmdale, CA 93590. Chapter III, Pg. 61-76.

15 **There are many good people in this world**, who are not Catholic, some of whom are very skeptical of the true and original Faith of Jesus. We lament that men have corrupted, over twenty centuries, the teachings of the Catholic Church. When considering

Consider here issues that center on economics, politics and theology, in reference to the present civilization and culture. Regarding such, Truth has often been mostly or partly denied our present population, which has been indoctrinated in monstrous forms of fabrication, projected as a part of vicious war propaganda. The consequence of such unfortunate story telling is impossible to determine. Hypocrites, who traffic in lies and deceit, propaganda and the destruction of virtue speak of goodness however, their own lives do not necessarily reflect what is goodness. Significantly not many know *"who is a Liar?"* Millions have been conditioned to accept a perverse form of political quackery,[16] whilst they reject the idea of sin and the existence of an Omnipotent being.

To remain pure, one must be completely good, chaste and holy, thus one may attain a state of grace. Unfortunately, millions have standards for everything except personal behavior. *One's behavior is often referred to as play-acting:* **playing and acting.** Individuals are called upon to fill some roll model, **fill and roll?** We need only to add the Rocks! We are encouraged to become politically correct in our thinking, what about truth? ***We are coerced to be broad-minded in the acceptance of blatant sin, social and sexual deviates and perversions, of all kind.*** We are admonished by powerful governmental forces as well as by a primitively alien instinct to accept all manner of deviate behavior and mortal sin, centered on the human body, prostitution, perverted sex, child molestation, pornography, group sex, ad nausea.[17] Who determines that all must accept sin as normal behavior, a fool or a wise man? Given the present circumstances, the trend is set. However, trends always change, the politically motivated fashion industry will encourage a new and different look. What is mostly silly and beholden to sinful behavior will be given a different name next Season, one could go on.

Mass media encourages youthful behavior to be venal, supercilious, pretentious, and gaudy. Clever salesmen, rely on sensuously displayed body parts, of beautiful young people, to stimulate sales, which in turn support mass media. Such tactics are clever and very profitable, however, not wise; or do they consider

---

all time in all places, that being eternal time, forever, one is wise who follows in the steps of our Lord, Son of God. We implore that the skeptic consider the nature and scope of reality, thus to better understand the meaning of the true Faith. The Gospels provide evidence, existing as *the unbroken line of an historic past,* directly from Christ and the Apostles.

16 **Knuth, E. C.,** *The Empire of the City, The Jekyll/Hyde Nature of the British Government.* The Noontide Press, P. O. Box 1248, Torrence, CA 90505. Chapter IX, Pp.59-66

17 **Reisman, Judith, PhD.** *Kinsey, Crimes and Cosequences.* Third Edition. The Institute for Medical Education, P. O. Box 15284, Sacramento, CA 95851-0284. ©1998–2000–2003. ISBN # 0-9666624-1-5

how children are influenced by them. Such tactics stand as symptomatic of moral decay; nevertheless many will do anything for a buck! Of course, sex entices, especially the young and curious, as it stimulates interest in the products being sold.

However, no one informs youth that much illicit innuendo is contrived and illegitimate. Truthfully, love, when decent, is more satisfying and is eternal, forever. Catholic doctrine forbids pandering in all forms, which might include much of today's advertising; not the least important of which concerns the adulteration of a product. One should not be encouraged to covet another man's wife, or lust for another man's daughter. One should seek permanent fidelity and return that which is given, till death calls to part. Here words have profound meaning; however, words do inflict pain upon the hypocrite and the unfaithful, the pornographer and the pimp, the prostitute and her John. So be it.

Guilt is the means whereby conscience is given to provide protection for the individual soul. Some experts may view this otherwise, for no good reason, for reasons which are suspect or for selfish and personal reasons. Amongst Psychologists and Psychiatrists, of which most may be positively inclined and attempt to do the best for their patients, it is certain that many are hypocrites hoping to gratify personal interests, some of which have a sinful connotation.[18] Practitioners often hide behind science and a professionalism that is often very suspect. *Many of our experts may very well be fools.* All of the elements combine in ways, which even for experts (so called), are difficult to communicate, even more difficult to comprehend.

---

18 **Reisman, Judith, Ph.D.** *Kinsey, Crimes and Cosequences.* The Institute for Medical Education, P. O>. Box 15284, Sacramento, CA 95851-0284.

Is this a royal flush?

Pregnant, by whom?

XII. Central Banking

Central Banks provide the means, whereby *the devious objectives of overt presumption may be achieved.* Central Banks also perform ordinary functions, concerned with the movement and use of money and various "other" instruments, which function as money; bonds, bank credits, checks, warrants, derivatives, calls, puts and other quasi-legal devices. It is not our purpose to submit a technically extensive critique of the banking system or the Federal Reserve System. Others, more able than we, have tried with little success; and, it is a very large subject, quite needlessly so. However, we do assert that the Bank of England and the United States Federal Reserve System are interlocking Institutions, which provide the means for much evil that is happening in the Western World.[1] Furthermore, that the capital Stock in the U. S. Federal Reserve System is held by an interesting consortium of mostly foreign Banking Institutions.[2] Actually, when known, truth is quite simple, whereas the lie requires a carefully woven and secretly maintained web of deceit.[3] *The Lie, the con and contrived Legerdemain has become as the political Sacraments of this modern age.* Our concern is that the Central Bank functions in favor of some very *clever and despicable hypocrites,* men who

---

1   **Knuth, E. C.,** *The Empire of the City, The Jekyll/Hyde Nature of the British Government.* The Noontide Press, P. O. Box 1248, Torrence, CA 90505. Pp. 27-28-30-35-57-59-60-65-66-70-93-97-98-99-100

2   **McMasters,** *The Reaper, Newsletter.* The controlling stock in the Federal reserve is held by: "(1) Rothschild Bank of London, (2) Rothschid Bank of Berlin, (3) Lazard Brothers of Paris, (4) Israel Moses Seif Banks of Italy, (5) Warburg Bank of Amsterdam, (6) Warburg Bank of Hamburg, (7) Lehman Brothers of New York, (8) Kuhn Loeb Bank of New York, (9) Goldman Sachs of New York, (10) Chase Manhattan of much of New York. Much of the staggering wealth of this international banking cartel is illegally and unconstitutionally extracted from the American people."

3   **Dillon, George. E., Mgr.,** *Freemasonry Unmasked as the Secret Power Behind Communism.* The Briton's Publishing Society, London, 1950. A short concise, very informative, provides a Catholic perspective into the history of Subversion (author's comment).

were and are of such nature as to completely despise their fellow man. We assert they are intelligent, comprise a new aristocracy and many have been generous in some ways however, not necessarily sensitive to the sadness, which is the product of much of their suspect efforts. Attempts by noble men, including President Lincoln, assassinated on Good Friday; Herbert Hoover, made to appear an irresponsible fool and Wright Patman, whose warnings were ignored, are met with the greatest ferocity in defense of a system perverse beyond comprehension.

Modern banking, involves many elements, the creation of capital, fractional banking, inflation and compound interest, to name a few. When one understands how the various components work together, one will know why things are as they are; and they will not change. Bet on it! Amschel Rothschild is known to have said, "give me control of the money and I care not who make the law". He was an intelligent, perceptive and clever man, no doubt and a good man as well. If he were living today, he might very well be ashamed of much of what has become of his legacy, but he would know that he was right. Also, he would know that every hypocrite serving in a public trust took advantage of his perceptive understanding. Certainly, his thinking in any case centered on ideas as old as the history of his people.[4]

The control of Currency is a most important issue. The reader should be informed from the very best and most accurate sources, ***not establishment sources***. Our officials, including past presidents (Wilson, Roosevelt, Eisenhower, Nixon, Bush, Clinton and still another Bush), have been unable, unwilling, or simply afraid of this issue. Our nation is deceived and is being plundered as no other nation in the world has been plundered. Other nations are being plundered as well. Astonishingly, stupefied politicians are guilty, of plundering others, even as we are being plundered. The difference is seated in reasoning and in the objectives being sought. Ill gained profits, including the fortune stolen from Czar Nicholas, are being used to destroy our Western Christian Civilization and our Culture; namely the Western, Catholic, Christian culture which has brought so much goodness to the peoples of this world.[5]

The issue of banking has become too technical and too vast to cover in any brief work however, *the reader is encouraged to inquire independently,* so as to verify some of the assertions made in so cursive a summary. Having said that, we call

---

4   Reed, Douglas, *The Controversy of Zion*, Veritas Publishing Co., Pty., Ltd. P. O. Box 20, Bullsbrook, Western Australia, 6084. ISBN # 0949667. pp. 1-6, 59-69, 88-98.

5   Webster, Nesta, *World Revolution, The Plot Against Civilisation*. 7th Edition, Edited and brought to date by Anthony Gittens. GSG Associates, reprint with permission of Veritas Publishing Company, Cranbrook, Western Australia 6321. ISBN # 0-85172-425-6

attention to an interesting observation. "...[T]he Philosophers were confident that democracy, government by the people, would bring about social perfection." *Did this really happen?*

"This prejudice was the fatal error of the humanitarians, the philosophers and the liberals. Men are not infallible they err very often. It is not true that the masses are always right and know the means for attaining the ends aimed at. Belief in the common man, is no better founded than the belief in the supernatural gifts of kings, priests and noblemen. Democracy insures a system of government in accordance with the wishes and plans of the majority. But it cannot prevent majorities from falling victim to erroneous ideas and from adopting inappropriate policies, which not only fail to realize the ends aimed at but, result in disaster. *Majorities too may err and destroy our civilization.* The good cause will not triumph merely on account of its reasonableness and expediency. *Only if men are such that they will finally espouse policies reasonable and likely to attain the ultimate ends* aimed at, *will civilization improve* and society and state render men more satisfied, although not happy in a metaphysical sense. Whether or not this condition is given, only the unknown future can reveal."[6] (Italics by this author)

There is much wisdom in the above quotation. We are encouraged to contemplate what is being inferred. However, we do not believe merely in the gifts of kings, priests and noblemen. We do not believe that Central Banks should or must determine the fate of Mankind. We do not believe that the present system of usurpation, fraud, vain supposition and covertly imposed control by a politically inspired messianic imposition, which resides in a moneyed Elite, is destined as necessary for the survival of Humanity.

We do believe in one God, Creator of Heaven and Earth, of all that is seen and unseen. We do believe in the Sacraments of the universally adaptive Holy Roman Catholic Church, especially Catholic Baptism, without which there is no Salvation.[7] This is mentioned in this context because, although money and wealth are worldly possessions, the Sacraments, beginning with Baptism connect man to what is infinite and eternal.[8]

---

6   **von Mises, Ludwig.** *Human Action, a Treatise on Economics.* Third Revised Edition. Henry Regnery Company, Chicago. © 1949 by Yale University Press. *Revised Edition* © 1943 by Yale University. Library of Congress # 62-17874. Pg. 193.

7   **Ferrara, Christopher,** *EWTN a Network Gone Wrong.* Good Council Publications, Pound Ridge, New York. Pg. 96.

8   **Ratzinger, Joseph Cardinal,** (Now Pope Benedict VI), *Theologische Prinzipienlehre.* 1982 Erich Wewel Verlag, Munich. Translation by: McCarthy, SDN., Principals of Catholic Theology, 1987 Ignatius Press, San Francisco, CA.

This exposition attempts to encourage the reader in acquiring a better under-standing of the value of holy Catholic Christian Tradition as it applies to politics, economics, money and banking. When all the numerous and titillating distrac-tions combine in a complex reality, many are confused. And with the boredom, that many experience, in their day to day endeavors it is understandable that we have come to where we are. What is required is an impassioned interest in the intricate workings of both the Truth and the Lie. It is possible to combine the insights of others in the formation of a correct and functional independently inspired understanding. To promote the understanding of what is true should be the purpose of education. It is understood that comprehension assumes a dif-ferent tenor as a consequence of the tremendous range of human experience. If Catholic Christian understanding is not within one's domain of reference, that one should at least attempt to understand the meaning of Christ-inspired holiness in the historic continuity and Tradition of the past two-Millennia. And, each one is encouraged to enact their own free will in correctly pursuing the life, which they enjoy, without the imposition of unfair bias or distractions meted by religious disagreement.

XIII. Compound Interest Again

Compound interest, earned on what is called finance capital, perhaps a better name would be *Monopoly Capital*, involves the relentless working of a mathematical formula to the advantage of the few who control the Capital. Furthermore, money <u>*created at the stroke of a pen*</u>, which bears interest, to be paid to the "supposed" owner of this same money, is presumed equal to the value of hard money.[1] The interest paid by a working man, one with several children for example, requires that he must spend a significant part of his life earning what will be paid as interest. Also, paying interest deprives one of the productive depositions of that same money. The poor man must utilize his very limited time to provide whatever he and his family will have. In contrast, wealthy men own assets, which generate income plus pay for interest and taxes as well. Those special few who control the nation's money and the institutions, which they inspire earn unimaginably large sums, simply because of their privileged position within our system. Importantly, such individuals have the full protection of the law, even though what they profit from is mostly unjust and, of course may be patently or *"somewhat"* illegal.[2] Admittedly, the rich do spend their money into the system and do create employment for those, less fortunate that work for a living. Nevertheless, our Constitution provides that only the Congress shall coin money. Unfortunately our Constitution is a document, which is mostly ignored, especially so by they who are sworn to uphold it, and the principals for which it stands, including some past presidents, congressmen and senators, all afraid for their own well-being.

The machinations of the Central Banks provide that *somewhat obscure billions of dollars* will be paid to an unknown recipient; that is unknown to those who

---

1   **Hard Money** is actual money upon which the tax has been paid. Personal savings are a form of hard money and exist as having true value. The bank has debt money, which is a form of fiduciary instrument such as checkbook money or a fictitious form of Reserve, generated by the fractional banking system.

2   **An Attitude of indifference**, having been unfairly assumed, assuages the conscience of they who are the robber Barons; or so we would imagine.

pay. This is a prime example of grand theft and is evil in action. Vanity, greed and covetousness [**all sins**] work in malignant harmony toward the propagation of deliberate, despicable and malicious consequence. What is capricious is *justified somehow, by those within the system who are both benefactor and beneficiary* thereof and, together with a controlled mass media, they are the primary players within our civilization.[3] Sadly, they have to a very large extent, also ruined our Western Culture, by means of the propagation of unnecessary wars whereabouts millions of the innocent have been killed. Furthermore, the genetic damage is incalculable. While Europeans and Americans of European descent, have been slaughtering each other, counting in millions, *backward countries have enjoyed a population explosion without precedent,* aided by western Technology. Presently we face the consequence, in the manner, until quite recently, of a silent invasion of both Europe and the Americas by aliens with contrary Ideas and overtly ambitious aspirations contrary to the host populations.

Our leaders are often involved in some manner of theft and, too often, are the beneficiaries of some clever albeit illegal operation.[4] Some others of our leaders do not understand what is happening, they are too busy working for re-election. Still others, who do attempt to change the conditions, which allow for the wholesale theft of a nation from its people, meet with all manner of obstacle, including intimidation (Lindberg, McCarthy) and assassination (Lincoln, Kennedy). To aid matters, the system is often so slow that the best part of a lifetime may pass before any remedy is made effective, in which instance it may be deemed unnecessary or outdated. In such instance the concept of "modernism" works as a distraction for those who might continue the search for truth and honesty. Even sex has its place, with the lecher and the homosexual, become the subject of blackmail and extortion, by those who pull the strings.

> *Oh what a terrible web we weave, when first we practice to deceive*
> *(Shakespeare).*

3　Pierce, William L. Dr., **Editor,** *Who Controls American Media, News and Entertainment?* National Vangard Books, P. O. Box 330, Hillsboro, West VA 24946. Cat. # 14, 1992. Reprint in Bulletin, #376, May 1993, Committee to Restore the Constitution. P. O. Box 986, Ft. Collins, CO 80522.

4　**Many men in government are 33 rd Degree Masons**. In principal, philosophy and aspiration they are anti-Christian and adamantly anti-Catholic. However, they are also hypocrites, sworn to uphold the secret and the lie and they have taken a blood oath to protect deceit and corruption, which is rampant at all levels of Politics.

Concerning money, Reality has been made to appear confusingly complex. Coincidentally, lies have been so carefully orchestrated that, honest leadership and intelligent participation in government and especially concerning money matters, is all but impossible. Any man who does not understand the machinations of money or who is unwilling to work truthfully to correct this parade of opportunistic malfeasance, should not be a leader of men. Nevertheless, until the public becomes aware and convinced that much is amiss, the public will continue to elect evil and/or clever opportunists to serve them.

This world is not as it appears to be, especially concerning the accumulation of wealth and power. Do you wonder why?[5]

That which we cannot see
Has more effect on us than that which is:
Apparently

All intelligent people should be aware of what the compounding of interest on "presumed" capital means to the poor. The poor will remain poor! The poor will become, as the recent past has proven, ever poorer.[6] Current studies of many of the world's poor, involving individual and family income (worldwide) have shown that *the humble and truthfully poor* are becoming increasingly poorer. In spite of any promises, by well-meaning, some not so well-meaning Politicians to the contrary, the poor will be joined by almost all of their children; beside which many such children will be killed before birth or they will be starved to death during their childhood. Many more will be crippled, as in the Middle East, by sophisticated however senseless warfare and turmoil. Importantly and tragically, large segments of the lower middle classes will join countless numbers of poor and starving people, coincidentally (?) they who have too much will acquire still more! *Present reasoning is based on sin; corruption, lust, vanity and greed, coupled with all manner of vice and outrageous inclination.*

Because of an aggressive and presumptuous cadre of influential alien Imposters, we are unable to exercise free speech unless we capitulate to pressure groups who harbor an unmentioned, nevertheless effective, religious imposition. Humanism is a religion! Unfortunately, in the public schools it is out of fashion to discuss the Christian religion, upon which this nation was founded and without which

---

5   **Disraeli, Benjamin, English Statesman and Writer,** Prime Minister of England (1868; 1874–1880). "My dear Conningsby, The World is governed by far different persons than you might imagine."

6   **LaRouche, Lyndon.** *In The Aftermath of January 28*. Executive Intelligence Review, Feb. 28, 2003. See Charts on pp. 18-19-20-21

it will fail. We dare not qualify good and evil, we cannot mention a sin, as a sin, rather it must be considered as a "lifestyle". It may not even be mentioned as a *sinful lifestyle*. It must be considered as an acceptable diversity not an unacceptable perversity. God the Father, maker of Heaven and Earth, is pushed into oblivion. What are the absolute and known understandings of the nature and consequence of sin are generally ignored. As a consequence of sin being ignored, serial murder, rape, pornography, vicious gangs; senseless graffiti and monumental thievery are the symptoms of decadence and the dissolution of a nation, culture and civilization. They are the obvious trail of the Beast.

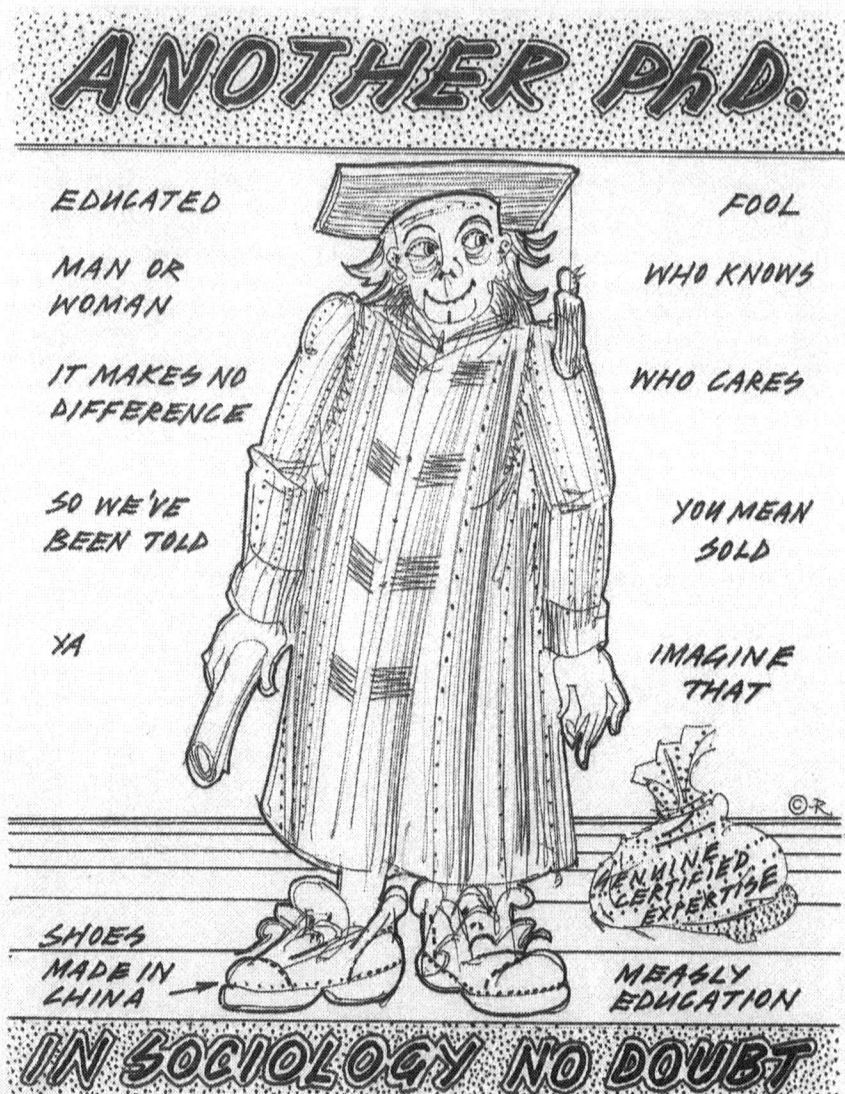

Another Ph. D.

College bound

XIV. Parental Rights

Every parent, mother or father has the right and the obligation to defend their children. Primarily, this is true because the child is an extension of the two parents. Rigorously, this is true in a biological and physiological sense and later in an intellectual, emotional, spiritual and psychological sense as well. This is axiomatic. One need not conduct any manner of study to prove this; common sense obviates what is, in fact, truthful. Parallel to this understanding, is that any Philosopher has a right to defend and refine an astute and pertinent understanding. And, Philosophy is related to the raising and nurturing of one's own children. One's disposition, emotional tenor, habit, manners and customs are a Legacy formed as Tradition, which one hopes to provide for and extend in time beyond now. *Children are the means for a pertinent and profound existential continuity.* Race becomes and evolves by the profound existential accretion of human fertility. Commonly we assert that the future belongs to the children. This is the truth. However, this is trivialized in the "it's a small world after all" mentality of they who patronize Disneyland or they who aspire to a One World Socialism. Both of which denies all children the right to grow, in the manner of their Tradition and to exercise a peculiarly formed free will becoming from uniquely experienced History as interpreted by an absolutely unique and individual being. Humanity is not a collectivity, excepting as is expressed in Tradition, which becomes of individually distinct participation. Collectively this is referred to as a Family, Clan, Tribe or Culture. Coincidentally, individuals respond to tradition in marvelously distinct ways. *No Dictator can admit to this fact, nor can a Central Bank or a Corporation, each of which Institutions depend on the subservience of the individual, to men as cookies,*[1] *stamped from the same set of dies, beholden to the salary which is*

---

1   **Consider Man as a Cookie.** Such men would be uniformly stamped, frosted, packed, boxed and shipped *to where cookies are consumed.* Who will eat the cookies are that buy them from those who control the cookie-making process. Wake up, smell the coffee or, enjoy your milk with real baked cookies, while you still can. As you do so, just imagine yourself being *"chewed up"* just like a cookie! We insist, as an aside that Girl Scout cookies, are not the real Thing. Real cookies are the ones that children

paid. The "set" is determined by how one is forced to believe one socialistic philosophy rather than another. In fact, all socialism is communism and all forms of Communism/Socialism are very much the same.

Certainly some manner of Law is required however it need not be repressive. Nevertheless the law must place in careful evidence some manner of force so as to be respected, not necessarily feared, by the citizen.

Concerning children, the parent has the right to defend the child against unwanted and/or unhealthy intrusion, including the impositions of public education. This is true in respect to both body and mind. No parent wishes for the rape of their child and no parent wishes that their child be deliberately subverted by the will of an unhealthy, devious, and self-interested Fool; a fool who would gain from the corruption of another man's child.

In the present sociological domain (a confused domain to be sure), their exists those forces which guarantee that many youngsters will be physically raped and that most, if not all, will be deliberately subverted for the benefit of those who wish to control them. Furthermore, the premium placed on self-interest in our schools, institutions, literature, and media guarantee that confusion and mayhem will continue, indeed, will become ever more problematic for a greater number of individuals in the future. Many will deny this, especially those in the most influential positions and who profit immeasurably or benefit most from what is the status quo. We call the construct of such individuals, the "Establishment." However, in the final phase of Civilization, gross negligence and blatant sin will somehow affect every living being. Ignorance and misunderstanding are an important part of reality and must be understood as such.

To return to our point, concerning parental rights, the decent and dependable parent is the best line of defense against sin and evil and all manner of consequence deriving therefrom. This is met, on the parental level, with the instincts necessary to survival and is entwined with the innate understanding of being who one is, *apparently no politician understands this.*

Do-gooders, pretending to know something important, would imagine that there are means, other than devoted, holy and sustained parenthood, which work more favorably in respect to the children. They are wrong. As such they project a bureaucratized manner of thinking, which has as an objective much of which is contrary to the best interest of another man's child. All large institutions are self-serving, growing ever larger and more onerous until such time as they, quite simply, collapse. *All of our institutions will, in time, collapse just as has happened in the past.* The greater the sizes of the institution, the more certainly harmful will

---

and dad smell baking in mom's own kitchen made by the loving and quietly disposed hands of she that loves you most of all. Bimbos do not bake cookies!

be the consequence. It is an Axiom that ever-greater numbers of people will be inflicted by the collapse of ever-greater controlling forces. *War causes suffering and Great Wars cause great suffering.* Ultimately, the earth will consume all that is upon it! To dust we will return, one way or another!

War involves demographic, social, economic, religious and political issues as well as issues that are always personal, especially so for they who will lie in a premature grave. *Those affected by events are always individuals; they are always, Someone's children.* Our World Trade Center Catastrophe is an example of this and demonstrates, conclusively, *why the sovereignty of any nation must and should reside in the individual, always destined to pay for the ultimate eventuality.*

Concerning children, individuals who opt for a one-world government are either *fools or they are mad.* **Who has the right to enslave your child?** It is of critical importance; parental rights are the first lines of defense against the usurpation of our civilization and the destruction of our Culture and of our Soul.

In a complex civilization, with huge cities and all manner of electronic and printed information, including words and images, protecting one's own children has become very complicated and sometimes quite impossible. The defense must begin very early, right after birth. The initial phase is referred to as bonding. The child is bonded to the parent, particularly the mother from whom (initially) the child receives very real nourishment. Such as mother's milk, is like no other. Mother's milk provides for the defense of the infant's body against disease and also provides defense against future afflictions. Nursing also provides the infant with a sense of security and well being. That mammals nurse their "very own" young seems obvious enough. However, in the case of human beings, there is often some manner of "formula" given rather than mother's milk. The reasons for this are various and it is not our purpose to discuss pediatrics. The reader can find all of the information necessary from other sources, some very competent ones and some not so competent. Noteworthy, in this respect, is the fact that Dr. Spock (of legendary fame) may not have been the best. Well-qualified professionals will attest to this fact.[2]Our concern is for the "formula", that mixture of milk (in the case of nourishment), which is provided for the child as a substitute for the real thing. Presently, whether a mother nurses her child or not is largely a matter of economics, fashion or convenience rather than for profound and justifiable reasons. Certainly, exceptions may call for a wet nurse or some manner of variation from what is normal and natural, however, they remain exceptions. The point is, mothers are denied a very important and satisfying obligation, when they switch to a

---

2   **Mendelsohn, Robert, M.D.** *How to Raise Healthy Children in Spite of Your Doctor.* Contemporary Books, Inc. 180 N. Michigan Avenue, Chicago, IL 60601. Copyright ©1984. ISBN 0-8092-5808-0.

formula as a substitute for what is biologically natural. *In so doing, they may (probably they do) allow fashion and expedience to determine how they make such decision.* Decision-making is very important, whereabouts children are concerned.

As children grow, they will be given various formulas (determined by others), which are supposed to be good for them. Of course, they will be constantly reminded of what is fashionable (advertising), what is politically correct (coercion), what is economical (commercial imposition) and what is convenient (salesmanship, product motivation).[3] Importantly, all must be stamped with the label of fashionable, politically correct, tolerant and [the] *correctly informed* understanding. What is determined merely for convenience has an appeal to ignorance and slothfulness, dumb and lazy. Just now, *dumb and lazy* is typical of great numbers from any given economically secure population. And, dumb and lazy will prevent anyone from developing truthfully significant understanding necessary for independent and pertinent thought in a politicized and desensitized world. It is important to understand that behaviors can be and are being trained for various reason. Therefore, it is important to understand the reasoning behind *any formula* that one may find acceptable. Most forms of conditioning are *"reasoned"* for the purpose of some economic, political or social gain.

The disposable diaper is perhaps one of the most telling examples of confusion in respect to doing one thing rather than another. The choice is based on what seems to be expedient and has become popular, even a necessity. The expense involved is considerable however the message we send is of greater importance. The procedure is almost totally unnecessary and is absolutely extraordinary. We wrap each bowel movement and transport it to a dump-site there to be buried together with millions of other bowel movements. Certainly the stuff is biodegradable however, to stress this misses the point.

We lament our forests are being plundered and trash and garbage are polluting the environment. Although, that forests are being plundered is probably a misunderstanding. Be that as it may, to contain the infant's bowl movements, we add billions of large disposable diapers to what are very large piles. We must not get our hands dirty; and of course there is the smell. Previously, mothers had perhaps several children, all of whom used the same five or six dozen diapers. Thereafter, the family was supplied with clean-up and polishing cloths for a lifetime. Our family still has some. In 1930 one could buy diaper fabric for $0.19 per yard and there was no sales tax. For an investment of perhaps $2.80 (20 yards) one would have had enough for all the children. That was when everyone was poor,

---

3   **Obesity in Children** is a consequence of the child's having been given too much of the wrong food, often as a substitute for what is healthy. Children, largely abandoned by working parents, do not eat properly.

so we are told, during the depression. One can understand that price is relative to an escalating minimum wage. However, the depression we are now approaching will be much worse; millions will never recover from the next really big one. However, the rich will become richer and the poor will continue to plug up the system with billions of unnecessary disposable diapers. All this for fashion and for convenience, of course!

Modern mothers, driven by a presumed necessity, are working outside the home, have too little time with their children. Children are pulled from bed, fed with haste and driven to a place where strangers watch over them, for a price. They are given a sugary snack, commercially prepared lunch and perhaps dinner. In the evening, they are picked up and driven home, in haste, so as to accommodate a working mother. Often there is no father, since he is chasing another man's wife, perhaps a younger woman, as Sigmund Freud, the good doctor, seeking to deflower a virgin. Perhaps he has a mistress, which he may share with others as eager and insensitive as himself. In such circumstances, his wife, mother of their children is stressed-out (as we say), and requires some loving attention herself however, such attention is not forthcoming. When the bloom is off the rose, the bee gathers honey elsewhere. There was a variation on this theme in the movie "The King and I" as one was informed that this is natural, the way it must be. *Marriage, an inviolate and sacramental partnership involving a profound mutual dependency, is old fashioned.*

Being together, (like you know) *"shacking up"* for a time, is more in "keeping with the trend" or "going with the flow." And "we must keep our options open". Even an occasional homosexual tryst is now considered, by some, as trendy, even a good idea. Do we consider, perhaps parents may be avoiding their truthful and profound responsibilities? Are parents too concerned, with imagined rights, imposed by shallow minded psychologists? Are parents driven by politically motivational dialogue? Who will bear in quietude the very unpredictable consequences? Is this a Tragedy? Are we having fun yet? Especially, not to forget, do we question the reasons for the absent partner having left spouse and children in search of something different? One can imagine that much of such irresponsible behavior is motivated by the tacky television shows, named situational and or real time events, and the overt display of childish, disrespectful and venal sensuality.

The questions enumerated above have significant economic, moral and social consequence. Unfortunately, individually many are not able to correctly understand the *profound value of marriage,* which provides many advantages, personally, socially, economically, emotionally and spiritually. Children with two loving parents are advantaged in many ways. Though perhaps well meaning, many adults are surrendering their most significant and existentially, profound rights and responsibilities to others, whom they cannot and will never, know. Nevertheless, "till death do us part" has a very significant and existentially profound meaning.

Procreation is at the center of Issues involving what we understand and define as Sociology. Keep in mind, Sociology is not a science being open to the inclusion of all manner of opinion. Opinion repeated often becomes understood as truth, which it is not. Sociology does present a format and attempts to address issues primary to human encounter. One would imagine that the sociologist would encourage correct behavior in reference to humanities most critical need. The most critical "encounter" is mating, which leads to the begetting of children. Nevertheless, under present Law women may choose to murder their unborn child.

Curiously, though somewhat cabalistic, certainly symbolic, abortion is given encouragement under this same tainted Law. The Law is in conflict with both common sense and intelligence, also it denies the accumulated Intellect and wisdom of Western Civilization. No matter what, the Government does provide protection for such practice, with no threat of penalty for this form of murder. It is "imagined" that mothers, being liberated women, have a right to kill their own children. Is this barbaric? Or, is this "enlightened" behavior?

Murder is perpetrated even as the government subsidizes illicit sex with food stamps and rent subsidies. There is much confusion in the "minds" of those that "suppose" they are Leaders of men (?). There is no moral defense for such behavior, which gives a clue as to why some continue to insist on a separation of Church and State! In a Democracy sin may be condoned as is inferred by consenting adult laws.

If one ignores the difference between good and evil bedlam is a certainty. Thus, with consent, sinful and socially debilitating acts are condoned, even encouraged by those that cannot understand what they are doing as the nation sinks deeper into a pit of politically contrived anguish. Perhaps some do understand very well and are making a deliberate effort to destroy the nation and negate the Catholic Christian Imperative, which supports all Christianity.

Dick and Jane

Dress for success

XV. Money and Familial Friendship

The accumulation of wealth, together with the Destruction of the individual person as a unique being, has been a subtle and to a considerable extent a carefully manipulated economic and political process. Manipulation is such as may be driven by two Cardinal Sins (yes, Cardinal Sins), Greed and Vanity. Additionally there is the phenomenology of the impact of technology on both economic and political processes. Individually wealth is a good thing as it enables a people to attain a better life. However, wealth in great accumulations has determined the political process and does encroach on all the little people one way or another. We have been admonished in the past, by no less than Christ, to not allow the influence of sin, and particularly sin of the most destructive kind, to dominate our being and therefore, to ultimately corrupt our soul. One should think carefully about this.

Sin and corruption, in the realm of economics and politics, as it bears upon and forms human consciousness is exactly what has caused our present dilemmas, as we have been warned. We see the consequence unfolding, carefully contrived on a monumental, worldwide scale (Webster, *World Revolution)*. Life has been corrupted because of the means of modern technology especially concerning the implements of War and the insistence of greed in the realm of economics. Nevertheless, simultaneously and interestingly technology contributes to the "betterment" of humanity in profound ways. Coincidentally, *the presence of boisterous ignorance, supported by great wealth, accumulated phenomenally, has a profound impact on thinking and knowing.* The phenomenology of the present epoch is largely determined by the sounds and message of music coupled with holographic images of brilliantly contrived make-believe as presented in the communications media.

Add to this that great influence is asserted by deceitful means, propagated over long periods of time and supported by the incessant workings of the compounding of interest, on debt considered as money. Also it might be assumed, as mentioned elsewhere, at least considered that the great fortune of Czar Nicholas, Trustee for the once great *truly Russian nation*, estimated, by some, at approximately two billion in 1917, is somehow factored in the equation.[1]

Additionally, there continues to be straight-foreword theft on a grand scale, made possible by the issuance of stocks and contrived paper transactions and (to some degree) taxation without representation, which has been awarded legal sanction. Beside, some face the gruesome possibility of confiscation by the governmental exercise of eminent domain.[2] Also, there exists an over zealous preparation for made-to-order wars, which kill and maim sons and fathers, for reasons not quite clear.[3] Bureaucratic rulings are put in place, which pertain to who may use the earth. Ultimately the earth is imagined or presumed to belong to a contrived collectivity, a curiously formed social domain. We know that reparation payments

---

1   **Mullins Eustice,** *The World Order, Our Secret Rulers*. (Pub. Ezra Pound Institute, Staunton, VA. 24401, Second Edition, 1992). **Czar Nicholas, Sovereign and Trustee of the Russian Nation had millions invested in Western Banks.** The Czar had 115 million in four English banks; 35 million in the Bank of England, 25 million in Barclays, 25 million in Barings and 30 million in Lloyd's Bank. The Czar had 100 million in Bankque de France, 80 million in the Rothschild Bank of Paris. The Czar had in Berlin 130 million in the Mendelsohn Bank, which had been bankers to Russia. None of these funds have ever been dispersed. Today, with compound interest this would be worth in excess of fifty billion dollars, *all interest free.* If that money had been invested for the good of Russia, the world would have had a very different modern history. (*The World Order*, Pg. 12.) In addition there were jewels, gold bullion and vast land holdings, thousands of acres, with a value, at that time of near one billion dollars. Who wishes to talk about grand theft? All, such "goings on" seemed of little importance compared to the destruction, which occurred during World War I. It, is tragically amusing that such theft was not punished?

2   **Smart Growth** (so-called) is a *euphemism for grand theft,* in violation of the Constitution of the United States. Smart Growth is little more than a scheme, devised by the clever men who trick an uninformed and distracted population into a One World Order, which will be an ultimate and final Tyranny.

3   **The Attack on Iraq,** a sovereign nation, the population of which is just as human as we and who, coincidentally, should be allowed (within their own country) to exercise their God given free will. Political hypocrisy obfuscates the real nature of the issues involved and the lie is used wherever necessary for effect. One can be certain that the main reason for attacking a sovereign nation, on the other side of the globe, had economic and political objectives, the attainment of which required the *construction of an adversary.* Who now, amongst our inspired leaders, will ask for the complete disarmament of Israel?

have been taken from a vanquished adversary[4] (as in blackmail). Finally, there are a number of variations on each of the above themes. All of this has happened slowly, often spanning more than one lifetime.[5]

There are many dynastic type beneficiaries of our system; for example the Delano dynasty (Franklin Delano Roosevelt), a prominent well situated family to be sure, can be traced to the Actii at about 600 B.C. This is an example of the true insider. There are the Rockefellers, the Mellons, the DuPonts, the Harrimans, the Peabodys and a host of others that comprise a ruling elite, all of whom have a distinguished lineage. Coincidentally, many of our present day population will never know who their father is or was. Woman's Liberation has produced an army of bastard children. They are called "Love Children", which is the politically correct euphemism! Where are the Roots? Branches severed from the root are destined to die!

The programs essential for ending the process toward complete domination, of a most confused population, will be somewhat difficult to establish. They who control the money also control the Law. Thus *the rule of Law*, honestly understood, is *the rule of Money.* Truthful co-operation is required to ensure freedom and the *right to reasonably exercise free will.* Programs should be initiated within the community, run by individuals within the same community, which would provide better conditions for their children. Simply, such effort should be directed against the apparent giants in the community, those entities, which represent finance capital and/or the existence of some form of cartel or monopoly. This, for many, may be difficult to understand (at first) since every giant financial entity has someone in each community who is a functionary and who seems to be, perhaps is, simply an ordinary citizen, successful in their subsidized endeavors.

It must be understood that *the ordinary citizen,* given special privilege, real or imagined, *will work for the house,* seemingly to better what is hoped for as a better life style. Make no mistake about it; *those who are systematically encroaching*

---

4   **Quigley, Carroll, Ph.D.** *Tragedy and Hope. A World History, of Our Time.* Macmillan Co., New York, N. Y. 1966. LC # 65-13589, pp. 267-312. Reparations extracted from Germany, as punishment for having fought in two World Wars, were not only unreasonable they were barbaric. Who then shall we call the Hun? The Catholic concept is to treat a vanquished adversary with some respect, knowing that circumstances might have placed the victor in a similar place. Barbarism has assumed a new form, with modern technologically advanced means of killing and is assumed as clinical in respect to the perpetrator of mass annihilation.

5   **Interlocking Corporate Structures and Directorships** assure that those who have most will be able to *pass the loot to a chosen people,* even as death robs the common man of the opportunity of providing for a meaningful inheritance for his children. (Mullins, *The New World Order, Our Secret Rulers*).

upon the entire Civilization are quite able to pay well for temporary service rendered. Antagonism between the sexes and the breaking up of so many families represent mortal wounds to the human community. Personal issues, involving intimacies and familial concerns, engender deep feelings. Such feelings may be joyful or sorrowful and some border on anguish and rage. Mass media news reporting makes this apparent. Not to be overlooked, the present milieu is fertile ground for all manner of crime, much of which is financed by huge amounts of ill-gotten wealth, in the form of money as a product of the very sins mentioned above. Importantly, legitimate business (so-called) is often tied together with criminal activities. The perpetrators may, in many instances, be quite innocent (in their ignorance) of what they are really working for and for whom they are working, and (of course) why?

In our great cities, millions of people are alienated one from another and in their alienation they become, each one, very much alone. Certainly there are many decent friendships as well. However, many imagined friendships are for convenience or some personal advantage. Dishonesty as it exists amongst *"consenting adults"* is rampant and will certainly invade the conscience of those who tell the lies. Additionally, many are dependent on communal institutions and various systems just to get along from day to day. Importantly, *"Singles"* must pay their own way, each, alone! This is a consequence of the destruction of the biological/spiritual family which, heretofore, formed (as it still does in many cases) a basic, fundamentally sound, social unit. *There is an economic principal here, which cannot be denied. All tangible assets are given more value, in absolute terms, when they are shared rather than used exclusively by one.* Furthermore, this allows for the functioning of both generosity and humility in acceptance of assistance and is the opposite of vanity and greed. If one person lives alone and is then joined by another, the place of residence has twice the value and represents only one half of the liability for each one. This exemplifies an important economic understanding. We are not encouraging *shacking up for convenience*, rather we are encouraging remaining in the home of the natural parents and siblings until such time as one is able to establish a biological family of their own. Even then, two or three tier families, son, father and grandfather could occupy the same structure. *Many Immigrants became wealthy as a consequence of applying just a little common sense,* sharing implies common sense. One can recognize this might not be the way for everyone however, it is worth considering.

In sharing what they have, graciously and with humility, poor people are given a very real economic advantage. This is especially true in our large cities where much of the housing is controlled by the government, speculators or the very wealthy. When poor people share a living space or home with family and friends, they put themselves in an advantageous position and are better able to save and to educate themselves with leisure time provided by shorter working hours. However, personalities being what they are, too often individuals are not able to function unselfishly, or they take advantage of each other in malicious ways. Television and Hollywood Entertainment, in large measure, function to encourage youth in the wrong behaviors, certain to be ultimately destructive. Well-known Actors, that comprise a celebrity-type moneyed elite, have millions to lavish on gaudy and pretentious accommodations, even as they encourage others toward a life of sin, a life of anxiety, barrenness and destitution. Bad manners and antisocial forms of behavior are encouraged in *mass media productions, which glorify the single, aggressive mom, pubescent independence, adolescent sex and the untamed free spirit, unchained by Tradition, convention, honor, or responsibility. **Especially targeted for abuse, by script writers become sociologists, are decent and kind hearted fathers;*** blatant nonsense, emanating from mass media, especially Hollywood, when truthfully considered, is obviously contrived bigotry against Christianity and especially Catholicism.

Co-operation can be a real and independent solution to many of the nation's housing problems, especially concerning cost. However, *in an environment where sex is considered a form of entertainment,* close accommodations often lead to promiscuity and unnecessary sexually engendered, personal entanglements, which can result in illegitimacy. This is a certainty where immorality is encouraged as a manner of accepted *performance.* Most importantly, it is absolutely necessary that mature adults do not prey on children, adolescents and young adults. It is important too to recognize that youngsters of eighteen are not mature adults. To pretend otherwise is to promote fraud and misunderstanding.[6]

Families with grown children have a marvelous opportunity to co-operate and to acquire what one could not acquire alone. This is very obvious in the now forming Chinese community in and around Southern California. With such attitude, the Chinese are able to buy our country, which is what they are doing. Most importantly, such alliance can reduce debts very quickly and because of the friendships involved such co-operation can generate inexpensive pleasures. We call this friendship, the familial kind. The real stuff.

There is a real difference between a stranger, a family member and a casual friend. Families should endeavor to be friends; thereby they create happiness amongst themselves and a feeling of well being and security. Given like-minded families, the ghetto is not a bad idea, meaning individuals are better able to share

---

6   **The young** are perhaps bright, certainly eager however they are not mature and are certainly not wise. The Administrators within Public Educators and the Schools of Education pretend that they are doing well in educating our children, which is simply not true. Such self-praise is simply not justifiable.

common interests. When one shares responsibility, some of life's pressures are removed from those who share. Most animals know this by instinct however millions of humans are too independent to understand that sharing enhances reality. *Hollywood producers, promoting venal and silly situational dramas, formed of stupid and malicious stereotypes create misunderstanding amongst youth and impressionable viewers.* Hollywood personalities, paid far more than they are worth, in respect to their real value to the community, are given too much attention, thus is formulated an undue authority, thereby to *corrupt the entire civilization with a display of shallow, superficiality and banal ignorance.* This could not happen without corporate encouragement and the great sums of money *given to the celebrity* to endorse a product. We all know them. The vain and obnoxious Celebrity can do irreparable damage to youngsters, who are in the process of forming character and determining their lifelong values. All of this is made even more complex by what stultified educators call *values clarification.*

The word value has a positive connotation, however, what is truly valuable is being stolen, from innocent victims day by day. Incessantly this process continues, and will continue, until the entire world is contaminated with the vulgarity and banality which is Hollywood; plastic men and venal, self-centered, playfully-sluttish women who pose as some form of sex symbol. *Rather, they are whores who preside at a destructive orgy, with pimps and lustful men who pose as the ideal for others to emulate.* Amongst good people most Hollywood types are certainly not proper and decent examples for behavior. In many of their performances, public and assumedly private, they are mortal enemies of every good thought and inclination known to man. Those guilty of promoting sin, blasphemy and excessive sexual exuberance excuse their own insensitivity's by reminding the audience that they are merely acting and as acting, *blatant sin is tolerated and encouraged for the imagined betterment of an art form*, or so they presume. Silliness and perversions of all stripes are pushed "in your face" as entertainment, without regard to the effects they have on those who are immature, gullible and weak-minded. In fairness, we commend all those who have done well, are decent and they who do not promote sinful behavior for money

> *The head of the Serpent is Money*
> *Any serpent can be killed, by cutting off the head.*
> *However, this is not possible, when the Serpent is a Hydra*
> *The head is money, when severed, becomes as two.*
> *What then shall the common man do?*

Every journey is made one step at a time. Therefore, what must be done (and soon) is that each one should take the proper first step. *Deprive the establishment of what it most requires, that being money.* Do not spend any more money than is absolutely necessary. Cut off the incomes of those who co-operate with all that is sinful and destructive to the mind, body and soul of another. *Do not aid and give wealth to those who distract with snide silliness, entice with pornography or enslave millions to the star-studded addiction of popular ignorance.*

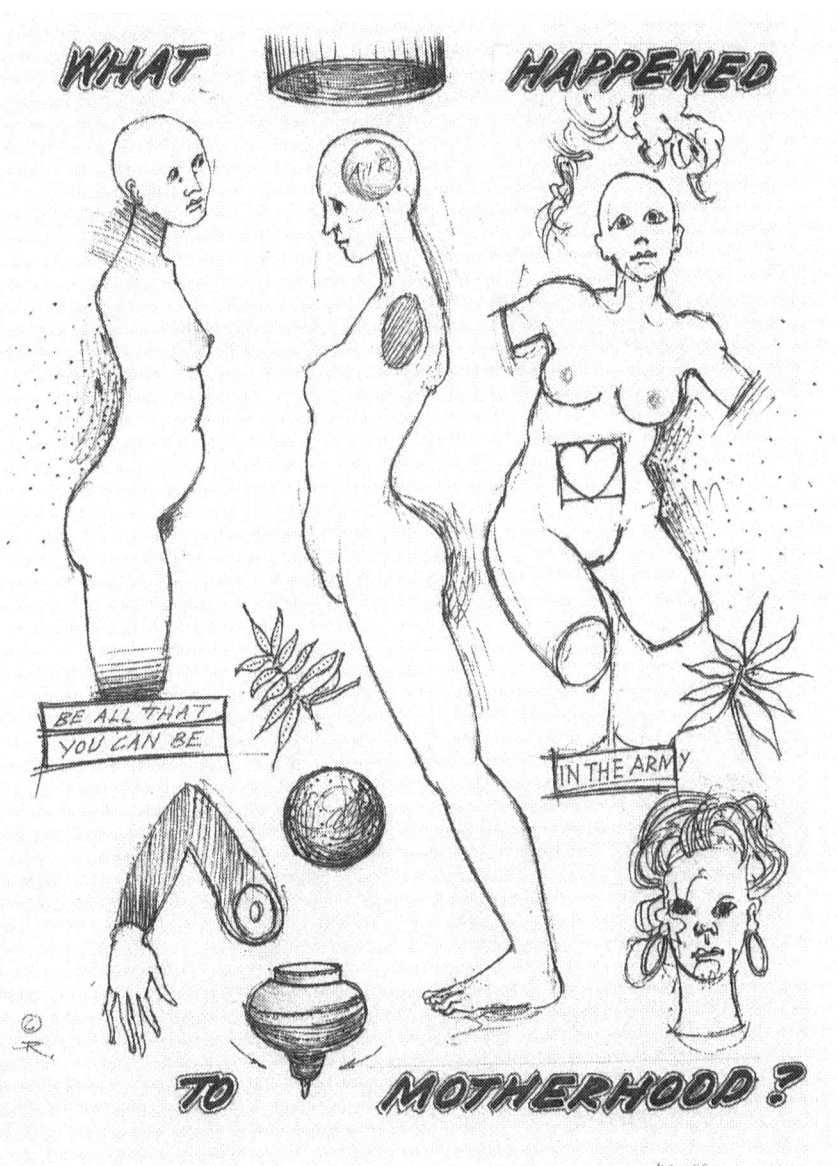

What ever happened to motherhood?

Bimbo

XVI. Being: Whom You Are

Individually, we are dependent upon a complex of phenomenon, which _cannot be completely and truthfully understood_. This is certain since man has only imperfect knowledge. Factors combine and are given to neurological, biological and psychological extension _in ways absolutely unique to the individual._ To imagine otherwise is to be a fool. In fact, education can do nothing to remedy this situation. Education, as the living of life, plus any and all forms of organized learning comprises just one factor in an extremely complex equation. The becoming of and extension of any human life resides in what is holy, mystical and transcendental. And, given the comprehension of individual intelligence, it is believed that there does exist a connection between **now**, understood as discreetly known **Time** and **eternity**, which is all time. The coming of the Christ, Jesus, provides easily understood reference that this is an important part of reality; very likely the most important part. And, in spite of the vicious and continued attacks on the Catholic Church, which he established, this most important idea persists.

Civilization is the foremost conglomeration of Humanity in the world at any time. A Civilization is a quasi-divergent complex, differing in where (place), how (in what manner), and why (reasoning) one does what he/she does. Civilization is an amalgam of complex groups and sub-groups, which may or may not work in harmony. Often there are millions of belligerents, antagonistic one toward another and, some few, toward all others. And, _there does exist small groups of schemers,_ which cause untold misery to mankind. Such as they have done irreparable harm to millions nevertheless, _some measure of gallantry is born_ in fighting the battles caused by the intransigent and malicious few.

Culture is a bit more homogeneous, however, may also be diverse. A culture is a part of the extant Civilization and as such is a component. A Culture has a more distinct personality, is more familial and shares common language traits (pertaining to origins) and probably is more localized in terms of where (European culture, while rather complex in total, does occupy Europe, just as Chinese culture is centered in Eastern Asia). This is obvious; however, in the recent past there have been greater movements of people from one place to another. Thus we witness a collision of Cultures within the Civilization. With this movement of persons, some problems have been solved (usually the simplest problems, those which may have been obvious in reference to cause). However, other problems have been encountered, given the nature of Time, such problems often have no precedent, are difficult to understand and even more difficult to deal with. Perhaps the most difficult issues are encountered as a matter of religion (pertaining to the nature and scope of ideas and reasoning), race and/or nationality, both of which have familial implications, biological, psychological, sociological and personal. Where money is an ingredient, animosity may find overt expression, fostered by greed and indignation.

Racism is one such difficult problem, which many now face.[1] Also, the annihilation wars, which seem to be attendant to racism or religion rather than land, or place, appear as very problematic. The anxiety over sex has a peculiar nature and is responsible for any number of crises in our present diverse societies. Millions of innocent children have been slaughtered because of an encouraged eagerness to become involved in illicit fornication. Particularly notable, in this respect, is how men treat their women in various parts of the world; this is a cultural as well as social manifestation and one, of course, which refers to some manner of education, learning and/or indoctrination, formal or otherwise. It also refers to how one value the life of another.

A Nation is a smaller unit than that of a Culture and, once again, Europe is a very good example, with an extensively documented history, spanning many hundreds of years, having a variety of Nations forming a complex Culture. The nations of Asia also have peculiar characteristics, which make them distinct nevertheless they are, to some considerable extent, culturally similar. They are Oriental in culture, however, are more familial in respect to nationality. We imagine that, the differences in the construction and use of language is an important element in how various cultures and nations are distinguished, in reference to the human mind, the thinking and understanding of reality. Also, Europeans did invade other places and have intermingled with the native population, which (in turn) was influenced in distinct ways. There are many fine distinctions, which only a native would recognize and there is some disagreement as to what is and is not valid in

---

1   **Everyone is somehow racist**, which may simply be the *inclination* of a positively inclined self-image. This is not a bad thing, when one has a decent respect for others, born to racially different Parents. Beside which, race is an evolving phenomenon developing coincident to love and mating. Love and mating may have distinct characteristics, depending on tribal, religious, moral and other considerations. Lust, a sin, may also play a part in the becoming of some children. No one can presume to knowing what has happened in every situation.

respect to assumptions. What is known or imagined is *thought substance*. *Thought substance determines how we will form our opinion, one way or another.*

Localities and Clans within a Nation, isolated because of geography, generally contribute to a more homogenized population. Also, Language can be and is an isolating factor, since communication is essential to socializing and to commerce. Linguistic dialect is a result of close associations and a minimal influence from the outside, however does maintain important similarities to a *mother tongue*. Interestingly, individuals can easily adapt, when they have a common language, and may possess personal traits, which provide entry to more than one national or tribal domain.

The Biological Family is a still smaller unit, however, is most fundamentally necessary to any and all of the others. This is true because of the nature of kinship, which is defined, *whether or not it is appreciated*, by one's personal being, such as a resemblance to a parent or sibling, that is to being, as embodied in the flesh. One's parents and children are biological and sociological absolutes. There are also many distinctions pertaining to how one may be imagined as being in the Image of God. *A God figure, humanly perceived, will have been formulated in a personal way*, which is defined by individual imagination, woven within the family, society, culture and civilization. Nations and Cultures form symbolism in a similar manner, with a consensual bias. When one compares Art forms, Christian, Asian, African, Eskimo, this is immediately apparent.

Corporeal Being, which has a genetic origin is responsible for the Individual, who is intimately formed, within the body of the mother, thereafter nurtured in a family. This nurturing begins at the earliest age, from right after birth, and continues during the most formative years. As such, this nurturing provides the basis for nation, culture, and civilization, from the bottom to the top. Language, manner, habits, customs, and religion are also directed from the very first by the behavior of both elders and peers. A manner of common sense is developed, within societies and groups, which is shared, in direct relationship to commonplace encounters, common in one place or another and demanding of some manner of responsibility.

If one is proud of whom one is, that one should be independent, good, well informed, dependable, and, above all, *not programmed to respond as one of an ignorant mob*. Watch any ignorant, militant and destructive mob, then ask yourself the question: "Is this how I want to be? Really?" At present, Television, movies and theatrical performance will influence, immeasurably, the nature of individual being. We admit, what is viewed and understood may have positive value. However, what is learned from unknown others will not provide the necessary ingredients for an well-understood self-determination, when there does exist, as is quite certain, an effort to sublimate the identity of the person as such. Individually, as a spectator, each viewer is vulnerable, *believing too much of what each has been programmed to believe.* We address a complex and intricate subject however, with the existence of mass communication and so many extraneous and anonymous inputs of information, it is reasonable to assume that one's thinking forms in ways unique in history. Not to forget the main issue, Money is generated, counted in tens of billions whereabouts mass communication is concerned. Indeed, such commerce as is attendant to mass communication is a very significant factor in present economies.

Our Public **Schools are, quite unfortunately, inextricable factors in the problems, which** we must face. *Public education is in many instances detrimentally causative as it attempts to be socially ameliorative* and succeeds more, in many respects, as being a cause rather than as being a cure for many of the problems we face. The structure and methods of Public Education guarantee that no significant changes will be enacted. There are too many individuals, in positions of authority dependent upon what exists. This assertion is made after having spent almost fifty years in public Higher Education.

Concerning Higher Education, much of what one might imagine has a positive connotation and in fairness there is much truthful effort in support of significant learning. However, beneath the surface all is not well. Concern is, in this instance, not for economics or the monies spent on silly programs, rather we are concerned for the immorality and overly competitive nature, destructively so, of some members of the faculties.[2] In fact much of what is done is simply a waste of time and functions primarily to create job opportunities. As such it tends to prevent serious learning for many, as it distracts students with needless information even as what is overly mundane often functions to obscure and corrupt the truth. The incessant longing of *some faculty members,* to engage in *"seemingly important research,"* distracts them from their principal responsibilities, which should be teaching and the dissemination of truthful and properly formed and understood knowledge with coincident truthfully supportive information. We suggest that Knowledge, formed and seated in Tradition, is trustworthy, whereas information, which accumulates in present time, piece by piece, as a part of present activities may be quite

---

2   **Immorality**, given the lustful nature of the more eager professors, is an issue in most universities. This author, after nearly fifty years of University teaching, can attest to the fact that many Faculty Members make a habit of fornicating with their students, and certainly many are adulterous. Concerning one Department of forty faculty members, more or less, fourteen are positively known to me to have been so involved, during a ten-year period. This is overlooked, for professional reasons and because, without photographs and personal testimony, it is difficult to prove such an assertion. Beside which, such behavior has become acceptable to many, especially to those so involved, who have a persuasive and intimidating position as regard young adults.

unreliable and difficult to place within the scheme of things. There is a time-space factor involved that is tricky to deal with. Present time is in flux and requires that elements be extended toward consequence, which can be studied and analyzed. As we live, day to day we learn from personal experience, from *"hard knocks"* as they say. Formalized Education provides opportunities to learn from a well-organized and competent understanding gained from the past.

Experience has indemnified, at least for this writer that, many faculty members presuming to be intellectually superior, look down on those who teach. In such instance Scholarship, or what is imagined as Scholarship is often assertively and negatively judgmental, as it condemns those who are attempting to do, what they are being paid to do. The way the system is structured is part of the problem and that Education is run mostly for the benefit of those in the *"Business of Education."* How this has come to be is difficult to imagine however, at the root is vanity, intellectual vanity. Those who are so inclined probably would be surprised at the inference. So be it. Such is an important part of University Politics, in the assumption of one who has spent his life, patiently teaching young adults, many of whom were misplaced, lacking the intellectual and experiential requirements necessary for serious learning.

Significantly, television and popular media have given college students standards, which they seem to have adopted with gusto. Shacking up, sex-in-the-dorm and spring break are some obvious examples. All this does relate to money and to economics, since entire industries have blossomed to serve all the nonsense, even as such nonsense distracts from and negates the effects of serious learning, which is brother to the acquisition of truthful knowledge. Obviously such behavior is transmitted by mass media, thus to relate to what is discussed immediately above, all for money. Furthermore, youth is encouraged to spend, spend and spend, thus to acquire things for instant gratification.[3] To repeat, Socrates did suggest that, "He is most content who is satisfied with the smallest portion". Who, in our overabundant land might believe Socrates? Thus, at present, youth is very likely denying the wisdom of one of the world's most distinguished and able philosophers. Youth is educated and trained, in both public and private venues, to embrace sin and all forms of vice, which will provide fatal consequence for those so compromised. Of ultimate biologic, social, moral and symbolic significance is the fact

---

3   **Credit cards** are distributed to young adults, who are unable to add a simple column of numbers and who are unable to evaluate true cost, when factoring principal, interest and the depreciation, sustained during a period of ownership. Automobile dealers pander on the university campus, enticing students to acquire significant debt, before they can comprehend what this means. Admittedly, cities have grown too large and seemingly what is done appears as necessary.

that millions of first-born children have been and are being butchered, killed rather than born by a loving mother.

Of great concern is the fact that we now have women in combat. Put another way, the men are not capable of defending the country, rather we should depend on our sisters and mothers. We have sent our young men and women too to the other side of the globe to protect what in truth belongs to others, albeit we do have some legitimate claims as well. Certainly there are economic and other issues regarding that our way of life may be temporarily threatened and they are of reasonable concern. Nevertheless, we seem to be pursuing the wrong course, especially since we have already been, to a considerable extent, conquered by those interested in enjoying what we have managed to accomplish in better times. We are being certainly conquered. Millions occupy our country without the necessity of force. Their force is their presence and that we have become dependent upon them to do what we cannot do or will not do. They perceive our weaknesses and will exploit them until we are overcome. And we should consider that our daughters are placed in a position of being run through with a bayonet, raped, tortured or blown up in the process. Before now this was a fate left to our sons. Who will occupy the body bags of the future, your wife, your daughter or your son.

Our "Salesmen Mentality" will guarantee that, ultimately, _all that is will be factored economically_, one way or another. And, the coins will roll in the direction of they who have captured the wealth of nations. ***Money goes, where money is!***

The world needs good soldiers

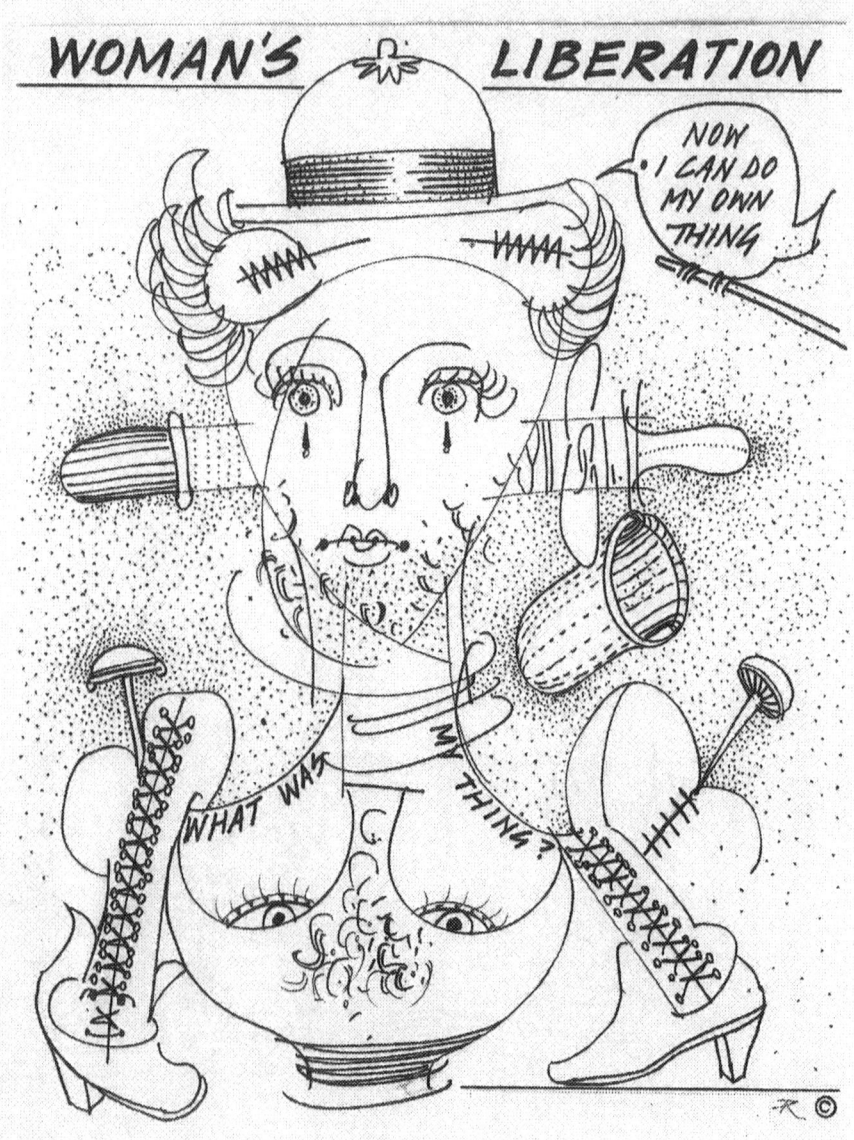

Woman's liberation

XVII. The Last Hurrah

Every step in the right direction will provide absolution for ten steps in the wrong direction, toward eternal salvation. Be good, decent, fair-minded, patient and humble then be proud of whom you are, without the unnecessary respect of those who would destroy you. Evil is woven into the garment of civilization in very peculiar ways. When you are truthfully able to act as God wills that you should, your entire being will be transformed with energy and purpose. You will never know this if you do not try!

What we witness, at the beginning of the twenty-first century, is the World-wide consequence of theft on a monumental scale. Without mass Communication, privately owned Central Banking and Computers, what is would have been unimaginable. Our Dilemma is absolutely guaranteed by the system, which we now patronize. If one considers fairness as a virtue, what we have is grossly unfair and a largely unworkable System designed and controlled by self-serving opportunists, hypocrites and myopic Politicians. Alien interlopers that despise the Ideals inherent in Catholic Christianity, which has provided so much for so many, do not even consider God. Thus we have a godless program, totalitarian, ruthless, insensitive, unholy! In truth, our system, including the most important money transactions therein, rewards theft, deception, cheating hypocrisy, vanity, lust and greed. This same system condemns virtue and all promise of goodness, thrift, prudence, patience and truthfully sustained love.

Nevertheless, misadventure and mayhem is in contrast to the many wonderful and decent things that do happen even as they conceal much of what is wrong. We postulate that this may be the necessary form of a great Civilization, perhaps it can be no other way. Nevertheless we do see much that can be improved for millions, those who would not understand the problem or the solution. And, we understand Greed as a primary motivation in the scheme of things, Greed being most obvious where money and the exchange of goods are the object of intent.

Who said, "Seek and yea shall find. Ask and it shall be given"? The world does need its entire people, all of its people. Not some or even most, all! Concerning money and the value thereof, no number of words, written or spoken for effect, will make any difference whatsoever to the man that is cheated by his government and by those who control the medium of exchange. Senseless conflict is made possible by the unimaginable scale of evil endeavor, which seeks to satisfy a perverted will to power. Many in power *have assumed, covertly and illegally*, to control that, which is not within their Jurisdiction.[1] Others *have been appointed* for having cooperated with the usurpers, thus played the role of a hypocrite in traitorous endeavor.[2] The Lackey termed Politician, together with their conceited, worldly functionaries, in government, media, banking, and entertainment (so-called), deliberately, conscientiously and consistently obscure or condemn the truth, so that few men are capable of understanding what is really happening. All this, in spite of the fact that we boast of a politically determined, overly expensive educational system, which has, in fact, abandoned the philosophy of Catholic Christian Civilization. When educational institutions *seemingly* value athletics over learning and the cultivation of the mind; when college students behave as lustfully barbaric morons during an Easter break; when the salesman's mentality dominates all levels of the educational system, be informed the Civilization and the Culture of Catholic Christianity are gone. All in this world will be victims, whether knowingly or unknowingly; the consequence will be the same.

We suffer from a strange complex existing of political domination in service of economic gain for they who mastermind the takeover of our wealth by a group with the object of determining fascist control over Agriculture, commerce and industry.[3] This is supported and youth are made ready, that is conditioned to accept and be in agreement with what they do not understand. The young, are bright, hopeful and beautiful however, they are not wise. They have been and are being conditioned to accept a form of amused and titillated servitude,

---

1   **Mullins, Eustice,** *The World Order, Our Secret Rulers,* (Ezra Pound Institute, Publisher, Staunton, A 24401, Second Edition, 1992). Pp. 50-64.

2   **Mendal House and Harry Hopkins (the Hop)** were appointed by Presidents Woodrow Wilson and Franklin Roosevelt respectively and were very influential in the lives of millions, nevertheless neither ever received a vote or were they known to the common man, except coincidentally. **Bernard Baruch,** made millions as a war profiteer and stock speculator, working on insiders information. **Joseph Kennedy** made a fortune in illegal liquor and another fortune as a stock speculator. Both men were inordinately responsible for the Crash of 1929. More recently **Henry Kissinger** (a foreign born alien) has had a too influential voice in America's foreign policy, both democratic and republican. At this very moment men, whom we do not know and can not know, are responsible for what is happening to us right now.

3   **Twight, Charlotte,** *America's Emerging Facist Economy,* Arlington House, Publishers. New Rochelle, NY. ©1975 by Charlotte Twight. ISBN # 0-87000-317-8.

perpetually in debt to they who control the money and the means of financial control. Amongst our population there will be many presumably successful at all levels that work for the established fascistic monopolies. This will make it appear as though everything is just fine.

All that we witness is as a consequence of political ineptitude and an inability to understand what made this a great country. And, it is still a great country in many ways, which no one can deny. Nevertheless the hypocrisy, traitorous behavior of our elected leaders, capitulation to vice and simple ignorance combine, to imperil our position as a nation. We have been and are being divided in various ways and we will be conquered by what is obvious and by what is unseen. Only God knows of all that is seen and unseen. Unfortunately, too many, perhaps most refuse to acknowledge the force of what is unseen.

THE HEAD
AND BRAIN
OF A POLITICIAN

STRICTLY REQUIRED OF ALL
SENATORS, CONGRESSMEN AND,
OF COURSE, THE PRESIDENT
AND ALL "IMPORTANT" GOVERNORS!

IT MAY TAKE A REAL WISEMOUTH
MANY YEARS TO DEVELOP, BUT
"LUCKY FOR THE REST OF US",
A "REAL" FOOL MAY BE BORN THIS
WAY. CAN ANYONE IMAGINE?

THE EYE, THOUGH PRESENT, CANNOT AND WILL NOT SEE CLEARLY.

TEAR DUCTS, ESPECIALLY EQUIPPED, FOR CRYING OVER SPILLED MILK!

NOSTRILS, ESPECIALLY EQUIPPED, FOR THE SNIFFING OF SOME PERSONAL ADVANTAGE.

THE SPINE, TYPICALLY WEAK, CANNOT AND DOES NOT SUPPORT A GOOD AND SOLID HEAD!

WHY DID YOU VOTE FOR THEM?

The head and brain of the politician

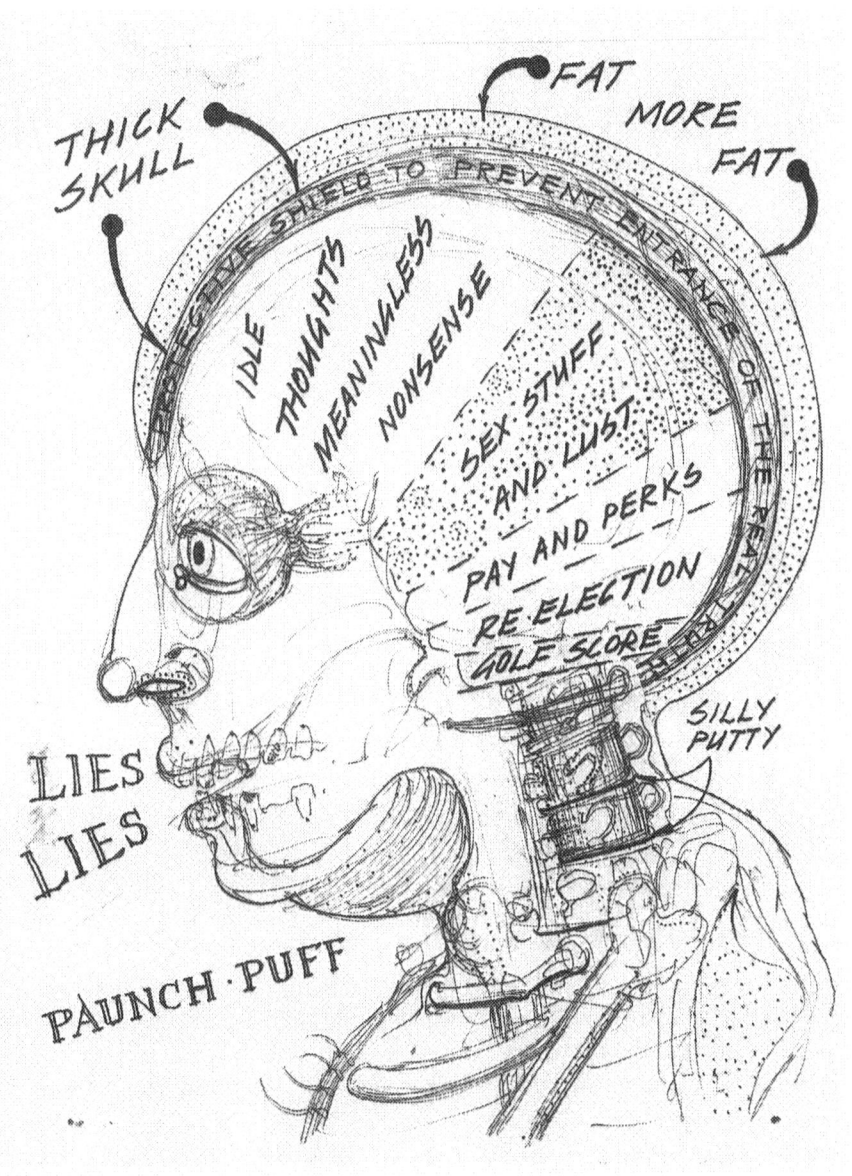

Fat, more fat

XVIII. What to do in Defense of Goodness and Freedom?

Actually there are a number of very simple actions, which might go a long way toward correcting much of what is sinful and evil. However, each will require some amount of self-restraint and, of course, many will have to discontinue those habits upon which the "elite" depends. The "elite" knows it is easy to control an eager follower, by means of engendering predictable behavioral patterns, which can be exploited. *Therefore, each one must become an individual, a real individual. What to do?* This need not involve any outrageous behavior or reverting to what is obnoxious, vulgar, infantile or savage. Youth is likely to revert to what is hereby inferred however, the young should be discouraged by the decent and proper behavior of the adults, those that set the examples. Adults must stop seeking to return to childhood in their manners and activities. Santa Claus and the Easter Bunny are for children. Being an adult does not preclude happiness.

Cancel subscriptions to some current newspapers and magazines, especially those owned by publishing conglomerates, which pretend to inform your opinion. The same few individuals or families own publications with the largest circulation and they are often greedy and mostly self-interested opportunists.[1] Therefore, spend whatever you might spend in support of those writers who write the truth and who are known to be enemies of Communism, Cradle to the Grave Socialism, The United Nations, The One World Order and the quasi-socialist entrenched political establishment. *Patronize men of integrity, who try to expose what is the greatest theft in the history of the world.* Support grass roots publications, those in your own community, which defy the existing establishments' presumptions and whose writers are, in fact, known to you. Do not be deceived by the appearance of well-financed publications designed to steal from you. *Every*

---

1 **Who controls the Media?** *Who Controls American Media News and Entertainment?* The Committee to Restore the Constitution. Bulletin # 376, May 1993.

locality in the world has a group of honest and well informed citizens, who will do what is right and will continue to act in your best interest, who are compatible with your own thinking and understanding. This will help to rebuild communities, which are being deliberately destroyed, especially rural communities, with spacious surroundings, those close to nature's wonders. Rural communities are where most of us would like to live. Keep in mind, the wealthy have country estates, with fences and horses and thousands of beautiful trees.[2] Compare this with an apartment next to the Freeway. Freeways function to destroy communities and make traveling a great distance a necessity, even as the community laments the cost of transportation. The time spent in commuting, sitting in the car burning fuel and going nowhere, is a certain sign that we have not always done the right thing? How great are great cities? Millions live in squalor, so that some can spend millions on several accommodations. We do not recommend a socialist form of wealth distribution, sponsored by corrupt government. We do recommend a more consistently Catholic Morality, a universal morality, which will ensure a greater emphasis on fairness and decency. When fairness and decency are given greater importance in any monetary equation, wealth will find all in need, who are capable of earning their own way; most individuals are able to earn their own way when given any small opportunity and they are satisfied in being able to do so. In addition they are happier, content and not likely to riot and to destroy what others have accomplished.

Turn off your television or simply limit the time you will spend viewing what someone else thinks is important. And spend more time with your family, your children and friends so as to better understand what is known and important to you, that which is in your immediate sphere. Spend your time doing what requires your intelligence, your skills, your participation and your ability to think. Especially, don't watch the news. Bad news impairs bodily functions, creates anxieties and causes illness.[3] *The news is carefully selected, contrived, edited and structured so as to inform, selectively, they who are mostly unaware and are susceptible to indoctrination.* All the news you receive from the "Biggies" is editorialized for effect, then folded in between commercialized nonsense, distracting from the meaning of the subject. The globe is not a village. *What is advertised as the "Family*

---

2   **The Dulles Brothers, Rockerfellers, DuPonts** and the like all have had magnificent estates, with gates and trees and woodlands, beside which they own millions of the shares of the great corporations. They own the Corporations! They have their own floor traders working every day to protect and enhance their holdings.

3   **Schulze, Richard, M. D.,** This assertion is made frequently by the good doctor, other Doctors as well.

of Man" is a euphemism for a uniformly controlled, obedient and economically subservient population. This alone is reason enough not to watch and read what someone else believes is necessary for your well being.

Know who is the someone-else that provides the information? Recognize that if you are spending a great deal of time watching television, you are also being denied the time necessary to access any truth, which you might discover better by your own "personally directed" efforts. *America is still a wonderful place. We do have wonderful libraries and serious works are available.* We suggest that you avail yourself to read some of the works listed in the bibliography, attendant to this work. Be assertive in your own behalf, not a docile "couch potato" certain to be made ineffective in your participation, as you are being indoctrinated into accepting the status quo and the concept of a One World Government, within which only a few will prosper. Actually, we do not believe this will happen, nevertheless, millions have died and millions more will die prematurely because of this *insane Ide*a. And, this *insane Idea* has been an important part of Civilization for five thousand years of known history. *Individually, we must understand that a One-World Government is primarily an economic undertaking, Politics is the handmaiden and Politicians are the Pimps.*

Certainly there are many great novels however, *don't be distracted by reading too many novels.* Many current choices are trash, appealing to lustful ignorance and to a *poorly educated, carefully managed population,* not unlike those that *participated* in the French and other Revolutions. Smutty books and indecent pictures will corrupt your being and your soul. *Do not let the ignorant, lustful and vain moron dictate what will become the nature and substance of your thought content.*

Don't eat in franchise restaurants! Patronize that proprietor, the little guy who owns his own building, who is independent, whilst you are still able to do so. Municipalities, together with state and federal agencies, the ones supported with your taxes, have made it difficult, if not impossible, for individuals to succeed in any business and, the restaurant business is no exception.[4] For example a bakery or a restaurant can be managed by a family and by small groups of individuals, that you can easily help with your patronage. Immigrant people, Chinese, Greeks, Polish and Russian have found restaurants to be an ideal place for their families to become wealthy. This writer has always found the concept of a corporate franchise quite repulsive. From a cultural standpoint, it is deadly on familial continuity and furthermore, the franchise is a rather subtle (nevertheless effective) first step

---

4   **Zoning Laws and Licensing requirements** function to frustrate individual participation and at times violate common sense. For example, the best bakery, bread and pastries that I have ever eaten were baked in a home bakery, in the basement of a duplex. Such bakery would be illegal today, for many *silly reasons* that defy common sense.

toward corporate domination. Mac Donald's perhaps is the best representative of this phenomenon. Mac Donald's has become a social illness and has led to millions developing unhealthful eating habits. Patronize the small entity so as to promote the smallest element in the society, that being the individual. It is better if the recipients of your patronage are local people, whom you know and respect for whom they are. They will have money to spend in your community. Put yourself in their positions and any question will answer itself. Be your brother's keeper. Thereby let your neighbor profit from you friendship, because you love and respect Him and what he is able to do, without mass-media advertising and the economic intervention and gregarious support of a distant and unknown proprietor.

Don't buy designer clothes. Remove the labels before you wear any garment. *Your identity is not enhanced because of someone's assumed name, sewn on an overpriced item.* If you have your own good identity, there is no use for a label that announces who made your clothing. The entire notion is childish however, has been created *in your mind* by hustlers and middlemen. Any intelligent person knows that the label is not the garment. *The idea of such need is a pre-adolescent one, abandon it!* Nevertheless, individuals are addicted to various labels and even small children are being conditioned to "prefer" that irrelevant attachment to what they wear. In extreme instances, youngsters are beaten, threatened and even killed over a jacket or a pair of shoes. Mothers should sew clothing for their own children, as was done in the past; thus developing a basic skill and providing an economically meaningful outlet for native intelligence.[5] In such instance, *the garment serves as a symbol of parental ability and respect for the child* who wears that same garment. Furthermore, this provides a significant opportunity for "bonding" (a rather new term, however, quite meaningful if properly understood) and allows the mother the opportunity to teach daughters a basic skill. Sewing employs motor reflexes as well as genuine sensibilities, which can and do refer to culture and to being who one is. Sewing should be taught in school as in the past however, many such programs have been abandoned as being unnecessary. Factory made "stuff" with some goofy label, made in a foreign country with cheap labor, does not do this. Such merchandise rather refers to someone outside the family, an athlete, rock-star, movie personality, that was paid for signing their name or to some non-person, with legal protection for a fictitious name. Actually, vain and greedy individuals would put their name on anything (for a price). Such as they, in fact, are pimps for the establishment and the millionaires who control the garment industry, including the control of the corrupt unions, subservient to socialist ideologies. Time, carefully and patiently invested in what has been known as "woman's work",

---

5   **Young women** might learn to sew, which is productive and provides an economic advantage. Instead we teach them to kick a ball, which is meaningless.

provides for the development and sustaining of a culture wherein the individual effort, purposefully directed with love and devotion (especially toward children), is rewarded in kind; with love and devotion.[6] No harlot in tight pants will ever know of such love and devotion, not from a child and not from a man. *Designer labels are just another rip-off. Face it!*[7] Then, ignore them in the market place so as not to make some opportunistic parasite wealthy on your own children's desire to conform. Importantly, what you do, for yourself and for your family, is tax-free: the skill, the labor, the art and (of course) the love. Think about it! Avoid Factory Outlet Stores like the *economic plague* that they are.

Move away from the great (so-called) cities if possible. How great are they? They are mostly congested, overdeveloped, dirty and noisy, have foul air and are riddled by crime (from top to bottom). Everyone might not agree with what is wrong, as so stated. In fact, in the great Cities there are too many individuals living in a too small space. This is exacerbated by the increasing value of land, which in fact, becomes less desirable as a site for an existence. Consider New York; a view of Central Park can cost millions, whereas on a farm the scenery is there for the viewing, at no extra charge. As cities are becoming more crowded they are more expensive and more certainly an economic trap.

Demographers inform us that the world's people live on just about two or three-percent (a bit more of less) of the earth's land surface. Our Christian Bible encourages us to spread over the earth and to multiply. To some extent we have done just that. Some may have been quite insensitive in the past, however, that does not preclude a more sensitive approach in the future. We need not encroach rather we should share in what is natural, beautiful and everlasting. For about one hundred years, perhaps longer, many men have known that much of our infrastructure, given a more restrained existence, would be quite unnecessary, especially so in respect to electric energy and the disposal of waste. The problems we face are caused by our not having peopled the earth in a more sparsely settled

---

6   **Woman's Work** is that, which does and always has sustained the family, the tribe and the culture. Mother's milk is just the beginning, followed by humble devotion to her children, progeny, which guarantee her future and that of her mate. If one is so disposed the children recognize this and respond in kind, which in fact provides the most honest and durable form of child-parent "Bonding". Often the children of the poor have much more respect for their parents than do the children of the Rich. Women have been encouraged to place their children in the care of strangers that work for money and have little long term interest in the child. This is because of the time and the love that is given, being understood for what it is. You can't buy love!

7   **Interestingly,** some retailers are bringing out their own brands, which are often better made and are less expensive thus they are better values. Albeit this is another corporate maneuver, taken by the Integrated Corporation, in search of greater profits.

manner; thus we have created what many see as an impossible situation. *For economic reasons, many millions are crowding together in huge cities, where millions live in squalor, or very near poverty.* It would appear the only reasonable option is to spread out where each individual and family can do more for themselves and for each other. In the past, hundreds of small towns functioned admirably with much less than we presently have. These same small towns have dried up, in many instances, and will no longer have children to supply the great cities, like New York, Los Angeles, and Chicago. Presently, the good stock of noble selfless and absolutely honest people, whom we could depend upon to bring vitality to an expanding metropolis, is dwindling. Admittedly, some prefer living in congested and squalid cities, especially they that profit most from the misery of others.

The "country bumpkin," willing to give an honest day's labor for an honest day's pay must be imported from another land. An Entrepreneur will recognize a good man; however; may do nothing to help him. Good men are, more often than not, simply exploited. We do not play on a level field. Therefore, do what you can for yourself and your family and friends, with your own abilities! Many of life's refinements, especially in the realm of dining, can be had for just a little effort and simple prudence. Prudence is a virtue.

Presently, Mexico supplies uncounted numbers of decent people, who are willing to work hard, for less than those born to freedom and prosperity.[8] Perhaps, their most important contribution to the great city is their moral disposition or their Christian ethic and fair-minded character, which too often, is never mentioned. Who understands and will admit to this? Europe too is being invaded by willing workers, however they are not necessarily Christian.

The above suggestion will require a century to implement and contradicts the objectives of the bureaucratic planners. Such Planners hope to position most of humanity in high-rise tenements, thereby to make room for the animals and the birds, which by some individuals are considered more important than our children. The sale of pet food is a good indication that some feed their dogs better than many can feed their children. With this apparent conundrum, their exists a very peculiar mind-set, one for which there are few precedents. Nevertheless, some children starve whilst animals are treated, by some, as a form of Deity. Animal worship is and has been considered a part of superstitious and primitive misunderstanding, which interprets that animals are just like humans in

---

8   **Legislation is being considered**, which will give preference to illegal and other aliens for doing what Americans, lacking both incentive and need are not able to do. Abundance has a way of encouraging laziness and a false sense of superiority. This will result in our undoing as a nation. We are following Rome, to an inglorious ending, financial ruin, intellectual bankruptcy, social and moral decay and to despoliation.

spiritually important ways. Disneyland, with its star, Mickey Mouse, has done much to promote this unusual misunderstanding; unusual in the light of what is known, given a so advanced and so "enlightened" population. It is not intended to develop this point completely, however, rather to suggest that *when people are "captured" in the cities, they are* without recourse concerning all vital and important necessities and are, therefore, *more easily controlled* and programmed toward "acceptable" behavioral patterns. This is exactly the notion, quite unfortunately so, which caused the becoming of the Ghetto, many centuries ago. The Ghetto is a place within the community, yet spiritually divided from that same community. Such divisions will manifest in the balkanization of an area, much as is apparent in Eastern Europe, whereabouts antagonisms, Riots and ultimately War is the obvious consequence. Serious beginnings were apparent in Los Angeles in 1993, more recently in some other of our cities. In New Orleans, even given an ultimate catastrophe many citizens were witnessed stealing from others, looting and causing mischief to selected "Others." Presently (2006) ethnic neighborhoods provide good examples of disagreement and violence, as in Paris and other Major metropolitan areas, throughout the Western World. And, Asia is not exempt from such occurrence.

Do not patronize the drug pushers. If you want to keep kids off drugs, adults must stop turning to all forms of sedatives, tranquilizers, sleeping pills, digestive aids, laxatives, hair dyes, and assorted formulas. The medical professions has been too aggressive in prescribing so many false remedies when, in perhaps most instances, common sense is all that is required.[9] And, it is generally understood that most ailments will be cured in a short time without any medication. Many Professionals believe that the human body will cure itself, just about ninety percent of the time, when the body is given the proper nourishment and is made free of toxic substances (Schulze MD, Douglas, MD). *The harmful ingredients in many patent medicines do more damage, in many instances, than the ills, which are presumably being cured.* Many patent medicines, so-called, required a prescription just a few years ago. However, when patents run out the same drugs become more readily available.[10] The issue centers on money, greed and the lifestyle of they who benefit from false expectations. The drug cartels reap billions from unwitting individuals who, because of ignorance or fear, contaminate their bodies with unnecessary, often harmful substances.

---

9   Privitera, James, MD., and Stang, Alan, MA., <u>Silent Clots, Life's Biggest Killers</u>. The Catacombs Press, 105 N. Grandview, Covina CA 91723. ISBN # 0-9656313-0-3. Chapters, 12 & 13.

10   Schulze, Richard, MD. Natural Healing Newsletters. **www.herbdoc.com**

<u>Most importantly, (if possible) send your children to private schools</u>, those most acceptable to you, the parents. To indemnify such assertion, this writer has almost fifty years experience in public education and concludes without any doubt whatsoever, *in too many instances, public schools are effectively preventing children from learning what should be learned.* Experience has proven that most educators, at the present time, well meaning though they may be, are poorly educated themselves. They are too often motivated by the wrong reasoning, <u>*devised for them by socialist schemers and pandered by the gurus of education*</u>, who are almost exclusively the enemies of free men.[11] These same gurus are part of the elite Establishment and presume to know more than everyone else. Generally, their programs are mostly failures, beside which though ineffective they prevent children from learning what **IS** important. For examples, look at what has happened to language, popular music, art, morality, and all serious learning; the best of every thing, with few exceptions, has been and is being removed from the curriculum. We concede in music and athletics, there are astounding examples of wonderful achievement. We imagine this is in spite of the System. Educators insist all is well however, the behavior, social aptitudes, sense of morality, sense of decorum and general manners of our children have been gradually worsening for fifty years. Many youngsters, deprived of proper parental guidance and the genuine decently inspired love given by family and friends, have formed vicious street gangs, which are a threat to the adult population. What is worse, the youngsters are proud of their vicious and savage behavior, even to the extent of inscribing their own bodies with silly retrograde imagery. They, imagine, quite incorrectly that, crudely inspired body mutilation is an art form.

The institution of learning, so called, is totally infiltrated by a cadre of self-interested and impiously motivated practitioners, many of whom have very little ability, however, who pretend to know how everyone should live. Teachers in establishment schools, that seek the truth, are generally ignored in their efforts. Appointed functionaries lead a system, which penalizes excellence and panders to ignorance and intellectual ineptitude. In contrast Athletics, which should be an extra-curricular function, often dominates the school year. The fact is, in the opinion of many brilliant scholars; the public educational system is a detriment to learning.[12] Public Education has been and is controlled by a force alien to Christianity, especially so regarding Catholicism. Having been under the control

---

11 **Sutton, Antony, (recently deceased)** <u>*How the Order Controls Education,*</u> Research Publications, Inc., Phoenix, AZ. 1984 © ISBN #0-914981-09-9.

12 **Blumenfeld, Samuel L.,** <u>*Is Public Education Necessary?*</u> The Paradigm Company, Boise, ID. Second Edition. ISBN# 0-914981-10-2. Especially page I, however one must take time to read all.

of an alien, socialistic philosophy, for just about a century, Public Education has almost eliminated Christianity, from the minds of the students, especially the moral and ethical aspects. Holy days of obligation are seen as time for fun and games, especially Christmas and Easter. They must be referred to as Winter Break and Spring Break, no mention is allowed of a Holy day of obligation. This is no accident, since _Christianity values the being of each and every person and regards no person or group as being superior to another._ Keep in mind, America was founded as a Christian nation, or so we believe, providing (at that time) an escape from what is apparently developing right here, right now. The enemy is following. Public Education and what it represents, in spite of the unseen efforts of decent and courageous teachers, may destroy what has been so carefully constructed, for the benefit of each and every citizen; One Nation, Under God, with Liberty and Justice for all.

Stop pandering to the cult of the athlete. What is called sports, in this nation, is really big business, encouraged by gambling (a vice), designed to sell expensive tickets, over-priced hot dogs, advertising, and all manner of outrageous behavior. If you prefer that your daughters not be raped, then stop financial aid to that segment of the population that might be inclined to do so. Formerly, the Law, to some extent, did protect you from being assaulted by the boastful lecher. This is no longer the case within a system where laws are meaningless, where certain individuals are excused for excessive behavior and where justice is twisted and is for sale to the highest bidder. Certainly, advise your sons to avoid all manner of whore, stop encouraging him, as so many young men boast, to "sow his wild oats". The _young lady conquered by an anxious young lecher,_ who believes this is how it should be, is someone's precious and lovely child. In the recent past, many athlete's (team players as they call themselves) have set the worst possible example for our young men. Although there may be a shallow effort to court decency, the very nature of what happens in a mob situation, chanting, vulgarity and excessive drinking guarantees much of what is so dreadfully apparent. Some of the most notorious athletes are vain, greedy, and lustful men who profit from the fact that too many individuals enjoy wasting their time in the observation of meaningless events, which, though sensational, have little or no significant value. _To remember the scores and the names of games is to be stultified in one's thinking or simple minded._

When one observes youngsters of ten "swapping" athletic cards, youngsters who will never learn to read a good book, youngsters who already are compelled by sensation, greed and the hope that they too can become rich playing a game, one wonders where will this all end? There are many fine, good, and decent men who are also athletes. We do apologize to the good men within the community of athletes, however, it is admonished that they should see what is apparent and not defend evil against what is good. We do concur that athletics and the development of a strong and healthy body are desirable ventures however, we caution the reader that there are limits to what is appropriate. Here the concern is for a complex phenomenon, the nature of which and the extent of which is difficult to comprehend, however, one may begin by being honest with one's self and by ceasing in the encouragement of what is over-valued, being merely simple-minded entertainment.

Condemn the Wrongdoing, protected by consenting adult laws, which are woven into the whole fabric of our society, to the prurient delight of some at great expense to others and to the societal body as a whole. The cities are full of the product of wanton fornication, protected as a right by consenting adult laws. The presence of militant, mean, boastful and dumb youngsters, who threaten the rest of the population provides a clear symbol of the presence of lust and the sins of the flesh. As individuals become more and more decadent and demanding of ever greater license to commit indecent and deviate acts, which are contrary to the best Christian, Catholic (universally sanctioned) wisdom of the past two thousand years, so too the Civilization and the Cultures within will be demoralized and ruined. The "Brave New World", represents only what is mischievous, old fashioned and unworkable. Nevertheless Sin is compelling on mischievously occupied imaginations. The men of alien conscience, who dominate the monetary and corporate endeavor and encourages large-scale events, including conflict and world war, must be challenged and brought to be accountable for what is happening. We do not believe any form of Socialism or Communism provides any reasonable solution. What is needed is that the moral order be re-established and that honesty, truthfulness and integrity be brought to bear on variously formed social, economic and political transactions. And this includes restoring sanity to what is supposed to be a game, fairly competitive, played for enjoyment and relaxation.

Demand good and proper action, from those whom you elect to govern, especially concerning expenditures of large sums of money. Demand that elected-Politicians restore our Constitution, which was written for the benefit of the sovereign American Citizen. And, *we must withdraw from the contrived and phony United Nations*, which is nothing more than a means to conquer the Civilization with the Wealth of our nation.[13] Demand that Traitors be weeded out and punished for betraying those who depend on honest and responsive government.

Incarcerate or punish those individuals who provide the drugs, which have addicted millions of unfortunate individuals. Those who are leaders, in this

---

13   **Bulletin,** *The Committee to Restore the Constitution,* Oct. 2003, # 503. Colorado, Non-Profit Corporation, P. O. Box 986, Ft. Collins, Colorado, 80522. Chapter XIII, Victory Denied, 306 page, by Archibald E. Roberts, Lt. Col., (then Major) Army of the United States, ret. LC # 66-20665.

enterprise, should be tried and if convicted (beyond a reasonable doubt), should be given the death penalty.[14] If our legal system can incarcerate individuals for calling someone a name, such *imagined as a hate crime*, Judges should also be able to implement the death penalty for fatally destructive behavior. If our computers can find a one-dollar error on an income tax statement, they should be able to find some moron that brings a ton of cocaine into the country. Who, is kidding Who? Drug pushers are responsible for ruining the lives of many individuals and as many families. Ultimately such irresponsible behavior will destroy our civilization and our Christian Culture if they are not stopped. When things get really bad, as they certainly will (and have already in some places) mobs will demand rule by force; total control of the population will be a fact of life, which affects hundreds or thousands of individuals. One should inform them self, of just who and how drug traffic was begun between East and West.[15] Coincidentally, many of those engaged in drug traffic may have been and are often engaged in many other forms of crime, including murder, Kidnapping and rape of women become sex slaves, so as to please and satiate the perverse "needs" and "savage brutality" of aggressively stupid and lustfully insensitive maggot-men.

Millions watch endless hours of "filtered" news of crimes being committed, which are presented as action entertainment. To be pacified and entertained by bedlam and speeding cars inveighs upon the collective psyche and does no good at all.

Lastly, keep in mind that *America cannot solve all the world's problems,* even though some imagine this is possible, America should not attempt to do so. Most

---

14   **The Death Penalty** need not be considered cruel and unusual. It might better be considered simply a legality, a fact of life. If a Nation can tolerate the *contrived legalities and suspect reasoning,* which allows for the killing of tens of millions of children, it is ludicrous for that same system to lament the execution of men for serial murder and other heinous crimes. If a man is able to murder innocent people, that same man should have the guts to pay an ultimate price. To be effective, the Law must have force. Without Force, there is no Law. The Force of Law should work in defense of a determinedly Christian, particularly Catholic Imperative, in that it would stress the Immortal nature of each and every human being. Nevertheless, the community and the Individuals defiled and killed by deliberately fatal anti-social behavior are entitled to a severe and final disposition of malicious Capital offenders. This does not negate the right to a fair trial, however fairness demands a sense of honor regarding the victims. The argument of sanity is a transparent attempt to capitalize on the confusion within the system. This being a broad subject, we cannot nor will we attempt to conclude the issues.

15   **Mullins, Eustice,** The World Order, Our Secret Rulers, Pp.53-55.

such problems have moral and social dimensions that are not understood by for-eign-born Do-gooders. We should set a better example ourselves for other nations to follow, then it would not be necessary that we move around the world blowing up another man's country. Politically inspired imaginations work for the destruc-tion of our Christianity as they steal our wealth in the most subtle, nevertheless effective ways. All men must be allowed the exercise of their own free will, pre-sumably this will lead to the best solutions for truthfully understood questions. We, as a nation, must solve our own problems as they pertain to our immediate sphere. We must free ourselves from an oppressive privately owned and operated Federal Reserve System. We must shut down the profitable and illegal counterfeit-ing, of our currency and consider more honestly the meaning of our monumental indebtedness. If we cannot become free in our own country, from an over-domi-nant alien influence then, *in spite of the millions of great Americans and the world's powerhouse of technical achievement*, America is still a very poor and barren land, a poor example for the rest of mankind. We will be overrun and disappear as a nation, unless more individuals become aware of the greater aspects of Reality.

If your have read this far, you have a good understanding of what to do. You will have many ideas of your own, which coincidentally can be brought to bear on the issues. There are many more pages, which might be written however; the reader must go beyond this to search, with heightened interest, through some of the works cited in the Bibliography.

Where Politics are concerned, we should all insist on a strict adherence to the United States Constitution. This is a critical document, now more than ever, one designed to protect all natural and legitimate citizens. If the Constitution is given to the status of a relic, every man, woman and child living in the next century and perhaps long thereafter will be given to a life lacking in responsible freedom and truthfully inspired Liberty. Furthermore, they will live in a politically controlled Corporate-Fascist State, wherein authority will be given as appointed, *to dupes in servitude to a vain and alien persuasion, in control of the nation's wealth.*

Individuals will be denied the most fundamental right; namely that right to own, use and dispose of real property which, under the Constitution is considered an inalienable right, primary and necessary. Various plans for land control are being implemented as this is written. The concept of native land, that is man on the land, man from the land and man for the land involves God, man and coun-try (or state) and is an important concept, perhaps second only to that involving heaven and eternity together with the existence of God the Father. Nationalism, as such, is an indemnification of the fact that man lives of and by the land. The biological family makes up the basis for Nationalism, which becomes as a Tribe, Clan or Community, thereafter grouped together as a peculiar Culture. Any per-son who is unable to understand this will, by nature of ignorance, be responsible for some measure of destruction of that which good men, in God's good time, have been able to accomplish.

The Family of Man is not some socialistic construct. Those who wrote the literature, which has brought us to our present circumstances were, to the man, vain and corrupt fools. Any who follow the dictums of their learned-ignorance and high-minded conceit are no better. It is time for good men to act in history, to erase the consequences of such wanton, foul and ignorant prattling. *__Innumerable discontents, for the past several hundred years, have written too much about what they did not understand.__* As a consequence, fools have been encouraged to believe that, which is simply not true, is based in mythology and comes from the minds of vain men determined to impose their will on the entire human race. The Catholic Church is discreet in the encouragement of prudence and in noting that human knowledge is imperfect knowledge, thereby flawed by the vanity of men. Thus we must be very careful to confine our leaders to well reasoned and well-understood endeavor, as outlined in our Constitution and as has been given by Christian Martyrs and Saints; all of which is embodied in the Western Christian Culture, woven into the fabric of a great Civilization. We are admonished by Christ that the truth will set men free! If they know not what that is, they will serve a brutal and unforgiving master.[16] Ultimately we choose between God and Satan, between good and evil. We have no other choices. There are no other choices.

---

16 **Manifold, Deirdre,** *__Karl Marx, a Prophet of our Times.__* G. S. G. & Associates, Publishers. P. O. Box 6448, Eastview Station, Rancho Palos Verdes, CA 90734. ISBN # 0-945001-00-2. *__Chapter XII, The Legacy of Marx. Pp.139-149.__*

Men of Amerika

Drs. Frank und Stein

XIV. So, What about Gold?

Just now (2006) there is much talk about gold, most of which is driven by anxiety over inflation. The dialogue is formulated in reference to the salesman's objective, which is to profit from the fluctuating price on the way up (or down). The big holdings are securely in place, having been acquired perhaps when gold was twenty to thirty-five dollars an ounce. Those that buy today for the purpose of hoarding a small amount where others may not find it will not benefit much from their acquisitions. Traders, working the market will do better and dealers will do the best of all. Having considered this brief introduction, let us continue, What is Gold?

In simple terms, *Gold is Ideal Money.* This has been known for millennia! Study ancient history and you will find mention of gold as a treasure. Archeologists have uncovered golden Treasures in the tombs and burial sites of many ancient Kings. Millions, especially, have seen the Egyptian Treasures, since they have been assembled, organized for exhibition and placed in a Museum. The gold appears now as it did then proving its enduring quality. Kings, Noblemen and Traders held gold, as *collateral against need* in future Time.[1] Refer to Chapter I, Money, What is it. Gold has all of the necessary qualities so as to make it ideal as money

Almost all of the gold that was ever mined is still in existence and is now exactly as it was when first smelted, the *intrinsic value of gold is* supported by this fact. Additionally gold is universally recognized as near indestructible and it is beautiful. Ancient Kings and Queens had solid gold jewelry however, what is sold today as gold jewelry generally contains very little gold. Much of the existing gold is found in large-bars, or ingots, which are stored in the vaults of some governments and the International Financiers. Over the course of centuries, all over the world,

---

1   Future Time is all time beyond this moment, beyond NOW. (Bearden, T. E., Col., *Aids, Biological Warfare,* Tesla Book Co., P. O. Box 1649, Greenville, TX 75401. ISBN # 0-914119-04-4. Time is forever! Time surrounds all events and will envelop all that live and will live in a distant epoch. This is an absolute fact, *supported by the presence of the Universe* and all that it contains. Use your own mind to ponder this affirmation.

millions of gold coins have been struck, many of which are exquisite in design. It is imperative that the reader seeks by himself some important information concerning the complexities of this issue, which are beyond the scope of this brief overview.[2]

Now we shall relate money with time. Concerning time *imagine* that in 1935 the minimum wage was 35 cents per hour. This provided that anyone working at minimum wage would be guaranteed 35 cents for one hour of their time. The 35 cents was redeemable in gold, which had a fixed price, which was dependable thus *indemnified their time in a tangible and sustaining form of money. The product of their effort* would be honored in the future as *having the same value as when the money was earned.* Then, the price of gold was $35.00 per ounce, greatly overpriced at that time (Larson pg. 203). Thus, 100 hours labor at 35 cents, equal to two and one half forty-hour weeks, was sufficient to purchase one ounce of gold. Poor people did not have excess capital to purchase gold, even at the low price however; assertively most do not have the resource to purchase at the high price. Presently, with a minimum wage of perhaps seven dollars and fifty cents, the price of gold should be $750.00 per ounce. This is close to the price of gold just now. Thus one could imagine that things are relative and price does not matter. This, of course, is a fatal misunderstanding.

A number of factors occur simultaneously when we have monetary inflation. *First,* the value of the currency declines in purchasing power, so as to rob anyone that *worked in the past and saved for the future. Prudence is a Virtue,* the consequence of which is nullified by inflation. As such inflation is an enemy of virtue. *Greed* becomes more apparent as individuals grovel for more and more of the easy money. Mass-market advertising encourages profligate spending and the vulgarizing of a population. Simply, *Savings are slowly confiscated by this process. Second,* the money value of all Things increases. Having to handle so much money for a simple purchase, the common man imagines he is rich. The imagination of the common man in this instance is formed by his near *total ignorance* of what is happening. The fox does not forewarn the chickens of his intention to visit the hen house. *Third,* Vice is encouraged *especially gambling and speculation* as individuals attempt to gain enough to keep up what is required of an excessive and profligate existence. *Finally,* excessive debt is contracted in the hope of paying with cheaper dollars; meaning in the hope of cheating whomsoever sold you something of true value. The *Idea* of paying with cheaper dollars is most appealing to who has the most debt. In large measure this is what motivate the excessive debt acquired on the Credit Card. Nevertheless the one with the most debt is the Government!

---

2   **Larson, Martin** Ph D. *The Federal Reserve & Our Manipulated Dollar.* The Devin-Adair Co., Old Greenwich, CONN, 1975.

Governmental debt is counted in *Trillions of Dollars*.[3] Keep in mind, not all government debt is bad. What is reasonably contracted as debt however, is co-mingled with what may be unnecessary even fraudulent spending. Much is admitted as being *"Pork Barrel"* spending. In addition, one can add hundreds of billions in "off-budget Items, for which the accounting is often fuzzy and confusing, even to the accountants that pimp for their pay. Who can tell the difference?

Assertively the value of money should remain constant. *Inflation is a governmentally imposed, economic, moral and social illness* the **product of political** *malfeasance.* This is exacerbated by the sin of greed, which sin is common to the general population. As structured, the system depends on a form of criminal theft however, not recognized as such by most citizens.[4] Governments seek to spend more than their people can afford and monies are often spent for that, which their people do not want, War, Foreign Aid, failing Social Programs and other excesses. Regarding inflation the government is the mortal enemy of the people. Admittedly the problem defies understanding however, in time, could certainly be corrected by decisive and proper governmental action together with a better understanding amongst the people.

It is important for the individual, with a limited amount of time on this earth, that the value of money remains constant. Everyone has more energy; vitality and strength when they are young, during which time they work hard and many save and prepare for their waning years. This is *a natural and very well under stood fact of life*, all are born, grow, live then die. Even some animals prepare for winter by storing food found during the summer. Preparation for old age should be the work of the individual, which provides motivation and a sense of attainment and contentment over having been prudent and wise, both of which are Virtues. An old age

---

3   How much is a trillion dollars? $1,000,000,000,000.00
     A first response for most is probably that it doesn't matter. Most citizens do not consider such a question, imagining quite unfortunately that those in government will take care of such money matters. Indeed, they will, most likely to their own advantage at the expense of the people and the nation. All Demagogues do this. Those that control us are no different! What might be done with a sum so large?
     Divide $1,000,000,000,000.00 by $200.000.00 the price of a new home. The answer is that you could construct 5,000,000 homes @ $200,000.00 each. That is correct, *you could construct five million homes each costing two hundred thousand dollars for one trillion dollars*. The numbers are so large that the citizen worried about paying a few dollars on a monthly mortgage cannot comprehend such magnitude. One can easily understand why the government wants an ever-cheapening currency!

4   **Mullins Eustice,** *The World Order, Our Secret Rulers*. (Pub. Ezra Pound Institute, Staunton, VA. 24401, Second Edition, 1992).

spent in contentment knowing one has done well leads to a quiet, peaceful death. A peaceful death is one of the most desired wishes of all men.

The Insurance Companies, use a theory concerning the understanding of the present value of money and the compounding of interest to determine how one may survive old age. Interestingly the insurance companies, with billions earned from the people, own many (perhaps most, in some instances) of the large buildings in the major cities. Whereas, *the elders must resort to a reverse mortgage because their lack of knowledge did prevent them from acting wisely.* One can place much of the blame on Public Education. Our State sponsored system is destined to deprive youth of the necessary opportunity for learning and understanding, what is most important. The fact that one can be employed *"pushing paper"* for the man, does not compensate for the subtle theft that is built into the System, hidden within the actuarial statistics, which few have been equipped to understand.

Millions are jumping up and down imagining that they are becoming rich as the consequence of inflation. This, is a fatal notion, for the individual and for the nation?

Inflation is the opiate of the masses.
Inflation will destroy this Nation and the Soul of Western Civilization!
Fiedler2006

Inflation is a consequence of having abandoned the Gold Standard, which indemnifies, in Time, the value of the currency in circulation. Dr. Larson and George Knupffer's books are excellent sources of truthful information and critical insight. Dr. Larson especially shows the necessity and the means of returning to a gold standard. A return to the Gold Standard is unlikely. It is most unfortunate, that those having a stranglehold on our Nation, our Economy our People and our Civilization are beyond the power of laws that assumedly are to protect the citizen.[5]

Keep in mind finance at the higher levels is largely dishonest or conspiratorial and is determined toward the benefit of those that structure *financial circumstance.* Particularly, governmental financial dealings are especially complex because of the magnitude of the transactions; the attendant political intrigue and the clever tricks employed to cover up the thievery of political insiders. In such cases it is intended that the citizen should not understand. *Billions disappear right under the watchful noses of those we elect to direct the affairs of the country.* Presumably the

---

5   **Mullins Eustice, Ibid.** *The Indictables.* One must review the entire text to understand who are indictable and why. Also one will be well informed regarding the institutions and methods that are used effectively to control the masses.

elected officials could understand however, they seek feathers for their own nest, which consist of various forms of attachment, intended to satisfy their former supporters and to entice votes for the *representative of some of the people*[6].

Being a hypocrite (Abraham Lincoln did remind us) in many instances, perhaps most instances, the politician does attempt to satisfy some of the people all of the time and all of the people some of the time. Therefore it is easy to understand that the politician is in large measure a political hypocrite. There are some exceptions. *Gold, having an intrinsic value,* inviolate and enduring, provides a currency (the circulating denominator) with a stabilizing factor. A new honestly conceived Gold Standard, would go a long way in preventing what is becoming as a fantastic attempt to *control the world by means of secretly contrived economic swindling.*

Economic swindling is made possible by the swapping of paper *assumed to have a value equal to what is known, tangible, honestly acquired and enduring.* Such means are commonly referred to as Financial Instruments. Wall Street, other Trading Havens as well, provide the venue for the most-clever theft ever conceived. It is likely that much could be improved if such monstrosities did not exist. There are other and better ways, for example a mutual company. A few money-grubbers scam billions from the honest efforts of others. A few small players do make money, often a great deal of money. However, this does not compensate for the destruction of a Nation, Culture or the Catholic Christian inspired Western Civilization. As this is occurring we are reminded, by lunatics, that the *value of money has something to do with the will of the people,* a strange notion, no doubt.

The greatest swindles so far, potentially, are in the Cyber-realm of Derivatives. Derivatives provide nothing intrinsic, tangible, recognizable, beautiful or enduring and there is an infinite supply thereby to provide forever-greater swindles. Derivatives provide a means for **(the)** ultimate Ponzi scheme. The participation of China and India in Western-world procedures and methods will, temporarily,

---

6   In our present circumstance, which is programmed to deliberately create diversity, one should consider that with politically motivated diversity no elected President, Senator or Congressman would be able to please their constituency. Therefore, decisions will be made more and more by appointed "Experts" that will bend to the wishes of our **"Secret Rulers."** The **"Experts"** will be known for their acquiescence, in favor of the One World Order's Agenda and will be rewarded handsomely for their compliant decisions. The United Nations is one such monstrosity. The people do not understand this and they will be powerless because of confusion caused by dramatic differences in Faith Reasoning and Aspiration. Beside which manner habits and custom do vary widely amongst diverse groups, having different linguistic, cultural and social propensities. We see the grave consequence in the war in Iraq and the in war on Terrorism.

cause some problems. However, human nature, being as it is, Asians will discover that *"some of them"* are most assuredly more equal than others are. The most aggressive amongst what will be an emerging cadre of Thieves protected by government will do very well and have easy pickings just like the manipulators in New York and London. Most recently, we are told, criminal elements are apparent in the newly emerging Russia. Few in the sphere of economics wish to consider Russia as one of the oldest and most devoted amongst the Christian Nations. We read much of Economics however, little of the Faith of Russia, one of the most, perhaps the most significant of the world's great Christian Nations.[7]

Financial Circumstance is a Construct built by those, educated to perform as functionaries, in a system built on Usury and Debt Currency.[8] There are eschatological and phenomenal components as well and Destiny plays some part in all great events. Nevertheless, the student that agrees with the objectives inferred in the instruction given by traitorous-professors, within our State controlled system of Higher Education find positions of influence and may rise to the top so to join a ruling Elite. William Jefferson Clinton as well as some others that the reader can name has done just that. Patriots on the defensive and honest people in general refer to this ruling class as the Establishment, those better informed call the conspiratorial leaders Traitors Mattoids or Miscreants.

And all persons *of presumed authority* work from a position of vain assumption and look down on the Proletariat, the peon, the Peasant and the Working Man. Neither, Karl Mar or his Nanny, Frederic Engles had any respect for the common man.[9] A fair-minded and decent man does not denigrate others. However, Sigmund

---

7   **Knupffer, George,** *The Struggle for World Power, Revolution and Counter Revolution.* 4th ed./, 1986. ISBN # 0-85172-703-4. Chapters 15, & 16 The True Russia and Some Facts About Russia. Pp. 128-146

8   **Knupffer, George, Ibid.** Chapter 4. The Political Consequences of Economic Power. Pp. 36-40.

9   **Manifold, Didirae,** *Karl Marx, a Prophet of Our Times.* G. S. G. & Associates, Publishers. P. O. Box 6448, Eastview Station, Rancho Palos Verdes, CA 90734. ISBN# 0-945001-00-2. Marx lived well, mostly on money that was given to him by others of similar conviction and by inheritance. Although, generally speaking, his income was very substantial he was in debt and his family suffered, at various times from depravation. **This supposed economic genius,** who was paid thousands of pounds per year, when the working man made perhaps two hundred pounds a year, was not even able to conduct his own business. Nevertheless, Karl Marx and **the nitwits influenced by his thinking, imagined** that they had (and still do have) the solutions to the economic problems of humanity. **Like all Revolutionaries imagining themselves as great thinkers,** Marx had imperfect knowledge. Tragically his **form of intellectual syphilis** did infect others with the same inclinations, which has resulted

Freud, the *"great doctor,"* had no respect for his patients, whom he referred to as Negroes, probably inferring simplemindedness. However, given authority and coupled with conceit, *small minds think stinky thoughts and do great mischief.*

Imagination, it is important to contemplae much of our understanding concerning what were noble, decent and good people. Our imaginations are directed by unknown others and are fueled or manufactured for us by Hollywood, by propaganda and by Entertainers that presume to correctly inform the masses. The ostentatious, vulgar and relentless productions substitute for the truth concerning the most important issues. And, *much of entertainment is the work of small nevertheless aggressive minds, thinking stinky thoughts,* blatantly dishonest and overly concerned with romantic nonsense. Imagined as entertainment, Hollywood and the Television programmers endeavor to change the way people think, what they understand and how they should behave. Especially, writers, producers and pretenders are at war with Catholic Christianity. Their business, it would seem, is the cultivation of vice and Eroticism aimed at turning youth into vulgar, insensitive or desensitized Pagans and Savages. Youth are thus prepared as to become Participants in a great big Satanic Orgy. Youth so conditioned will not be equipped to understand the value of a sound and honestly functioning monetary system.

Hollywood and Television Programming have done great harm to the truthful understanding of History and the role of a medium of exchange, as an objective denominator, and (generally speaking) the world we live in. For example, all the Cultural beauty of Islam was rolled into a few spectacles, The King and I, Lawrence of Arabia, Kismet, and The Arabian Nights and, of course Sinbad the Sailor and Sabu the Elephant Boy. The golden treasures are reproduced in plastic, abandoned after the performance, or sold at auction for ridiculous prices, whereas the real thing does sustain for thousands of years. Someone is fooling the peons. Great Spectacles are reinforced with orchestral music written for the hypnotic effect it will have on the viewers. Much of the music is plagiarized, from great composers of the past. All such presentations are for the purpose of acquiring a profit, in money and many are determined in converting the masses to Paganism, Satanism, Witchcraft and the ways of a savage.

The artifacts, symbolism, culture, religion and indigenous habits were offered for viewing, first for a dime, then a quarter, then fifty cents, one dollar and now 6 to 8 dollars for one (often) quite bad movie. Movies are harmful because they are

---

in the killing and maiming of hundreds of millions and the mass destruction of much of Europe with the Architectural Symbolism, which in concrete terms defined our Catholic, Christian European Culture.

Interestingly both Marx's daughter and his son in law did commit suicide, over the kind of thinking that this **self-imagined Genius** bestowed upon them.

clever deceptions given to an uncritical population hoping to be amused, distracted or erotically stimulated. Entertainment as such, given humanly acquired restraint may have some value however, in present circumstance Hollywood and the entertainment industries, *"capitalize"* on all forms of vice, existing as an endemic social and mental disease, heretofore unimaginable. No one would deny that the special effects are phenomenal however the effects, for sensation and distraction, are never Art. And one must be aware of the reasoning of those so interested in entertaining others.

Civilization has been dissected, by authors, screenwriters and newspaper reporters, thereafter conveyed to the population in bits and pieces, chosen for unknown reason.[10] Woven within an often-delicate fabric is the lie, misunderstanding and personal prejudice. Just now all of Islam is supposed to be our enemy. We are told that the enemy is being freed from cultural and social ineptness so to be like we are. Is this a good idea? What might we do if someone invaded our land so as to make us over in another image? As a matter of fact, for money, this is happening. *With every illegal entry we loose a bit of our identity and acquire a liability that few understand,* all encouraged by corrupt men that take profits from their nefarious efforts. Lawyers and Judges are amongst the worst offenders since they do understand something of the law. Nevertheless, they *"embroider"* Ideas, which are destroying the nation and the Culture, with meaningless words given to the dialectic of subterfuge.

One can suspect the value of oil in reference to gold and a sound monetary system. Who understands the value of a gold-backed currency in this instance? Who knows how much gold Islam holds? Who understands that prior to the brutal butchering of the Russian Imperial Family, the Russian currency had one of the strongest gold backings of any world currency at that time?[11] "Russia had the world's biggest gold reserve and the issue of paper currency was more than covered by the holdings of gold."[12]. This included the very same gold that was stolen from the Imperial Treasury by thieving hypocrites. Thieving hypocrites, brutal assassins ordered to kill and destroy innocence by a cunning form of savagery unknown amongst noble men also murdered Czar Nicholas, his wife, children and servants.

---

10 **Marvin Olasky,** *The Anti Christian Bias of the American News Media.* The Prodigal Press. ©1988, Marvin Olasky. Crossway Books, Westchester Illinois, Publisher. ISBN # 0-8910476-7. Chapt 4.

11 **Knupffer, George, Ibid.** Pp. 142-145. On these few pages one will learn more about the Russia that was than they would learn in fifty years, studying in most American Universities, excepting who are in a Department of Russian History.

12 **Russia also did have and still has one of the world's most significant oil supplies. It is a certainty that in Russia, a vast land, more oil will be discovered**

They were butchered, murdered in cold blood, without compassion driven by lunatics nurturing an insidious instinct to overcome the Christian West.[13] Such as committed this horrible atrocity were aided and encouraged by Traitors in Western Governments for nearly a century. Where will this end?

Who now worships at the Altar of the Anti-Christ and is poised to capture the Golden Calf? Who now labors to create dissention and turmoil, to upset the peaceful existence of mankind? Who now files the coins in ways never before conceived of? Who now does attempt to incite conflict with the intention of enslaving humanity? Who now poisons the minds of youth with the promotion of vulgarity and pornography? Who now steals millions, one dime at a time? The answers to most of such questions the readers must find on their own. The following paragraph should help to set the tenor for understanding.

Prostitution, gambling, the Lottery, drugs, narcotics and pornography are, some of the most profitable enterprises, all are vices! The young are the most easily corrupted lacking in experience and wisdom. Once habits are formed they are difficult to change. Wild animals and some human beings seek the tender flesh of youth to consume, to defile and to denigrate. Sin seeks companionship.

Our first concern is that not all believe in sin. Secondly, youth do not understand why sin is so destructive. Third, millions refuse to believe what is obviously true, many of who are part of the problems. Fourth, each individual is morally obligated to responsible and decent behavior however, may not take such responsibility seriously. Fifth, it is important to avoid all occasion for sin. Blatant sin is disrespectful of certain individuals, party to an illicit affair, notably children and any faithful spouse. Sixth, support should not be given to anyone known to be immoral and sinful, in his or her behavior. Seventh, don't buy tickets to productions that reek with sinful episodes. Unfortunately, much of what exists would certainly be ruled out for participation. Finally there can be guilt by association especially, when one tolerates who is involved in sinful activities, so too ignores important safeguards.

---

13 Wilton, Robert, *The Last of the Romanovs, How Tsar Nicholas II and Russia's Imperial Family were Murdered.* Copyright © 1993, the Institute for Historical Review. First British Edition, pub. 1920 in London by T. Butterworth. First U. S. Edition published 1920, in New York by George H. Dorn. French Edition, pub. Paris 1921. Russian language edition, pub. Berlin 1923. ISBN # 0-939484-1. Chapter 9, Cavalry.

All such serious questions are somehow related to a precious,
Enduring beautiful and intrinsically fine metal, that metal is

GOLD.

Intrinsic Value

Never Changing

Beautifully enduring

Immutable, substantial

Inflation

Is an opiate?

Inflation is [THE] opiate of the masses.

Inflation can, perhaps will, destroy this Nation and the Soul of Western Civilization

The End

Appendix A. Speaking of Money

The following quotation is from <u>The World Order, Our Secret Rulers,</u> by Eustice Mullins, Pp. 11-12.
It is significant enough to be considered as primary in the present world situation, especially since money is the means whereby they who would control the world could and very likely will succeed.

"After the fall of Napoleon, the Rothschilds turned their hatred against the Romanoffs. In 1825, the poisoned Alexander I; in 1855, they poisoned Nicholas I. Other assassinations followed, culminating on the night of Nov 6, 1917, when a dozen Red Guards drove a truck up to the Imperial Bank Building in Moscow. They loaded the Imperial jewel collection and $700 million in gold, loot totaling more than a billion dollars. The new regime also confiscated the 150 million acres in Russia personally owned by the Czar". *(Fiedler, comment; we wonder why the New York Times and other great (so-called) free-press papers and American Public Education had not made more of this most tragic event? Over the past nearly one hundred years, there was ample opportunity to do so? This most profound theft and absolutely, brutal murder, of innocent men, women and children, the complete Romanoff family, stands as a point of departure for much of what has followed? The same type of Idea is now harbored in the minds of different men, anxiously working to rob and pillage the rest of Catholic Christianity, the entire people of the world as well. Vain and evil men, presuming and arrogant, have robbed and defamed our Christian faith and our bountiful heritage and continue to do so under the condescension of a corrupt law. All such atrocities, under whatever disguise, have the control of money, power and landed wealth as the objects of their most evil endeavors).*

"Of equal importance were the enormous cash reserves which the Czar had invested abroad in European and American banks. The New York Times stated that the Czar had $5 million in Guarantee Trust, and $1 million in the National City Bank; other authorities stated that it was $5 million in each bank. Between

1905 and 1910 the Czar had sent more than $400 million to be deposited in six leading New York banks, Chase, National City, Guarantee Trust, J. P. Morgan, Hanover and Manufacturers Trust. *These were the principal banks controlled by the House of Rothschild, through their American agents, J. P. Morgan and Kuhn Loeb Co.* They have held control of the stock ever since." *These were the six New York banks, which also bought stock in the Federal Reserve Bank of New York in 1914 (author's comment).*

"The Czar also had $115 million in four English banks. He had $35 million in the Bank of England, $25 million in Barings, $25 million in Barclays, and $30 million in Lloyds. In Paris the Czar had $100 million in Banque de France, and $80 million in the Rothschild Bank of Paris. In Berlin he had $132 million in the Mendelsohn Bank, which had long been bankers to Russia. *'They parted my garments among them, and upon my vesture did they cast lots.'* (Mathew C. 27. V. 35.)[1] **None of these sums has ever been dispersed; at compound interest since 1916, they amount to more than $50 billion.** Two claimants later appeared a son, Alexis, and a daughter Anastasia. Despite a great deal of proof substantiating their claims, Peter Kurth notes in *Anastasia* that 'Lord Mountbatten put up the money for court battles against Anastasia. Although he was Empress Alexandra's nephew, he was the guiding force, behind Anastasia's opposition.' The Battenbergs or Mountbattens, were also related to the Rothschild family. The did not wish to see the Czar's fortune reclaimed and removed from the Rothschild banks."

"If the American people had been more truthfully informed, at the beginning of the twentieth Century and, if they were more truthfully informed at the present time, they might better understand. As early as 1894 the Russian Christian nation had reached a high level of attainment. Russia was an advanced nation, a leader in the world, in many respects. And, Russia since the Civil War, was a friend of America. There is a very great distinction between what was Holy Mother Russia and what became of it. *Bolshevism was not a product of Christian Russia, nor was Communism.* Any such political monstrosity is in absolute opposition of Holy Mother Russia, the Russia of Katherine the Great and Czar Nicholas." An authoritative, albeit quick and brief, insight and overview can be found in the book by George Knupffer.[2]

---

1   **Vesture,** relates to belongings, garments, etc., whereas **Investment** relates to money, gold or a call on the future. There is a subtle nevertheless profound relationship. Both Christ Jesus' and the Czar's *call on the future* was usurped by an evil persuasion, which continues and has created a mortal problem for all of humanity.

2   **Knupffer, George,** *The Struggle for World Power, Revolution and Counter-Revolution.* 4th Edition, 1986, ISBN #0-85172-703-4. pp. 221-232.

"No matter what has been fabricated in thousands of "historical" works to the contrary, it is an irrefutable fact, visibly illuminated by the subversion against the United States on the part of the British-Zionist conspiracy nowadays, that without British involvement in subversion against the Russian Empire, there would never have been a revolution at all, the Imperial Order would have been maintained and the Great War against Germany and Austria would have been for Russia a victorious one".[3]

"Surely to no nation has fate been more malignant than to Russia. Her ship went down in sight of port. Every sacrifice had been made; the toil was achieved. *Despair and treachery usurped command at the very moment when the task was done.* The long retreats were ended; the munitions famine was broken; arms were pouring in; stronger, larger, better-equipped armies guarded the immense front; the depots overflowed with sturdy men. Moreover, no difficult action was now required, to remain in presence; to lean with heavy weight upon the far stretched Teutonic line; to hold without exceptional activity the weakened hostile forces on her front; in a word to endure—that was all that stood between Russia and the fruits of victory." (Sir Winston Churchill, and, no friend of Russia was he).

---

3   **Imperial House of Romanoff, Role of British Royalty in the Revolution.** Reprint in Bulletin, June 1976 Committee to Restore the Constitution. P. O. Box 986, Ft. Collins, CO 80522.

<u>The Masonic Pyramid</u>
Grand Architect of the Universe

The
Eye   of
The Pyramid

Council   of   Thirteen

Council of (33) thirty   three

The 300   The 300   The 300   The 300

B'NAI B'RITH   B'NAIB'RITH

Grand Orient   Grand Orient   Grand Orient

COMMUNISM   COMMUNISM   COMMUNISM

SCOTTISH RITE SCOTTISH RITE SCOTTISH RITE

YORK RITE   YORK RITE   YORK RITE   YORK RITE

White Masonry,   Rotary,   Elks,   YMCA, etc. etc. etc. etc. etc.

Blue Lodge   Blue Lodge   Blue Lodge   Blue Lodge   Blue Lodge   Blue Lodge

<u>"Masons Without the Apron"</u>   <u>"Masons Without the Apron"</u>

Secular Humanism   Secular Humanism   Secular Humanism
Secular Humanism   Secular Humanism

Debt ans Taxes

Appendix B. Speaking of Sin

The following is excerpted from Chapter VIII,
The Last Days of the Romanovs, by Robert Wilton

"Isai Goloshchekin, the intimate friend of Yankel Sverdlov, took charge of the prisoners on their arrival. Isai played the part of the Bolshevist Pooh-ba, being a Komisar many times over, but above all he loomed largely in the local *chrezvychaika.*"

"When, three weeks later, the other children and the remainder of the household arrived, the same procedure was adopted.—the person in charge being Rodionov.—It was raining heavily and the platforms were slimy with mud. He would not permit anyone to help the Grand Duchesses to carry their own luggage. Nagorny, one of the Imperial servants, was knocked over for daring to extend a hand to Anastasia, dragging a heavy bag."

"Nobody had permission to share the new prison with the Romanovs except the physically weak or mentally underdeveloped."*(Author's comment; One can imagine Isai and Rodionov were ignorantly vain, venal and sullied personalities, perfect representatives of the caliber of misguided revolutionaries, that would delight in the torture and humiliation of one of higher and noble countenance, especially so regarding Christian Royalty. Was ever thus. It is important to realize, imagine at least, that deviate personalities are suited for the atrocities, which were committed).*

"Around the house, a wooden hoarding was put up to the windows of the upper floor. Soon after the prisoners arrived, another hoarding was put up, completely screening the whole house up to the eaves, and enclosing also the front entrance and the gateway. There were double windows, as usual in Russian houses. Both panes were covered with whitewash, rendering it utterly impossible for the prisoners to see anything outside—even a crow flying."

"Prison fare of the poorest kind was provided. Breakfast comprised of stale bread from the day before, with tea—no sugar. For dinner they had thin soup and meat, the latter of doubtful quality. The ex-Empress could eat nothing except macaroni".

"The guards sang revolutionary songs devised to hurt and shock the feelings of the prisoners, containing, foul words such as no man would dare to utter in the presence of innocent girls....revolutionary warriors delighted in wounding the modesty of the Grand Duchesses in this and in still more repulsive ways, by filthy scribbling and drawings on the walls and by crowding round the lavatory—there was only one for the prisoners and the warders." *(Author's comment; We are wise who would recognize the avalanche of pornography, deviate behavior and vulgar language is a prelude to ignorantly arrogant and repulsively revolutionary behaviors, which are just now being formulated in the minds of they who imagine what is not true. And, we are much more conditioned to accept what our Masters tells us is true, than to inquire of our own intelligence into history and the meaning of words).*

"Now we come to the final phase that proceeded the murder. It is full of significance. Every step had been taken by the occult powers of the Ekaterinburg *chrezvychaika*, which it must be remembered, did nothing without orders from the central institutions in Moscow...Sverdlov, being in direct communication with Goloshchekin—*(concerning each event)* falls into its natural appointed place as part of the cruel fate reserved for the Romanov family."

From what is excerpted (written above), it is clear that every means, at the disposal of ***ignorant and vitriolic hatred***, was employed to shame, embarrass and defame a noble family. Every one of noble countenance, including five helpless young people, was made to suffer totally and completely, each in view of the others. As is asserted in Appendix E, which follows, the Personality is perhaps the most important element in forming individual behavior, regarding both attitude and disposition. Once understood, the personality of a simple minded Dolt can be easily harnessed to commit various forms of action, even to the extent of the most atrocious activities. Vain, warped, aggressive and anti-social personalities are responsible for the World Revolution. Every century produces individuals that will continue the atrocities and the theft, which have sustained, century after century. Revolutionaries, though some may be somewhat intelligent, are, among the following:

1. Sullen hypocrites involved in religious fantasy and an aggressive fanaticism, which they do not and cannot understand (suicide bombers are the most recently obvious)

2. Disenchanted romantics, unable to satisfy selfish personal-desire (Hemingway). Such men boast of the carnal pleasure and elicit fornication that they knew.

3. Over educated and presumptuous malcontents (Karl Marx fits the description). Scribblers, their evil has lived after them, which evil persists placing millions of innocent people including children, and the elderly in silent graves.

4. Vain and evil practitioners (both Hitler and Stalin may be considered). Nevertheless, present thinking would employ many of the same methods as Europe's butchers.

5. Greedy seekers of wealth (the International Bankers)

6. Eager Lechers, that desire intimacy with youthful beauty.

7. Lastly, there are simple-minded and ignorant fools.

Our good reader is encouraged to determine the personalities that fit the assessment as enumerated above. Then fill in the squares, with your own selections.

Appendix C. Why Fight at All?

All Wars and Revolutions are fought for just a few reasons, all of which have their origin in sin. Vanity and Greed, both considered Cardinal Sins by Christianity, have been the most conspicuous.[1] Vanity stems from a feeling or sense of superiority, or from a *belief* that one has been chosen by God. A feeling of superiority is personal whereas a messianic imposition is more tribal, and may have religious and philosophic implications, spanning the past twenty-five centuries, more or less. *Revolutionaries assume to know how the rest of the world should behave.* This assumption, to be fruitful, requires considerable power and *wealth, so as to be able to buy, if not force, others* to do what is *imagined to be in their own best interest.* Greed, as was obviated by Christ in admonishing the Moneychangers, has both monetary and political implications, as well as those of a more spiritual nature, which have sustained through the centuries. Christ was aware that "All in this world is vanity". *Lust, envy and avarice* may be included in the equation, as *personal vices,* however they have fewer political implications, excepting that beautiful women often compromise the *"politically minded hypocrites",* that are *"elected"* to rule the lives of others.

The Political posturing and vicious propaganda, which accompanies Revolutions and Wars is generally for effect, that being the effect it has on enticing the population, so as to accept outrageous measures and increased spending, *for the good of the people.* Of course! The same techniques, as have been refined over the centuries, are always employed. Mass communication makes the job more complete. Ultimately *we the people will pay the price in blood and Treasure, as they die, one by one, in pointless endeavor,* for whatever mistakes are made along the way. And, flatly stated, War and Revolution are always a mistake. In the past three centuries, England has endeavored to maintain the balance of power in Europe and, to some considerable extent, globally as well. In protecting her own

---

1   **Ideas become of Ideas** and once implanted, Ideas sustain for long periods of time. The Idea if significant will outlive the man. Revenge is born in the mind of they who ponder the past and do not understand the present. Those who seek revenge value the past more than the present, which anyone can make joyful with a small effort.

interests, England has adopted various allies, purely pragmatically and for political and economic reasons.[2] Two World Wars have been fought, nevertheless onerous problems remain and some others are being generated right now. A third World War is a distinct possibility, as many now believe and may be a final apocalyptic struggle between good and evil; or so it would seem. All understanding emerges, dependent upon which side one favors. Any antagonist in a conflict may have what seem to be sound reasons. Ultimately dialectics will encourage participation, thus the "Pen [**is**] as mighty as the sword."

Preparations for War are an obvious waste of resources, especially when the War is engendered for economic and political purpose *in defense of what is only imagined.* This is difficult to contemplate, more difficult to understand. With only imperfect knowledge, any man has command of only part of the truth. Truth should set us free however, thousands work incessantly to obscure, twist and denigrate the meaning of truth. Often, gender plays a conspicuous role, especially at this time, when so much attention has been given to outrageous and prurient sexual practice. With tongue in cheek, considering the irony of social consciousness, it is asserted *that too many present-day warriors fight between menstrual periods,* unless they are impregnated as part of the action. The statistics from the Gulf War might be quite interesting in this respect. When valor and a sense of noble action were in vogue we imagine half the population was at home tending to the requirements of Children and of Culture. Presently, young women fly airplanes and kill the sons of they, whom some have been taught to hate. All imagine this is some kind of defense, against what they cannot comprehend. Comprehension requires specifically truthful information, which is difficult to obtain. Most of what is truthful history is never recorded, thus is not available for consideration. And, of what is known, truthful and correctly understood, much is carefully hidden from those that *"might be incorrectly influenced"* by that same truth. Newspapers and magazines, in spite of some serious and decent effort, cannot help being, as it were, significantly engaged in the dissemination of untruth, half-truth and the Lie. Interestingly, both Douglas Reed and Robert Wilton, quoted in this exposition, did confirm that much of what they sent to their newspapers for publication was never printed. Obviously, from such assertions, we can deduce that the *"great Newspapers"* (so called) were in on the act determined to destroy the Catholic Christian Culture of Russia and the World, most certainly so. The truth should set one free, nevertheless the truth must be known.

Civilization is very complex. Thought forms can be engendered by propaganda, thus individually we are not truthfully informed. And, *Time leaves factual truth*

---

2   **Knuth, E. C.,** *The Empire of the City, The Jekyll/Hyde Nature of the British Government.* The Noontide Press, P. O. Box 1248, Torrence, CA 90505. Pp. 12 through 16.

in its wake. Much is overlooked as being inconvenient and generally people are not inclined to search for meaning. And, there have been and are groups, determined to upset the moral order, that work incessantly, to destroy what decent men have accomplished

One might consider that the Russian Revolution was not a Revolution of the people, most of who, except for their own suffering, were not truthfully aware of what was and what did happen.[3] The facts suggest great subterfuge and hypocrisy of unimaginable scope. *The Russian Revolution, other revolutions as well, were really staged programs.* By means of scheming, lying, criminal intrigue and grand-theft, the Russian nation was stolen from the nobility and from the people, whom the nobility did honestly represent. The Nobility was dispossessed and the population came under rule of a Fearful Master.

One can imagine that the definition of the word nobility has an origin in noble actions, for the benefit of others. Politicians and various schemers, Moneychangers and Bankers have corrupted the meaning of this and other words. This has been done and continues, as an important part of an attempt at complete world domination, by just a small group of powerful and wealthy men. If one studies the interlocking Directorships of the World's great Corporations and Industries, who is important becomes immediately apparent.[4] Keep in mind, some fish are bigger than others, the really big fish are few!

The following is from, *The Last Days of the Romanoffs*, by Robert Wilton, Pp. 186-190.
It is important as substantiating assertions above, concerning the Russian "Revolution"

Speaking of the Parties, which were involved in the *take over of Russia for the benefit of the International Banks*, Robert Wilton, had this to say. "These parties, in appearance opposed to the Bolsheviks, play the Bolshevik's game on the sly, more or less, by preventing the Russians from pulling themselves together…No matter what may be the name adopted, a revolutionary government will be Jewish. [Although the Bolsheviks permitted these leftist political groups to operate for a

---

3   **Fahey, Dennis, C.S.Sp. Rev.** *TheRulers of Russia and the Russian Farmers.* Omni Publications. Hawthorne, CA 90251. First printed Sept. 1948. Reprinted 1987.

4   **Mullins, Eustice,** *The World Order, Our Secret Rulers,* (Ezra Pound Institute, Publisher, Staunton, A 24401, Second Edition, 1992)

time under close supervision and narrow limits, even these pitiful remnants of organized opposition were thoroughly eliminated by the end of 1921]".

In his book, Robert Wilton names all of the players in the "Council's of People's Commissars (also known as the "Sovnarkom"). Without comment, because this writer is not an expert historian, the reader is encouraged to review the Appendix of _the Last Days of the Romanovs_. Pp. 186 through 190. Rather than present a reiteration of the material, I urge the readers of this exposition to avail themselves of Wilton's writing, giving his first-hand experience, as a London Correspondent, including photos of the site of the atrocity and burial of the victims. Unfortunately, the mind content of the men who would order some of the most brutal murders in the history of the world, carries ideas forward, such as to be a curse and a pestilence on the future of the human race.

It is said, the love of Money is the root of all evil.
No doubt, any atrocity that has happened in the past,
Is as a consequence of such evil in action.
It is imperative that we teach our children to know right from wrong.
Education must include a Universally functional moral Imperative.
Learning must be a companion to holiness.
Meaningless prayers in public, uttered by hypocrites, are not enough
Holiness must be confirmed within the mind content and psyche of every individual.
If we cannot accomplish this, we should not presume that we are a great nation.
We cannot imagine we are good, when we tolerate, even encourage, evil ways.
We must not travel the globe pretending to help in situations, which we do
not and cannot understand.
It must be considered that politics, religion and human behavior are welded
Simply put, they are the important elements, in a broad and ongoing continuum.
We must understand this or, as a people, we will have sacrificed our Soul.

Appendix D. How much are you worth?

Abortion is the unbelievably cruel killing of innocent pre-born Infants!
Nevertheless, it is an industry, a business run for profit.
Abortion is Infanticide, (1. The murder of a baby, _Webster_),
Which delivers the soul of the Mother to the arms of Satan.
We address a critically profound aspect of our
Present existentially circumstantial dilemma.
Our dilemma is a consequence of ignorance in concert with vain aspiration,
Cowardly deception, conspiratorial imposition and intrigue.

Abortion is a form of ritualistic murder, a form of cabalistic Mysticism, having origins in a distant past, which are for the most part misunderstood. _Abortion, in most instances involves the sacrificial murder of the first born_, which _opens the womb_ of the mother. The sacrifice, when considered comprehensively, becomes necessary as a consequence of improper behavior and may be as a form of Satanic-worship, or a sinful dependency on technologies. One must be aware that the _Ideas_ apparent in Satanic-worship have been promoted as entertainment aimed at youth and adult ignorance, all in good fun, of course. _Sex is the Golden Calf of Modernism._ common sense should obviate this in light of the Golden Rule, which states (explicitly) "Do unto others as thou would have others do unto you". However, an anciently conceived dark force, a Satanic force has been carried forward in the minds of some men, and has compromised common sense. A modern version of this same dark, atavistic, force controls the subject matter, content and attitudinal inference of much of the mass media. Mass media imposition and public education form, albeit with some subtlety, the Ideology and Libido of the present population. The imposition of mass media is fundamental to the goal and possible success of Communists, world Planners and Satanists that impose their will (to power) on humanity. *All are guilty of conspiring to overthrow what decency has done,* that promotes the notion of a Satanic One-World Order. Importantly, the Tower of Babel has risen to unimaginable heights due to the phenomenon we name mass communication. Mindless chatter is a hallmark of contemporary Civilization; and, the Telephone!

Not without significance is the fact that abortion that is socially organized, ritualistic murder, is *a multi-billion dollar business,* thus many are concerned with abortion relative to economics. Abortion is a convenient alternative, like condoms front and center, which allows as it promotes and encourages promiscuity. Promiscuity *stems from sharing,* in a **communal sense**, especially the bodies of *poorly educated, eager and ill-advised young women,* (spelled modern, liberated woman), with as many men as the young woman is able to *engage in performance, thus to entertain,* or to *admit within her physically, intimate being.* And, given the serial encounter, there is room for many. **Communism,** that is communal living, of a politically motivated species, **grants sexual license.** When one embraces this tainted anti-family and patently absurd philosophy one sacrifices a unique and special sexual nature, which would be better served in a permanently monogamous, humanly fulfilling and decently conceived manner. The Idea of familial continuity is as old as known time and has biblical as well as social, philosophical and political connotation. *From such continuance children are born, within the family-group-tribe-culture-nation, not butchered, like the lamb,* nor sacrificed in some meaningless or ill-inspired, albeit technically and socially accepted ritual. Western Civilization, other Civilizations as well, depend upon a decently formulated idea concerning the value of motherhood, children and of familial continuity.

Homosexuality, which can be somewhat understandable, may be pitied, however, is, nevertheless, an adamant denial of fruitful mating and the begetting of children (progeny), necessary to sustain the human race. Notwithstanding, aggressively silly, blatantly disgusting and idiotic parading of "gender denial", by those **who could know better (?),** is a deadly form of an otherwise *somewhat perplexing as well as amusing* Charade.

From the position of a Catholic Christian, Communion with an Infinite Being is delivered as the Eucharist, the Body of Christ. Thus we become *one in being with the Father,* from whom all good things come, and are thereby joined with what is infinite.[1] Such Communion places the receiver in the presence of Christ, by means of the Holy Spirit. This aspect of Theology and *Profound Learning is infrequently discussed, never in a public school.* Catholic, Christian Theology and Dogma are in total opposition to **technologically clever infanticide, motivated**

---

1   **Blatant Sinners** cannot become "*one in being with the Father,*" who is infinite and perfect. God has higher expectations than some might imagine.

by an anciently conceived and formed cabalistic ignorance. Indeed, to discuss a Catholic, Christian (that is universal) Holy Communion, in a public school, would very likely be cause for legal action, on behalf of those who might disagree and those that worship the anti-Christ or Satan. Those who are simply unaware would back the loudest noises. Consider, what has happened to the Christmas Season and to Easter. Also consider the burgeoning interest in Halloween, with Witches, Goblins and Satanic Ritual considered as party fun! Please understand, regarding good and evil, they are in absolute opposition! Of great significance is the fact that "evil doers," in large measure control governments, which control the wealth of the nations! To control the wealth of a nation, by means of a contrived banking system, is to have opportunity to steal "legally" from every productive effort of an entire people.

The Savage and the renegade take no part in the building of Civilization, rather they would destroy what good men have accomplished. This is exactly what Savages do. There are no "noble savages." *By definition savages are ignoble!* Sex is assumed, by the savage, the idiot and the moron (and there are millions), to be a form of performance for immediate gratification, in a transient encounter. The cult of the Athlete, to some degree, encourages this, as do the girly magazines and pornography. Pimps (most know who they are) and Prostitutes, who should be in jail (or hiding in the dark), are interviewed on Television and given the status of a celebrity. And to *enter the crotch of a maiden*, of course, is the goal of most Revolutionaries, middle-aged Reprobates, young fools and all irresponsible fornicators? Even Sigmund Freud had a longing to deflower a virgin. *Satan and those who are "on his team," become as the progeny of evil delight in the rape of innocence.* Literature is full of examples of such behavior and entertainment reeks with insinuation. Check out the Internet for the latest attractions, then, make your own judgement! Give this some thought; *Are the young women who are being exploited perhaps your daughter, your mother or your wife?* Is your daughter or your grand daughter ready for an ejaculant facial? Wake up, old man and smell the coffee! Or, is the aggressive man (to use the word with indiscretion) engaged in bestiality and lustfully degenerate forms of perversion, your father your husband or your son. So what might one think of this? The inference, at this point, is attendant to the Golden Rule.

All forms of sexual sin and perversion are tied to the body of a woman or a man. This is reality. Abortion, fornication, adultery, voyeurism, deviations from what is normally procreative, perversions of various forms, bestiality, pedophilia, drunkenness, rape, birth control, ritualistic sacrifice of children and suicide, comprise a list well worth any intelligent man's attention. Who has the guts to challenge the establishment? Who will make the call? Or, would our *"uniformly educated citizen"* rather have another beer and watch another football game?

The emotional well being of young women, older women as well is compromised by the conscience, aware of what has been and is being done. Thereafter, life has a different meaning. How the young lady deals with this has blossomed into a business, like everything else, for money. Psychologists, Educators, family Planners and Charlatans of various stripes are lining their pockets, on the products of Sin, without acknowledging that Sin does exist. Furthermore, Sin is given a different name, so as to encourage the sale of a service, a drug or some program imagined/assumed to mediate circumstances.

The fact that advertising, which earns hundreds of billions of dollars, depends on the display of beautiful body parts is coincidental to this phenomenon, which has swept the entire Civilization. Such aggressive imposition and exploitation of the intimate aspects concerned with mating, family and nurturing of children have been _fraudulently promoted_ for money. The men and women, who engage in the promotion of venal, _sexually ludicrous_ and silly advertisements, for all manner of stuff, comprise a cadre of overpaid and despicable pimps and whores. The problem is that very few will admit this and almost none are capable of understanding. Keep in mind, **_what is written immediately above is the message_**, not the Messenger!

To this add the fact that we formulate medications, various creams and lotions using the body substance and fluids of unborn human beings that have been butchered. We are informed and constantly reminded that a murdered child was only a fetus. In spite of any contrary indignation, such behavior and the procedures, which have been found necessary, deserves no accolades. Rather such as this is evidence of a **_technologically driven savagery with no precedent_**. Such procedures may be scientifically interesting and technically clever however, are they wise? Evil will find a way.

We ask; what then shall make us proud? For what shall we receive some earthly reward? Why have we abandoned the Intellectual framework, of this Godly inspired (universal) Western, Catholic Civilization conceived by Christ, Saints and Martyrs and brought through the ages by some of the most learned among men?

Where Satan Stalks the Virgin's dead, gentlemen are no more.
Shall every father's daughter be a whore?

And

Silly man, with itching gonads, stupid banal glee.
Your prick a stick, sing to your mother, in concert with a flea

Or

With mother's milk and loving kisses
And many soft places to touch
My heart is yours, indeed my Soul,
To me you mean so much

With you I spend my yearnings
My substance and my life
I'll hold you close eternally
My faithful wife

Appendix E. The Secret Will to Power

One cannot consider money without considering the multitude of conspiracies, which form around the attempt to steal the wealth of individuals and of nations.

Almost every thinking person, in the Western World, has considered whether or not there does exist a Conspiracy to overthrow the existing social order. We assert that **the will to overthrow does exist** and is that, which is of our most important concern, whether or not it forms as a Conspiracy (as, in many instances, it most certainly does) is secondary to the dominating Will. It is the **Will to power**, which commands our interest. And, the Will of the dominating money and financial interests, is centered within the International banks, controlled by just a few, who seek ever-greater wealth, hence control of all others. We define this as Consolidation. We understand consolidation, as the implementation of [**the**] **Will to Power.** Some others may have differing-opinions. However most well informed persons do understand what is inferred. Carol Quigley, in his monumental and phenomenally comprehensive work, _Tragedy and Hope_, makes this quite evident. Spengler, in his profoundly penetrating _Decline of the West_, was aware of the the political, cultural and social tenor of the modern existence of the Western and other Civilizations.

Human Will is centered in the individual personality, which becomes of experience, by that is meant what is learned from others, what is encountered as event and what is imagined as fantasy. The numerous _Independent Factors combine in unimaginably complex ways_ as well and such _combining_ is in a state of flux, altered as new experience is introduced into the manifold.[1] However, in the recent past, perhaps three hundred years and especially the past one hundred years, entire

---

1   **Thinking** is always in a state of flux, a consequence, of a continuum of the incidents which bear upon the human mind as a product of experience.

populations have been overcome with propaganda.[2] To some extent, variously informed persons have similar objectives and are **willing** to accept one form of understanding over all others. Such Individuals form into _small revolutionary groups_,[3] _which function, for a price and become well known,_ thus to aid the clever in conquering the goods, as money and property, of the multitude. If a few control the money supply and the government, they are well positioned to control almost all of the rest. Submission to illegal imposition, one way or another, may be as a consequence of fear, complacency or a product of imaginary reasoning, encouraged by misinformation, as disseminated by a _presumably controlled_ mass media. When people are uniformly convinced, _as in a democratic society,_ **they will attempt to insure compliance and service favoring an unknown master's will.**[4] The war in Iraq, considered from either side, is a current example, of such blind capitulation, imagined as patriotism and altruism, misunderstood of course.

We do not imagine there exists a single Conspiracy, rather submit that there are many. We assert _many co-incidental conspiracies_ have common objectives and that one group of Conspirators can profit from aiding and abetting the work of similarly engaged Conspirators. The young have not heard mention of the most important groups of Conspirators, men who rule over the lives and fortunes of an entire Culture and Civilization. The Illuminati, The Council on Foreign Relations, The League of Just Men, The Pilgrim Society, The Round Table, The Club of Rome, The Bank of the City of London, and The Bilderbergers, have led Civilization

---

2   **Populations**, to some considerable extent, are similarly informed and may be easily directed into accepting what is good for a well placed elite, that control the means of communication, the privileged few, rather than for the civilization as a totality. What we define as a _Population_ may be of geographic, religious, linguistic, hence ethnic, and more recently categories defined by age and sex. There are innumerable sub-groups, which coalesce into distinct larger groups, for example American, Asian, European and Islamic. In turn larger groups may be antagonistic toward others.

3   **At present,** locally formed street Gangs, groups of dissident militant aliens and some internationally involved criminal syndicates fill this role.

4   **Slavery,** in fact, is being imposed with the consent of they who will be enslaved, economically and socially. This is difficult to understand, since there does appear to be a vibrant and productive economy and millions of individuals are _seemingly_ prosperous; albeit most are hopelessly in debt and the nations are being _bought up by their own indifference to the meaning of debt._ Ultimately the sovereign Beings, that includes all the people of the nation, must submit their lands as collateral for whatever debt has been contracted. This must be understood as an ultimate Bankruptcy. Inflation only works for a period, after which it becomes unmanageable; so we are told.

to the brink of disaster. This is simply a **monetary and political Concert;**[5]with many different *instruments* [*legal and illegal*] playing the same tune. Contrived legality and capricious governance combine, thus to have allowed and to encourage this formidable network to have been established. Men in public office knowingly and unknowingly have aided and abetted this tragic farce. It is important to understand the implications of the meaning of a word, for example **Concert**. In a political sense, there was in the recent past a "Concert of Europe."[6]Language, which should provide for significant and truthful knowing and understanding, can be confused, meaning altered, by overrunning truthful content with the cliché, the slogan and the banal and incessant imposition of cleverness, destined to subdue truth. The clever Hypocrite uses Mass Media to obfuscate and confuse the meaning of words. Certain words such as racist, bigot, Niger, anti-Semite, Nazi, Skinhead and some others are generally known are trigger words. The object of the trigger word is to defame, to incite, to ridicule and to discredit an opposing point of view. All such attempts are generally mindless and depend on emotion and some manner of defamation of an adversary's character and mental competence; coincidentally objectives and methods are certainly condemned.

History is full of examples of what has and is happening regarding the conspiratorial take-over of Catholic Christianity,[7]our Culture, our Western Civilization and our prosperous way of life. Other Nations, Cultures and Religions will suffer in due course, as the next victims of monetary pressure, having as a basis, the tremendous wealth of the Western Culture, which has been concentrated in the hands of a few of the Conspirators. We will mention only a few pertinent

---

5   **Concert** (kan-surt' ; *for n & adj.* Kon-sert), **v. t. & v. i.** [Fr. *concertere;* It. *Concertare;* L. *concertare,* to contend. Contest < *com-,* with + *certare,* to contend, strive; meanings influenced by consort & L. *conserere,* to join together], to arrange or settle by mutual understanding; contrive or plan together ; devise **n.** [Fr.; It. *concerto,* agreement, union < *concertare*], 1. Mutual agreement; concord; harmony of action. 2. Musical consonence. 3. A performance of vocal or instrumental music, usually one in which a number of musicians participate. **Adj.** of or for concerts. in **concert**; in union; in agreement; together.

6   **Knuth, E. C.** *The Empire of the City, The Jekyll/Hyde Nature of the British Government.* The Noontide Press, P. O. Box 1248, Torrence, CA 90505. Chapter IV, The Concert of Europe. Pp. 23-25.

7   **Dodd, Bella,** *School of Darkness.* The Seminaries of the Catholic church, were invaded by a cadre of malicious young men, perhaps a thousand or more. This was done with the express purpose of conspiring against the Faith, Catholic Dogma and the Structure of Church Tradition. They have, to a great extent, accomplished their devious and malicious purpose.

examples. The interested reader can find others merely by searching through some of the works listed in our bibliography.

The French Revolution was a consequence *of conspiracy, which flourished on ignorance, vanity, pride and greed.* Thousands were killed, murdered, beheaded and raped, so as *to satisfy the imagined needs of they that presumed all were being treated unfairly.* Nevertheless, *the perpetrators are all dead,* (Shakespeare) then, what did they accomplish? Encourage more of the same! We suffer to this day from the clever deceit that was propagated for the purpose of instilling the necessary anxiety and rage in the subject population. We are told by our Informers that the French Revolution brought equality, fraternity and freedom. Wow! **Nesta Webster's,** two very important books, _The French Revolution_ & _World Revolution_ would be the place to begin a serious inquiry. Mrs. Webster's intellect and understanding is far beyond and superior to most all politicians, whom the simpleminded have elected to govern this or any nation. Interestingly, her works are not generally suggested reading, in the public schools of our cleverly contrived Democracy, even though many search for women, whom they hope to prove are more capable than white European men. Certainly, Mrs. Webster was far beyond most of her peers, men and women and fearless beside.

The Russian Revolution (so-called) was, without question, a conspiracy. The Conspiracy included politicians (Wilson, Lloyd George), New York and European Bankers (where the Czar's fortune was deposited), and rabble rousers from the United States and Europe (mostly non-Russian and non-Christian). In a brief and concise work, Fr. Dennis Fahey obviates who ruled Russia, during the period coincident with the *Russian Revolution.*[8] The whole lot of, _ignorantly scheming, traitorous cowards plotted_ toward the destruction of Christian Russia and the Imperial Romanoff Family, especially the Czar and his wife and children. Millions have died prematurely as a consequence of theft, deceit and fraud, without precedent. **Robert Wilton,** a London correspondent and eyewitness to the ritualistic and cabalistic atrocities, has a very extensive overview in his _Last Days of The Romanovs_. Although published in several editions in various languages, right after the event this work is scarcely known. If our public education is so good, we wonder why this book has not been widely read. The events obviated in Mr. Wilton's writing have shaped the course of the economics, politics and the social and intellectual tenor of the world, especially so regarding the Western World, for nearly a century.

The Federal Reserve, our controlled money machine, was planned and executed by men alien to Christianity and the Christian way of life whereabouts all

---

8   **Fahey, Dennis, Rev., C. S. Sp.** _The Rulers of Russia._ **Cum Permissu Superiorum Religiosorum.** First Edition, 1938. Twentieth Edition, 1975. Printed in USA.

men could profit from the plentitude of this world. Together with the separation of Church from State, the private control of money, which leads to the control of government, is a fatal flaw in our present legal and political system.[9] The control of money will be followed by the control of the minds of the people, ultimately the soul as well. At this moment the thinking of humanity is being flooded with sentimental and romantic trash, illicit, silly and perverted sex presented as entertainment. Lie upon lie is promoted covering a valiant search for truth by just a few, brave enough and intelligent enough to understand the reality that surrounds us. In this respect the word *currency* has profound implications. The Federal Reserve System combines with the graduated income tax, a socialist notion, to guarantee that eventually all money and property shall fall to the control of a politically dominant elite.[10] The United Nations provides the format for this eventuality, which is becoming more of a certainty, as this work is written. Well-informed citizens understand this and have attempted, generally with little success to take back control of money and banking from a worldwide banking Cartel.[11] The solution, actually quite simple, is to follow to the letter the Constitutional provisions concerning the issuance and control of money and credit. Only the Congress has the authority "to coin money and regulate the value thereof", that is to print/strike and disburse money for the use of the nation. Private racketeers should be prevented from engaging in this endeavor. The problem is made very complex by contrived legalities and the fact that the usurpers have control of the money and are able, aggressively, to defend their illegal manipulations. Usurpers can buy whomsoever is of any importance, including politicians and the intellectuals who are their Pimps. Who are not for sale, are destined to obscurity or confined to an early grave.

The United Nations, it is imagined, will be the framework for the New World Order, a socialist construct, which is the brainchild of various conspirators, *"especially for a harmful or unlawful purpose"* alien to Christianity. They hope to _collect and control the loot_, which is as the Capital Stock of the International Banking Conglomerate, together with the Capital Stock of the multi-national

---

9   Knupffer, George, _TheStruggle for World Power, Revolution and Counter-Revolution,_ 4th. Edition 1986, ISBN # 0-85172-703-4. Chapter V, The Nature of Capitalism and Banking. Pp. 40-45.

10   **House Banking Committee,** _Elite Group Dominates Nation's Economy._ Chart I, Pg. 4, Reprint in Bulletin, #371, January 1993. Committee to Restore the Constitution. P. O. Box 986, Ft. Collins, CO 80522.

11   **Larson, Martin A.,** _The Federal Reserve and our Manipulated Dollar._ The Devin-Adair Company, Old Greenwich, Conn. © 1975 by Martin A. Larson. ISBN # 0-8159-5513-8 (cloth) and 0-8159-5514-6 (paper).

Corporations, together with title to and control of the land (as collateral for the mountains of debt that are piling up). They aspire *"in acting together"* to create a Fascist Worldwide Empire, ruled from London (The Empire of the City, The Bank of England) and New York (Wall Street and the New York Federal Reserve Banking Cartel). *The United Nations is rammed* into the consciousness of every student in all public schools, some private schools as well. The Conference in 1911 on Jekyll Island, at which the fate of a nation, possibly Western Civilization was determined, was almost never mentioned during this author's rather extensive public education. Technology alone cannot and will not compensate for the ignorance, the moral decay and the misunderstanding of the Universal Christian [Catholic] Philosophy, which brought the Western Culture and ultimately Civilization to so high a level of achievement. *The United Nations is a Socialist Communist Scheme, the plan agreed on,* an anti-Christian *plot* or scheme, conceived by Alger Hiss (a Traitor) and others like him. *Fools in the past harbored great hatred for the Catholic Church and for Christianity.*[12] Presently Revolutionaries, vain Politicians and Nitwits harbor the same **bad Ideas**, which haunt the Culture and the Civilization; all are formulated in the United Nations Charter. An ill-advised cadre of clever faculty and wide-eyed students continue in the fatal charade, for example at the London School of Economics and at our great Universities (so-called), notably Harvard and Yale (see footnote Anthony Sutton, *The Order*, Four volumes. I. *An Introduction to the Order* II. *The Secret Cult of The Order* III. *How the Order Creates War and Revolution, and* IV. *How the Order Controls Education.*

    The Masonic Lodges comprised of men, who have taken an oath to destroy Christianity and especially the Catholic Church,[13] have been active secretly and openly in all Wars and Revolutions. The members, up to the 32nd Degree may have some things in common with the general Population, however the 33rd Degree Masons, having been chosen for very special and/or covert purpose, are of a somewhat different stripe. Many men in governments belong to the various Orders, especially the 33rd Degree and, in effect, they combine to form a secret and all-powerful force in world affairs. They are sworn to protect the interests and person of each other, which supercedes all other *pledges of allegiance.* And, various individuals belong to one or several of the interlocking secret and hidden groups, functioning in favor of they who would rule by deceit. Some men,

---

12 **Manifold, Deirdre,** *Karl Marx, a Prophet of our Times.* G. S. G. & Associates, Publishers. P. O. Box 6448, Eastview Station, Palos Verdes, CA 90734. ISBN # 0-945001-00-2. *Chapter IX, Pp. 95-109*

13 **Wardner, James, Ph D.,** *Communist Infiltration of the Catholic Church.* Video Tape. Most Holy Family Monastery, 4425 Schneider Road, Fillmore, NY 14735. Tel. # 1-800-275-1126.

we may imagine, as being individually weak in character, without honor, deceptive, hypocrites at least, depending for success on cheating and lying, work in secret to accomplish what they imagine is good for this world. *What is imagined as good for this world yields large profits for they who do so imagine.* Especially so, when they who imagine control the various governments and the money and credit of the Western Civilization. An attitude of vain exclusiveness is in exact opposition to Christian charity, decidedly so concerning Catholic (Universal) brotherhood.

The Illuminati, The Council on Foreign Relations, the League of Just Men, The Pilgrim Society, The Round Table, The Club of Rome, The Bank of the City of London, The Masonic Lodges and The Bilderbergers, comprise *"The Group" that is taking part in a worldwide plan of conquest, driven by the will to power.* Presumably there may be others. Conspirators all. Given the definition of Conspiracy[14] and Concert, there can be little doubt in respect to what has been and is happening.

---

14   **Conspiracy** (Kan-spir'a-sy), *n.* [*Pl.* CONSPIRACIES (-siz)], [ME @ Ofr. *conspiracie* < L. *conspirare;* see CONSPIRE], 1. A *planning and acting together* secretly, *especially for a harmful or unlawful purpose,* such as murder or treason. 2. The *plan agreed on, plot.* 3. *The group taking part in such a plan.* 4. *A combining or working together:* as the *conspiracy.* **SYN.** see **plot.**

Appendix F. An Idea Born of Genius

Money must first be considered as a reciprocal for whatever else exists
as tangible.
This understanding is necessary, if the world is to be more decently governed.
Governments control the economic, political and spiritual futures of all people.
It is absolutely necessary
That honesty and a sense of fairness be returned to all government transactions, which must not continue to be dominated by selfishly motivated, secretly contrived, vainly inspired, private Interests.

The *Idea* of Money is *formulated of genius*. It is a concept, which enables all parties in any transaction to be treated fairly and equitably.

Money must be more reasonably and fairly utilized:

1. Money provides a *means of instant accounting*.

2. Money is a *store of past time;* it equates with and should be equal to Time spent in gainful endeavor.

3. Money is or may be *symbolic* of decently formulated accomplishment and truthful success.

4. Money provides a margin of *objectively factored value* against adversity, famine and hard times.

5. Money, in many instances, can have *an almost magical value.*

Narrow-minded, conceited and possessively greedy beings[1] have corrupted the meaning and function of money, which in the eyes of the common working man is beyond comprehension. Only a few, who have made a business of money transaction, understand the nature of what is happening. Nevertheless, Inflation guarantees that every dollar a man may have saved will be stolen one penny at a time. *Money is a reciprocal for time spent in the past, providing that past effort will have current value.* Keep in mind, past time is gone forever, thus it is wise to be able to *store* what value was accrued *yesterday*, thus each man can provide some substance for tomorrow. Hence the term *currency*. The problem we now face is that *a few clever individuals have usurped the monetary process,* thus are able to swindle billions from the process, which billions have the same value dollar for dollar as money legitimately acquired. We have Currency, as money. Currency implies a sense of timeliness and is simultaneously as being up to date (so to speak). *Money compresses and stores time in a recognizably symbolic form.* Thus, it is of the utmost and critical importance that money has a constant value. When the value of money declines, the purchasing power is reduced and every individual holding that form of money [Currency] is systematically robbed, even as the greedy and the clever are given positive opportunity. The Inflation, that is a consequence of the ever-declining value of money, functions as a surrogate to appease the population. Profitable Opportunities are mostly enjoyed, in Time, by scheming Politicians and treacherously deceptive Manipulators of Events. The names of Bernard Baruch, Avril Harrimann, Joseph Kennedy and George Soros come to mind. Actually, what is called Inflation (the erosion of the purchasing power of money) is a cleverly devised means by which, *governments and a favored few are able to consistently and certainly rob the people of the product of their past efforts*. Admittedly, the greed of men is also a factor. Imagination plays an important role

---

1   **Alien Beings** are herein defined as they who have **Ideas** contrary to what are universally beneficial, that being defined as Catholic (from the Greek; meaning, universal). **Ideas** separate men, often into mortally antagonistic beings. Keep in mind, an **Idea** can reside in any single mind. And thinking is a phenomenally changing continuum, being altered as new elements are introduced within the total. Where there are many, holding the same **Ideas,** a complex consensus will/may develop. Most important is how individuals interpret and act on ideas, one way or another. Religion, Race and Nationality do not hold an exclusive right to any **Idea**. Rather **Ideas, shared by many, whether for good or for evil,** are woven within the fabric of familial, tribal, cultural, racial or religious *habit* and become as the dominating **Idiomatic**. This is personal, nevertheless any response may be a consequence of intimidation by the seemingly strong over the weaker and/or less aggressive **personality**. Certainly, we do learn from each other and are more inclined to learn from those who are most outspoken, aggressive or simply persistent.

as well, in that individuals *imagine they are becoming wealthy*, when in fact they are being pauperized. Certainly, some few individuals do benefit from inflation, *especially they who work in concert with the Governments* scheme, in a tacit form of Conspiracy. And, Inflation begets more Inflation, even as a feeling of prosperity is heightened by false expectation. An Inflation Index, which is built into the system, insures that this will continue, in a seemingly ordered manner, indefinitely, or until such time as populations understand how and why they are being robbed each and every day.

Unfortunately, Inflation has been *advertised in mass media* so as to give the notion that individuals are becoming wealthy. We hear speak of how many millionaires there are, at the present time, compared to the past. However, most things cost ten, twenty or a hundred times more than in the recent, median or distant past. Every adult knows this, however *few understand the meaning* of what is happening and *fewer still would believe how this has come about*. We witness *the monetary take-over of the Civilization*, by just a few people and institutions, by hypocritically subtle means. This is, in fact, what may be defined as *Americas' Emerging Fascism*.[2] The *International Bankers and their paid Toadies* are they who profit from the *giant deception and unmitigated fraud* of clever alien interlopers.[3] By this is meant they who are alien to the reasoning and methods of divinely inspired Catholic Christian Civilization. Christ was the first Catholic! He drove the Moneychangers from the Temple however, men with the same inclinations are back, with greater cleverness and ingenuity than even He might have imagined. Many of these same Scoundrels are given the status of being high class, wealthy beyond the dreams of Noblemen, legitimate Royalty and Genius, only because of their ill-gained wealth, not because of any noble or decently inspiring human attribute. Some appear as being quite philanthropic however; even then the tax write-off and their public image are primary motivations. There may be exceptions. At present, we are unaware that any, in fact, do exist. Keep in mind, evil seeks company, where evil dwells.

Malcontents despise and hate the Catholic Church. The Catholic Church is the Conscience of the American Culture and of the Western Civilization and suggests that much, perhaps most, of what we are doing is wrong, is sinful and should not be done. War is wrong, adultery, fornication, embezzlement, lying, usury, and

---

2 **Twight, Charlotte,** *America's Emerging Facist Economy.*, Arlington House, Publishers. New Rochelle, NY. ©1975 by Charlotte Twight. ISBN # 0-87000-317-8. Chapters 1 and 2, Pp. 13-50.

3 **Steinberger, Calvin** (deceased), *International Banking Comes to America.* Reprint in Bulletin, #377 & 378, June 1993, Committee to Restore the Constitution. P. O. Box 986, Ft. Collins, CO 80522.

many forms of behavior that we accept as normal. Read Christ Jesus' Sermon on the Mount and the Ten Commandments, then, follow the Directions. Simple as pouring water from a glass! The Catholic Church expresses, albeit abstractly, the Will of an Omnipotent and Perfect Presence. We are encouraged to have Faith in such Omnipotent will. Since no man is perfect, we all find some difficulty in living up to infinite perfection. This is, in fact, the most profound Human Dilemma. When one imagines they are good and decent, fair and honorable, then, much is expected of them; so as to prove any *truthfulness of such imagination*? If one imagines he is a believer then, to not offer such proof makes one simply a hypocrite.

To be exclusive and generally antagonistic is to remain apart from the family of man. As an outsider one is inclined to be suspicious, fearful and unduly aggressive. Although there is certainly some agreement, most of the World's significant Religions do not accept the entire Catholic faith, which includes the structure, symbolism, Sacraments and other requirements of the Catholic Church, as formally instituted. Millions are antagonistic, some are merely skeptical others may become as fatal enemies. What Pope John Paul II has done, a few others before him, is to *give up elements of the Faith*, in an attempt to satisfy a stubbornly determined opposition. Such *"giving up"* is a submissive or condescending action, is Heretical and is rigorously, Blasphemous. *Any Philosophy can be destroyed, by inserting thought elements and removing required strictures, until such time as it becomes ineffective, without meaning, secular and mundane, as is happening just now.*[4] Conversely any Philosophy can be inserted one idea at a time thus to modify and to eventually overcome the structure and nature of the accepting system. This is exactly what is happening at the present time in the minds and thought-structures of the Catholic, Christian Culture. As the Bride of Christ, the Catholic Church must remain inviolate, unchanging, as is (forever) thus to fulfill the expectations of Perfect Being.[5] This should be easy to understand, however the *Will to understand* is lacking in most, since such understanding requires a prop-

---

4   **Pope Pius XI**, *Encyclical Letter, January 6, 1928.* Gregorian Press, Most Holy Family Monastery, 261 Cross Keys Road, Berlin, NJ 08009. Pg. 2. "They presuppose the erroneous view that all religions are more or less good and praiseworthy, inasmuch as all give expression, under various forms, to that innate sense which leads man to God and to the obedient acknowledgement of His rule. Those who hold such views…distort the true **Idea** (bold inserted) of religion…falling gradually into naturalism and atheism."

5   **Pope Pius XI**, *Encyclical Letter, January 6, 1928.* Gregorian Press, Most Holy Family Monastery, 261 Cross Keys Road, Berlin, NJ 08009. Pg. 10. "Therefore, since the foundation of charity is faith pure and inviolate, it is chiefly by the bond of one faith that the Disciples of Christ are to be united. A federation of Christians then is inconceivable in which each member retains his own opinions and private judgement

erly formed attitude and the correct holy disposition, thus determines the universally acceptable perimeters for human existence, as being Christ-like, including all forms of personal behavior. Not to be misunderstood, *much of what an individual will view as entertainment places him outside from the acceptable perimeters of decently formed participation, within a sacred and holy Tradition.*

Disagreements, between religious factions, may have been small initially, however have been fanned into hatred, often for a profit rendered to those holding the Fan. We have come to understand this as international Banking, Finance Capital. Modern History provides countless examples of *fanning for profit.* All major Wars, as well as the present minor Wars, are fought for *profits tendered to avarice and greed,* with funds extorted from good and decent citizens. Malcontents and Scribblers, offer weak explanations, with strong secular appeal, which are catapulted into the psyche of most in this world altering the attitude and disposition of millions. Patriotism, nationalism and religious fervor are harnessed in support of obscene and decadent activities, deemed as an appropriate use of modern and advanced technologies. Dead Heroes are the young, who do not understand what they are doing or why so many are returned home in body bags, or buried in an unidentified grave. We are informed, by the American Legion, that battlefield casualties are less likely to die because of wounds inflicted. So what! *Thus, in fewer instances the community laments what never should have happened.* This is not surprising in a nation, culture or civilization, where the attitude and disposition of a people is formed by movies, television, pornography, special slanted news reporting, Disneyland, Mickey Mouse, Bamby and Talking Muppets, like (you know) in the Land of make-believe. Albeit, some of mass communication is uplifting and decently inspired, such as is, is exceptional. Certainly, the well-staged Presentations are captivating, one way or another, for the minds of millions. Mayhem, bedlam, overt sexual displays, noise, ignorant prattling, Rapper's wailing, advertisements, country, rock, Lawrence Welk, new cars, motor-cross, athletics, body-makeovers, the sales pitch for creams, ointments and salves. Finally, the subtle brain washing continues incessantly, slowly forming attitudes and dispositions in an attentive population. There is no escape!

An attentive Population, attitudinally disposed and addicted to what is mostly unnecessary, meaningless and inconsequential is slowly being strangled by its own excessive prosperity, even as debt loads continue to rise to heretofore unimaginable levels. In their distraction, this same population is allowing the take-over of the wealth and property of a Civilization, by *an alien attitude, an international imposition* that is robbing individuals and nations of both wealth and heritage. An

---

in matters of faith, even though they differ from opinions of all the rest." Also read Plato's Dialogues.

attitude and disposition alien to most of humanity is in control of the wealth of the nations, built by the Western Civilization. Albeit many will deny that, because of the Catholic Christian Ethic, *a divinely [inspired] Imperative* underlies the good that has been accomplished by millions of individuals over the course of twenty centuries to help Humanity. Decent Catholic and Christian men and women, millions of others as well, have been willing to share their goods and prosperity with others less fortunate. Who now is leading the Band of Thieves that will enslave the Families of all Men? Truly, the Family of Man becomes as a consequence of one's being in communion with God the Father, from whom all good things come. We suggest that "The Family of Man" as advertised in slick magazines by the usurpers is, at best, a contrivance and represents mostly profound misunderstanding.

Addressing the Skeptic, the disbeliever or the antagonist, in reference to the assertions made in the above paragraph, the Catholic Imperative resides as an *Idea*, quite independent from the institutions and established order of the Western Civilization.[6] However, the *Idea* is persistent and will not go away.[7] **Ideas coalesce to form what is referred to as an Imperative.** It is important exactly what is meant and inferred by the use of this word.[8] Those who, by their attitude and

---

6   **The Idea is a phenomenally functional ephemeral,** albeit quite elusive, obviously not always and everywhere apparent. Nevertheless, **Ideas** are presented as the focal point of this exposition. Ideas can combine in ways which are difficult to conceive and even more difficult to understand. How the individual mind has interpreted, a phenomenally and existentially complex time/space cluster of neurological inputs, is what is responsible for any **Idea** or act engendered thereby. Historically, extensive occurrence, such as war, the building of a city or the conception and use of money, forms the **warp of history** as certain as the individual acts are as the **weft**, becoming as the **fabric** of Civilization.

7   **Pope Pius X, *On the Doctrines of the Modernists. Pascendi Dominici Gregis. &The Syllabus Condemning the Errors of the Modernists. Lamentabili Sane,* July 1907.** St. Paul Editions. Whether or not one is Catholic, even if one despises the Catholic Faith, it is wise to read this profound work, the understanding of which will help to clarify our present dilemmas, one and all. Additionally, it will help any parent to better understand, in certainly defined terms, by what means many of our children are becoming as savages, uncaring, vain, irresponsible, decadent, untrustworthy and violent. Whatever happens is a question of just a few ingredients: attitude, disposition, understanding the meaning of words and confronting the nature and meaning of the most important **idea.** *All Ideas function in accord with or in opposition to other Ideas.*

8   **Imperative,** (im-per'a-tiv), **adj.** [LL, *imperativus,* **commanding** < pp. of L. *imperare, to command, order* < in-, + *parare,* to prepare, order], **1.** Having the nature of, or indicating, *authority* or command: as an *imperative* gesture **2. Absolutely necessary,** urgent; **compelling:** as it is *imperative* that I go at once. **3.** In *grammar, designating*

disposition, deny the existence of a singular, divinely inspired complexity, which we witness as ultimate reality, are unable to make the necessary connections or perhaps they are simply stubborn

It is important to keep in mind, philosophically speaking, what [IS], **is as it [IS]**! Universality must be **exactly as it is**, or it would not be at all. In the Sciences, this is an important principle. Biologically, you must be who you are or you would not be at all! Each person is a singularly unique and irreplaceable Human Being.

Psychologists, in concert with those who gain from conveying falsehood, have confused the thinking of millions on the Idiomatic of Western Philosophy. Many important Writers (so-called) have *"piddled"* their romantic nonsense over an entire Civilization, they have confused millions with imaginings and nonsense and a pubescent understanding of reality. Thousands of venal Novels are written, which distract from serious learning and understanding as they expound flawed information and sexually perverse innuendo. It is impossible to determine the damage that has been and is being done on the simple minds of those that read them. What is worse, falsely formed imaginings have covered the psyche of the entire Civilization, as snowflakes cover a meadow. This is not all bad, to be sure. However, it is important to understand the tremendous influence of the **Stargazers**[9] and *assumed professionals* who formulate **Ideas** and combine them in various ways, for common-consumption.

Dialectic can be formulated to confuse most, even as it is contrived so the insider does understand the true meaning of utterance and what is written. Controlled confusion is part of all Conspiracies and Modern Revolutions in general (Nesta Webster, *World Revolution)*. Additionally, it is easy to confuse with spoken words since the listener is trapped by the speaker's inference, which may or may not be understood and may be seated in truth or falsehood. The Orator with clever use of words, intimidation and the *threat imposed by "others"* incites the Mob. Any Mob can be stirred to violence against what exists or is only imagined to exist. Revolutionaries capitalize on a *"lets pretend"* mentality, and fear of the *"Boogie Man",* left over from childhood. Indeed, many assumed as adult are in fact overgrown children, those in need of some outlet for their childish animosities.

---

*or of the mood of a verb that expresses a command, **strong request or exhortation**. n. 1.* A command; order. **2.** In *grammar, a) the imperative mood.* b) a verb in this mood. Abbreviated **imper., imp., impv.** (Rubric for emphasis)

9   **Human Life** and what is of truthful importance is right on this planet, at this very moment and we must do whatever is possible to enhance the life of all that live, here and now! Too soon we reach for the Stars, which too is an extreme form of Vanity. In reaching for the stars we find new technologies, which will no doubt be utilized for the development of even more sophisticated means of killing our fellow man.

One may witness thousands parading on the street, for effect and for the excitement generated by being *"finally"* a part of something [important?].

Where serious issues are involved Vanity always plays a part. One is reminded that *vain assumptions* do exist. And there is indignation, when dearly held assumptions are brought into question, especially so when the question obviates some falsehood or discrepancy, real or imagined. It is important to encourage that the Skeptic, as well as they that hold contrary views, must consider others fairly, thus to share reasonably in this world with those who deserve to live with dignity, with some prosperity and in peace. This touches on the existence of Indigenous People (a subject too broad for this presentation) and all that are somehow different in one or many ways. One can appeal to goodness and to fairness, as it is an important part of individually determined action.

Appendix G. Sin is the Cancer of All Civilizations!
Usury, Fornication, and Deceit are Cardinal Sins

An Analogy to clarify some significant assertions

Cancer is chosen for our analogy for various reasons. The most important reasons have to do with a statistical analysis from the Medical Profession and to compare this with the products of deviously inspired forms of social engineering, incorrectly conceived public education and crime rates amongst various segments of the population. Finally, the level of personal, corporate and governmental debt must be considered as bearing upon much of what is considered. Certainly, the medical profession, the drug cartels, the insurance companies and the political impositions, as tax on all manner of endeavor, add up to putting big money in the many and very deep pockets of those that play the game well. Such is **the _disposition and nature of a nation riding a wave of covertly engendered prosperity._** Expensive cars, mountain homes, yachts and big bank accounts are the rewards greed pays to sin; hypocrisy, usury, fornication, pornography, narcotics, bank fraud and child desertion to mention the most obvious. _**Educated fools refuse to put the parts together since millions are involved in the swindle.**_ And for many the swindle is considered good business providing a comfortable existence right here on earth. Who needs Heaven?

To begin, let us consider three primary factors. 1). **Regarding Cancer,** in the year 1900, the rate of cancer was considered to be that about one person in twenty-five would contact the disease. This was not good news however present news makes even such bad news as that sound good. How out of control is Cancer? "Cancer is a raging epidemic, every other American male will get it and every third female. What that means is if you don't get it, or don't have it growing

189

in you right now, then the person sitting next to you will."[1] And, because cancer is a fatal disease contracted because of a corrupt life-style, you will receive no help from *those who corrupt you* or from the *Medical Profession*, which profits immensely from unnecessary and dangerous (often-fatal)[2] procedures. The thought alone, of having Cancer, is enough to scare many to death.

2). **Regarding Social Engineering and Education**, in the land of the free, many well-educated Medical Doctors, that seek effectively proven alternative treatments, have been silenced, for speaking the truth, concerning an undeniably expert opinion. *Remember, some medical opinions "are more equal than others".* Nevertheless, *pressure groups,* such as the American Medical Association, Hospital Administrators, Lawyers and Politicians are given full authority to *dictate* how shall a patient be treated. Insurance forms, disclaimers, consent forms and corporation presumption on common sense confuse all but the professional who deals with a small part of what is in fact largely a charade or simply a fraud. The expensive buildings comfort "All who enter here" (Dante) even as it is known that hundreds of thousands *become ill or die from the best treatment* (Contrares, MD. Internationally known Oncologist). And, much of what happens is as a matter of acting, a performance, playing a part, assuming a role or is an expression, seemingly significant, of an unknown other. And there is the anxiety that dwells near as death may be approaching. In many instances, corruption of the language plays an important part and who has been chosen to play the part?

The Educational System has failed to properly inform children on what is good health and what are proper eating habits. The **Children's Desires** are *laid on the dear little ones* by corporate enterprise, featuring nonsense-creatures on television, which push the *sugar coated crap* that lines the isles of the *conglomerate-monopoly-cartel* food industry. All the name brands *one has been conditioned to recognize, thus to choose,* could line up for an award, *the award for encouraging bad eating habits and ruining children's health!* Of course, the children, we imagine, being so very

---

1   **Schulze, Richard, M. D.** *Natural Healing Newsletter*. January 2004, Vol. 5, Issue 1. Natural Healing Publications. The Voice of Dr. Schulze. Pg. 1.

2   **Iatrogenic Disease, that disease caused by treatment**, is a leading killer in America. By some, Medical practitioners, **Iatrogenic Disease** is considered to be the leading cause of death, keeping in mind, regarding the cause of death, many deaths are assumed natural, which may have (in fact) been caused by some form of *treatment.* Also, keep in mind that the Medical establishment is engaged in the *treatment of disease or the containment of a disease* and rarely, if ever, is heard mention of an attempt to cure, especially where cancer is concerned. Extraordinary profits, hundreds of billions each year, are gained in an *often-fatal* pursuit. *The term Fatal is used with discretion.* Never in the history of the World, in spite of totally unnecessary technologies, have so many paid so much to die an excruciating and debilitating death.

bright and much wiser than their parents ever were are given to make their own choices *"by tantrum"*, thus to *"encourage the condescending, bewildered parent"* to meet the demands of both ignorance and greed. In our analogy, the Child represents ignorance the Cartel personifies greed.

3). **Outrageous spending habits and the accumulation of debt** have _compromised the emotional tenor_ of an entire people running to stay in the same place. Unreasonable expectation and failure to meet the fiscal demands of excessive spending (private, corporate and governmental) are part of an equation, which includes self-imposed anxiety. Add to this the emotional stress of Mortal Sin, which multiplied has enveloped almost every aspect of our existence. Mortal Sin and Perversions of various sorts are considered normal and are acceptable to millions, a **way to go** (so to speak), nevertheless, we are certain that the individual human conscience is paying a high price. This is in spite of whether or not one may be aware of what the price really is. One might consider that Alzheimer's Disease is that disease caused by a persistent conscience. The past catches up and it seems convenient, indeed necessary, for victims of excess, disappointment and social blundering (in one form of another), to withdraw from reality. This may seem an unfair or absurd assertion however, should be considered and not be undermined by sentiment and a misunderstanding of Catholic Christian theology. It is well known that spousal fidelity, which is monogamous and sustaining without interruption and truthfully formed love is an aid to good health and long life. Thus one might conclude the opposite is certainly true as well. We are placed in a position of living modestly and faithfully with the one that we have promised will be *till death do us part.*

Now we draw our analogy.

Cancer invades the healthy body in subtle and seemingly unimportant ways. First just a few cells are apparent as being malignant. However, Cancer Cells divide quickly choosing to harbor in those areas, which are weakest and have the least effective defense. Often such areas of the body have been under stress caused by some manner of excess and function poorly. They are unable to meet the demands of the human body.

Sin[3] **invades** correspondingly a healthy society in seemingly harmless ways, just a few liars, thieves, pornographers and hypocrites. We term their slow

---

3   **Sin**, it must be emphasized, is any act which violates God's commandments or that which, perhaps as importantly is contrary to the Golden Rule. Sin is aggressive and

encroachment as *gradualism.* Sinners are anxious and eager, thus to entice others to become, as they have become, enticing the eager and the vain, with earthly rewards, money, power, prestige and self-gratification. The power of mass communication is awesome providing that sin may be transmitted at the speed of light, to all parts of the globe, by Television and the Cinema. All know that Sin multiplied seems less as Sin, thus may be considered merely as entertainment, fun or a necessary, harmless and healthy diversion. Drug pushers create millions that are physically and emotionally impaired. The Medical Profession, Doctors, Psychologists and Psychiatrists respond by attaching the name of a disease or impairment, which must be treated. The diseased and impaired, *become patient,* must be treated, or they will simply withdraw of their own accord into a myopic stupor. Are we having fun yet? Overt Sinners become, one by one as Serpents in the Garden of Eden.

Cancer Cells multiply quickly and ultimately may become a tumor, or they spread (metastasize, *thus to be "place(d) in another way* [Webster]), within the blood stream, they are carried to other parts of the body. It is believed there are many forms of cancer, which may be true. Nevertheless, Hulda Rehger Clark believes there is a *"Cure for All Cancers"* and has written a book on the subject, known by that title. Such writing is shunned by many of her peers who imagine they must continue looking, thus to gain funds from the government so as to enjoy more extravagance during their leisure.

Sin multiplies quickly and spreads, especially when given to the near-speed of light as is common in the mass communication industry. One stupid, silly and vulgar comedian or a porno queen can be seen *simultaneously* by millions *instantaneously,* like [*you know*], really fast. And **Sin multiplied** is not considered as sin. Everybody does it. So, what's the Big Deal? Youth learns quickly and *sin is easily peddled.* And, we do have "Consenting Adult Laws" so as to protect (?) We are not sure, the Consenting, the Adult, or, the Law? We, totally confused, can't decide. If we did decide in favor of the traditional understanding of Sin, no one would listen, if they did most would shun our opinion.

Cancer cells form as in tumors, clusters or colonies of cells, which deprive the body of necessary nourishment, even as pollution is given to the blood stream.

---

stains the person or the character of the person that is involved in Sin, whether as perpetrator or condescendingly as accepting or condoning what is sinful. Sin is a difficult subject, which becomes nearly impossible in (for example) a familial, political or economic discussion. Sin, importantly, gives rise to indignation and an aggressive behavior in defense of what is wrong. The admission of Sin, as in a Catholic Confession, requires humility and an openhearted and fair-minded spirit, and is dependent upon truthful repentance. "Go and sin no more," (Christ).

Cancer emits *death photons*, minute waves, almost non-discernable, which invade the surrounding tissue.[4] ***Death photons are as an emission of a death dealing spirit.*** As the cells divide, the number of cells is increased exponentially. At one point there become so many cancer cells that the body of the person is over-whelmed and succumbs to death. The death is generally painful and can be very slow, debilitating to the spirit and to the will to live. A foreboding and evil sense are present in advanced cancers, whereabouts the victim knows the certainty of the consequence. Even the smells are "very scary". The fact that expert (?) opinion can warn of an approximate date of death *indemnifies an understanding* of how the disease advances *throughout the whole body.* Interestingly, if the patient dies *there are never any refunds* for malpractice, hospital-induced (entrogenic) death or the Practitioners incompetence[5] or as a simple courtesy. Lawyers may get rich attempting to gain some settlement for a bereaved family member, however this does not bring back the dead.

The Great Cities (so called) are as tumors, that contain the ingredients for terminating the Biological Family, the Christian Culture and the Western Civilization.

One could imagine them as being *sociological tumors of sorts.* For convenience, our great cities appear to be a reasonable harbor for human life[6] however, as Cities

---

4   Bearden, Thomas, Col., USA, Ret., *Aids, Biological Warfare*

5   **Patients** have been treated for the wrong disease. Others have been treated, using the wrong lab reports. Some have had healthy arms and legs removed, because of the con-fusion, within those departments committed to a critical task. Regarding Cancer, *the exploratory operation is necessary* when the surgeon does not comprehend exactly what may be a problem. Not to belittle all decently formulated effort, one does appreci-ate some of the rather wonderful things being accomplished by the present medical establishment.

6   **The Town House,** of the past, was perhaps *an ideal place for winter or for special occasions,* as a retreat from a vast country Estate. As such, it provided better access for friendship and to attend those functions, which were considered fashionable, theatre, opera, political events and grand socializing. At such time servants maintained the country house. Today few have a staff of *honest and dependable servants* upon who they might rely. Presently, in America, married couples attempt to enjoy some such comforts, however with children and a myriad of domestic and professional respon-sibilities it is mostly a dream. Beside, in a Democracy (of presumed equals) who then will be the servant? The servant may come from another land, so as to escape to freedom, opportunity and consenting adult laws. Today, men who collect trash or do manual labor *presume to be professionals.* In such and similar presumptions, the meaning of language is being constantly eroded. Even a hooker imagines being in a legitimate business!

become more and more congested, some are beginning to comprehend the ultimate disasters that will confront us. We face violence at this very moment: riot-
ing, gang warfare, murder and unimaginable crimes. We photograph mayhem
and project it upon a stressed population, for the moneys gained from advertising, imagining it as entertainment. Millions spend their evenings watching what
properly, in a dignified and sensitive adult community, should not be shown.
Actors, really pretenders, deliver curious examples of _"Sex in the City, Desperate
Housewives, Grays Anatomy, Boston Legal"_ and other _cute, horny, stupid or just
dumb_ presentations. The pretenders are paid millions. The programs are offered
as entertainment, which they are, for those that do not read one good book in a
lifetime. And, the contrived and outrageous behavior of one's _favorite Character,_
encourages the simple-minded and those that are dissatisfied with their own self
to adopt curious, aggressive, silly or vicious forms of behavior. And, nearly every
talk show is filled with the presence of the Celebrity making the politically correct
comments, as we hear of their sinful adventures, especially concerning fornication
and the illegitimacy of their love child, all for mass ingestion. Television is the best
form of Behavior Modification, ever known to man.

Directors punctuate bad acting with images of explicit sex. Bawdy, tacky and
vulgar representations are interspersed with _million-dollar-a-minute commercial
messages_, appealing to a consumer's instincts, destined to place one deeper in debt.
Everywhere; advertisements for automobiles, insurance, pharmaceutical drugs,
intimate products, vacations, tools, sun screen, schooling, the hamburger, the
taco, French fries, weight loss programs, real estate scams, coke and diet foods are
"in your face." Nipples and crotches are cleverly exposed to entice the prurient
curiosity of the moron, the dolt and a young savage looking to get laid.

Great concentrations of indignant, vicious and arrogant individuals are centered within the crowded and congested cities and more are becoming the same.
Animosities have often been engendered and incubated over the course of many
centuries or perhaps are just recently imagined as a response to the Idea of a
Sociologist seeking a government grant. Sin is encouraged by a lack of respect for
holiness and by a government with the full intention of destroying the nation,
which it pretends to serve. Coincidentally, the greater part of the Nations wealth
is harbored in the huge metropolitan areas, as ownership of real estate and infrastructure demand greater payment in debt currency. Interestingly, wealthy individuals and institutions that are centered in the metropolis hold title to vast
rural lands as well. The Franchise reaches every small town and village from the
financial centers within the great (?) cities. Wealth has been drained from the

countryside. The Franchise Restaurant *seemingly* has made every kind of pro-cessed, dehydrated, frozen and *adulterated* food available to all.[7]

The roadways connecting the center with the hinterland are as (veins and arteries), which carry an often-questionable commodity (the nation's tainted blood) to and fore. Many of the foodstuffs are not fit to eat. Conglomerate food suppliers supply an endless variety of stuff, imagined as food that often requires more energy for digestion, than that gained from eating the food. And, obesity is as an epidemic. The plastic gadgets, created for our convenience, are largely unnecessary; nevertheless *they enhance one's lifestyle* we are informed. The great cities are complex clusters of smaller communities that have grown together com-pletely filling all the space in between, much as a Cancer consumes the victim. Or, cities have simply expanded and spread (metastasized) upon all useful land sur-rounding what may have been an *ideal place for habitation*. Ugly signs, defended by an outdoor advertising lobby, blot and corrupt the landscape, like tumors on the colon or warts. At the speed of light (by means of minute waves) we receive messages, the news of events worldwide, for most individuals mostly meaningless. Unfortunately, gruesome messages may be stressful depending on one's level of empathy for those, who have been tormented, tortured, murdered, pillaged and raped. Stirring up the population is a business, which calls for solutions as other businesses, form to meet the challenge. This creates employment, we are told, even as it draws mothers away from their children.

Mickey Mouse and The City of Hope are two of the World's most recognized Institutions. Certainly Disneyland gives some relief from day to day boredom. The City of Hope, one can imagine, may provide the *therapy/treatment of choice,* peddled as main stream medicine. Such business augments the seriousness of the Rose Parade and Super Bowl Sunday. Christmas and Easter are under attack by Zealots that believe in freedom for some even as they would curtail the freedom of others, leading to rule by a minority coalition.

Tarzan and Jane are back in *porno flicks on the Internet* encouraging the spreading of a social disease that shatters the lives of millions. One can imag-ine that Tarzan and Jane practice safe sex. However, *Pornography is a form of visual Cancer* and is a sociological as well as a mental and medical infliction, infecting the mind as well as the body of those that participate as certainly as it destroys the soul of the perpetrators. *Pornographers are certainly reprobated.* Pornography, besides being disgustingly explicit encourages the imagination

---

7   **Thou shall not commit adultery** is one of the Ten Commandments. Check the labels on your foodstuffs. Cancer is largely a consequence of what we eat, breath, drink and that which is *seemingly* pleasurable. Aids is the Classic Disease of sexual excess and misunderstanding, a consequence of an immature sense of self.

of the viewers to fantasize in future time. Such fantasizing, one could imagine, leads to the variously conceived and executed forms of overt perversion, as in criminal assault, directed especially against young and beautiful women. We imagine Pornographers as giant, foul and oozing Maggots, which suck up the body fluids and *pustules,* from a decaying Civilization. *And of course, their image of Jane is that she always gets the shaft, one way or another, from some eager Nincompoop!*

Gender-confused *Persons* have assumed a political attitude, which intimidates those who have no recourse within a fluid and inconsistent legal system. Women hope to marry women as men hope to marry men, ignoring the meaning if words so to further corrupt what is already failing. Such Unions, is certainly a form, of diversity, perhaps perversity however, not necessarily so. There are many variations in respect to how and why individuals do exist and it is reasonable that all should attempt to be in a manner of harmony. And, presumably, there may be much that is good in light of what might be an alternative. Nevertheless one should not abandon the proper meaning of words, to do so makes correct understanding impossible. Having chosen a *questionable option* such *persons* fulfill their *Role in society*, or *Act their part*, or *Perform*, so to imagine a *normal* and productive life. As such, they (may) represent a manner of metastasizing from the parent pornographic tumor. It is understood that some such assertions are difficult to deal with however, *"in an era where truth is relative"* one must expect that there will exist such antagonisms. Be that as it may, hundreds of millions of *Persons* do consider perversion to be perversion in spite of any skewing of Definitions.

Our patient Reader can go on from here certain to see the picture, without the rose-covered glasses offered by apologists, those earning a living from maintaining and furthering the status quo.

Finally, to repeat, **most of what happens is good** however, the bad, ugly and the sinful are what one is expected to correct. Corrections demand a change in the attitude and habits of a distracted population. This is a difficult assignment in a social complex where contradicting ideas are given equal authority. *Plato* was quite certain that sin progresses from father to son as does all form and manner of sinful excess. We believe Plato was right. And, *Dante* did make a good case for a Monarchy imposing truthful, viable and decently inspired leadership, the best kind.

It is apparent that the Democracy, which is being fostered as a political contrivance, suffers from learned ignorance, philosophical ineptitude, racially inspired contempt, anxious greed and a general misunderstanding of reality in a failing system. The *Third World,* which is a euphemism for what cannot be explained in simple terms, will very likely overcome and consume the Western Civilization, which coincidentally is engaged in political, economic and moral suicide. The

United States has made two attempts to aid the Western European Civilization, both of which were orchestrated by deceitful hypocrites. In the second instance the hypocrite presumed to chase a madman away. Of significance is that the burgeoning Third World countries do see a decidedly formed religion as part of politics and their quietly aggressive, often illegal, invasion of another country. When they arrive at their destination as in the United States and Europe the alien, almost immediately, builds his church and insists on the right to worship as he sees fit. This is done even as the alien despises the host that has offered them opportunity to prosper and to live in peace. In time the stronger of any two opposites will overcome by means of force, or conquer by means of infiltration. Since they have survived for so much longer than we have, perhaps there is much we might learn from the Indian and the Chinese Cultures.

My Peace I give you (Christ).

Most of what happens is good! However

Cancer, is an illness of the human body

CCCCCCCCCCCCCCCC
CCCCCCCCCC
CCCCCCC
CCCC
C
Corruption and Sin are illnesses of the Soul

SSSSSSSSSSSSSSSSSSSSS
SSSSSSSSSSSSS
SSSSSSS
SSS
S

Lets be Ann

Lets be Men

Appendix H. Power and Influence

Power and influence are increasingly in the hands of fewer and fewer individuals. This is as a consequence of the, grow or die mentality. Corporate mania, that is the consolidation and buyout of commercial enterprise is, among other things, a destructive force that most probably leads toward a form of collectivism and ultimately Fascism.[1] Ultimately a few dynastic families will control governments and the peoples of this world. Such concentration of wealth, with attendant material and land holdings is not unlike a Monarchy, except it is a product of political and economic usurpation, without precedent.

We will enter into a new Feudal System, wherein the power will be in the hands of those that control the debt currency, from a privately owned consortium func-tioning *in concert* *as a central bank.* This is a form of Collusion and may be con-sidered as a Conspiracy, a Concert *"performed in secret."* Only some will be invited, who will be given free tickets (?). Ultimately it is possible that the usurpers will attain total ownership of all lands, beginning with what are now considered public lands, which will be pledged as collateral against our enormous deliberately con-tracted debt. The State as a matter of subterfuge, will impose taxes thus guarantee that all *commoners or peasants* will remain in a position of economic servitude beholden to the State. The State will be dominated and controlled by the same families and individuals that control the money. The dynastic families, as is now generally the case, will continue to benefit from generous provisions in laws gov-erning taxation. To a great extent this is what has already happened.

Inventions, technology and communication marvels will assure the becoming, of new rich. The new rich will co-operate, politically, with the regime or they will be ostracized and eventually consumed, one way or another. Total domination is not a certainty to happen however the possibility does exist. What is here written should help to prevent such occurrence.

---

1 <u>Twight, Charlotte,</u> *America's Emerging Fascist Economy.* Arlington House, Publishers. © 1975, Charlotte Twight. ISBN #0-87000=317-8.

The creation of money provides that they who oversee the creation and control of the money will also create and control the law. What is now termed rule of Law, being driven into the collective psyche, is rule by those who make the law. Dialectics will make it possible to convince the citizens that what happens is in their best interest. Humanism will be, actually is right now, the state Religion. *Functionaries can be bought to perform any task, from child-care to murder and everything in between.* Presently the power is consolidated in old families and a few new ones, which because of the phenomenal characteristic of mass consumption, combined with the increase in money value of urban real estate and the ability to trade stocks in a controlled market have made giant fortunes. The shrewd amongst the new rich will retain what they have however the unwary will lose to stronger and more determined adversaries, those that will organize for the purpose of eliminating undesirable contenders. In other words, big fish consume the smaller ones. The various governments will be the biggest fish in any given pond. The Ponds will be given to those that will cooperate with the International Bankers. This is exemplary of the dog eat dog mentality of a politically and economically driven market place, which lacks a truthful and holy moral imperative. Listed are a few of the most prosperous families, allowing the reader to better understand the nature of the dilemma. It is a dilemma.

Below are listed some of the most powerful and influential families in the world. There are others as well.[2]

The Rothschilds, *** The most wealthy "Clan" of all. They have been and are at the Apex of International Finance and Banking. European Bankers (London, Paris, Frankfort, Hamburg), Money lending (The Bank of England, City Banks in the US), especially they are known to have financed War and Conflict. They control vast amounts of Real Estate, Precious Metal (Control price of precious metals, especially gold), Mineral Deposits (Rio Tinto). *In the instance of War, the Rothschild interests are notorious, financing both sides of a conflict, so as to profit from the defeated, by means of confiscation and milk the victors, by means of usury.*
The Sassoons, *** Far Eastern Trading Company, Finance, Narcotics Trade (especially Opium), Real Estate. The Sassoons were beneficiaries of the Opium Wars in China.
The Windsors, *** Prominent in England since fifteenth Century, they have an entire nation and much of the world, _beholden to a notion_ of the superiority of a corrupt and opportunistic Nobility? They are Associates in the Bank of England,

---

2   Lundberg, Ferdinand, _The Rich and the Super Rich._ Bantam Books, 271 Madison Avenue, NY. © 1968 Ferdinand Lundberg.

Land, Fine Art (there collections number in the thousands of very important works, drawings, paintings, books, suites of armour, etc.), Jewels, Thievery, Gold and Real Estate.

The Rockefellers, ** America's Rothschild Associate. The Rockefeller Foundation works to socialize and communize the American people. They are engaged in Transportation, Real Estate, Banking and Philanthropy aimed at changing the nature of our Nation, Culture and Civilization.

The Du Ponts, ** There are many. Their wealth is in Manufacturing, Chemicals, Synthetics and Drugs. It is understood that many synthetics are responsible for much of the poor health and disease (Schulze, MD) currently obvious to they who understand cause and effect relationships. Philanthropy destined to change how a nation thinks.

Warren Buffet, * Stock trading, Finance, Stock Funds. *One of the New Rich, obviously, a clever and astute trader of stocks.* **We note** *present stock manipulation is largely fraudulent and is effectively controlled by a few giant players. Recently the US Government has acted to maintain a false sense of security within the system. Timing is important and they who "set or mark the time" (so to speak) benefit immeasurably more than they who are gainfully employed in production, barely able to meet necessary expenses and debt obligations, those who's pension funds and retirement funds are being robbed, coincidentally, by sophisticated stock trading techniques. Admittedly, some of the profits enjoyed by the big players, Insurance Companies and Pension funds, for example, find their way to the pocket of the little guy.*

Walton Brothers, * They are most prominent among the new rich. Retail merchandising and **_exploitation of the Third World._** Truly an example of phenomenal circumstances come to assistance of greed served by monumental insensitivity. Wal Mart is, in fact, a social and economic disease. Because of modern transportation and Communication they are able to rob one side of the World, those paid a pittance in wages, even as they rob the other side of the World by dumping boatloads of foreign made merchandise on an eagerly consuming population. They have benefited, phenomenally from the globalization of commerce, co-incident with the aggressive spending habits of an anxious population hoping to share the American Dream. There are other dreams as well. It is true they keep prices somewhat lower however, this cannot last. **_Landfill bloated with commercial crap dot the nations landscape._** Some believe this is progress. So it is, right to the dump, where mountains of junk are put to rest. It is true much of this can be recycled and some is biodegradable however, this begs the issue. The issue is a gluttonous need for what is ugly, oversized, temporary and cheap. Such exploitation as is evident in mass marketing is thought of [only] as good business. Admittedly, some good is evident from what is happening, however, much such [good] is only imaginary and is offset by the [real] damage being done. Few would comprehend the nature and scope of the damage and most would not have it any other way! Generally speaking, the common man does not participate except as a wage slave or a misinformed consumer.

Industries need not rush to *"who knows where (?)"*. The world will be here for a very long time, unless we destroy what is necessary for healthful living. The present confrontation between Moslem and Western Culture is one step in such destruction, which should obviate a cultural disparity, which begs for better and a more truthful understanding of the world's people. It is probably wise and certainly more prudent to move with fair-minded caution, so that more individuals can prosper, rather than the few that are being encouraged toward the scalping of an entire Civilization. That same well-placed few can [milk] millions or billions from a corrupt and decadent system, which is in fact a combination of *corrupt Socialism* fed by a just as corrupt *perverted Corporate Capitalism*. The corporate headquarters buildings are as Cathedrals for those that worship money, wealth and power. There are occult insinuations, where great fortunes reside. Satan is proud of those vain and despicable men, who do form a cadre of opportunists, profiteers, liars, adulterers and thieves.

Many speak of good business however, good business has a different meaning for an honest man or for one who is generally selfishly interested in his own well being. And, whatever else may be, there are some good things happening within any giant system. Any such system has some honest and decently inspired participation. Nevertheless, the problems reside at the top and in the relationship between politics, economics and sin.

Appendix I. Who Does call the Kettle Black?

Those who worry about Moslems cutting off heads of a few other Moslems and a few foreigners, in addition to maiming some of their own citizens, might better inform themselves about some of the [noble] actions in the past, committed by they who we imagine to be the good guys. Who does call the kettle black?

English Sailors, others too, were often *beaten to death or forced to walk the plank,* just as a matter of sustaining discipline amongst they who were beaten and kidnapped to server in [Her Majesty's] Royal Navy. Interestingly the present [Her Majesty], is celebrating her eightieth birthday this year; eighty years of splendor, *living off the fat of the land.* And we did mention above that the Windsor family is a Dynasty prominent since the fifteenth century. Under such "Royalty" young men were subject to one hundred lashes for some infractions on discipline. All this did happen as Royalty, seated in their Carriage, (?) did parade about London and many other parts of the World.

The Indian Sub-Continent was systematically plundered so as to provide the "Benefactors" with unimagined and often undeserved wealth. This was done for the good of the victims, of course! And, as might be imagined, there was collusion between the ruler and the puppet that would cooperate as the intruder *"pulled the strings".* One wonders what India might be like if it had not been subject to so much imagined *venerable attention?* Especially, we wonder since India had been in existence, with a complex culture, long before England had a navy. Certainly the people of India probably did suffer in various ways as any populated area did so suffer. Nevertheless, the number of Indians attests to a high degree of familial success, especially as they now move about the world and fulfill many of our responsible occupations, especially those requiring superior intelligence; pharmacy, medicine and dentistry. Interestingly they speak better English than Americans.

The Enlightenment in the thinking of many has set the groundwork for the destruction of Western Civilization. Because of this strange form of Light, numerous wars have been fought, killing millions of people, thereby altering the genetic structuring of our Western Civilization. The Nordic races especially have been slaughtered, Germans, Poles, Russians, etc., following the direction of lunatic politicians that did crawl at the feet of the money-men, placing their citizens in servitude to whom they did never know.

The French Revolution is notorious for the *beheading of the innocent as well as the assumed guilty,* that were judged so by lunatics, opportunists, traitors, criminals and other mean and niggardly Citizens. Certain forms of mayhem have been romanticized by Professors and by Public Education. Nevertheless, many honest French Citizens were laced on rafts and drowned in the Loire. Propagandists and demented scribblers have had a field day with a Tragedy that is generally misunderstood, even to this day.

The Illuminati, since 1776 have been engaged in crime of the most vicious kinds against the Christian nations, using secret methods to weave incredible Conspiracies throughout the Western World. Unfortunately the details of many important illegal undertakings are not given much attention, by the mass media. Rather eager Commentators prefer to discuss the minute aspects of football, basketball, golf, gymnastics and other more important issues, as though humanity depended upon the outcome of a basketball game.

Karl Marx has inspired murderous Rampages within an otherwise quite decent Christian Civilization. Nevertheless many of our *learned Men (?)* imagine him as having been the Savior of mankind. Actually, he envisioned a Political Disneyland, complete with the subservient rodents (not unlike Mickey the mouse) that would be formed and developed at the various Communist Internationals. Such leaders would guarantee that every man wore rags, except the "Leaders of Men" of which he presumed to be one.

The Civil War and the First and Second World Wars contained many atrocities perpetrated by the [good guys], whom we imagined were us. It is not generally known that the *Types* that were [presumably] leading our country orchestrated all three conflicts. In all instances, the men with the money pulled the strings. All Wars are filled with atrocities nevertheless Nations are beholden to the miscreant and the bankers and are incited by lunatics, those imagining to be wise, leaders of men. Those presume to *work fearlessly as well as piously for a better world.* All this from behind a desk, guarded by young men who could not write a meaningful paragraph about the situation. **Dresden** an unarmed City filled with women and children, the wounded from a fallen enemy that was not allowed to surrender with honor however was placed in bondage, because of the vindictive nature of Winston Churchill. Dresden was bombed, unnecessarily, after we had won WW

II. This was [assumed] as some form of lesson. What were we teaching? We taught that it is noble to commit a brutal atrocity, to shame a *defeated* enemy. Know, Total War is total Insanity!

Hiroshima and Nagasaki were annihilated after the Second World War had been won. Why? Might it have been because they were the most Christian Cities in Japan? Why was a Catholic pilot chosen to fly the plane? Even that pilot imagines he did a wonderful service for humanity. He should consult with those still surviving who were the victims.

Why did we not drop the bomb out in Tokyo Bay? The "Japs" were smart, they would have gotten the message. We hear of an imagined invasion of Japan that would "presumably" have cost a million lives. Might we not have tried a trade embargo?

Franklin Delano Roosevelt, *our noble puppet president,*[1] deliberately allowed Pearl Harbor to be bombed inciting the United States into World War II. No decent, honorable man would have done this (Curtis Dall, *deceased,* Roosevelt's, one time, son-in law).[2]

George Bush, our current president imagined that Iraq had piles of *"Weapons of Mass Destruction"* that were never found and *following his imagination* he invaded a sovereign nation. The United States is being blanketed with propaganda concerning his (also imagined) *"War on Terrorism,"* Honestly speaking, just who are the terrorists? What about the tens of thousands of illegal aliens, that invade our country? We are overcome even as we attempt to destroy another country for our convenience so as to have plenty of fuel to waste on mindless movement.

The Romanoff Dynasty was slaughtered, including the Czar, Czarina, their Children (5), all Relatives, servants, loyal friends, even the Czarina's dog (Eustice Mullins). They were slaughtered by men in the service of wealth provided by the *"scrupulously honest"* banking Establishments of the United States and Europe, especially those associated with the Bank of England. Hundreds of millions in gold Rubles were stolen from the Russian people and their nation suffered tens of millions of deaths. All in defense of freedom [?] so to serve an imposing cadre of monopoly Capitalists, Socialists, Communists, Atheists, Sniveling Politicians, and a now-corrupt Leadership. Insane political Idealism and Ideas stemming from the Illuminati informed a despicable cadre of evil men performing a heinous crime.

Inflation is a Cover-up, and encourages profligacy in the light of the eroding value of "hard earned" money. Astonishingly, everyone at the party believes they are becoming wealthy as the **"debt value"** of all things escalates, more or less, in

---

1   Beaty, John, Col., PhD. *The Iron Curtain over America.* 1968 Ed. Pub. By Chestnut Mountain Books.

2   **Dall, Curtis, Col. USA.** *My Exploited Father in Law*

tune with inflation. Such misunderstanding stands as the most phenomenal fiscal, economic and political Blunder, that is possible at this or any other time!

Pig-rat

Appendix J. Affordable Housing

To buy or not to buy, that is the question?

Many individuals very enthusiastically consider their home as a good invest-ment, which it may appear to be. Considered more realistically, one's home is a liability, which must be maintained (quite likely) for a very long period of time. Mortgages are written for as many as forty years, others for a shorter time however, a fifteen or thirty-year mortgage is standard. One's home does provide some hedge against inflation however, it would be better that we had no inflation.[1] Inflation provides for an individual to refinance his home so as to have money to spend into the economy and to pay for charges attendant to the transaction. It is reason-able to assume that much of this notional wealth has migrated to Asia, where it becomes real. Such *"converted assets"* will, very likely, be returned to this nation as we are being overrun by alien beings. For millions refinancing may yet prove to be a disaster, it is somewhat like spending your future yesterday. However, the failing system requires ever more inflation to keep up so to perpetuate what is the greatest fraud in the history of the world. And, this inflationary incentive may continue, certainly until the inevitable collapse hits us.

One must also consider other related factors. An increase in the minimum wage will cause all prices to rise proportionately. There are a *greater percentage* of poor people now than before. Nevertheless, even a poor man living in squalor is

---

1   **Government** allows this procedure thus to encourage the citizen to assume greater debt than is prudent. And, government is then able to track families, in respect to their financial activities. It is complicated, being tied in with an onerous income tax and the need for the inflation, which provides a subsidy for the Government. Additionally, greater money-value provide local and State governments with ever increasing revenue. Keep in mind however, those who loan money own the house until the mortgage is satisfied, the banks loan the money, which suggests that the banks <u>in fact</u> own most of the nation's housing stock.

aware that his hut is worth more *shrinking dollars* now than at any time in his life. Simple-minded citizens see this as an advantage however it will be short-lived. The inflation, which we now experience, is part of a greater plan of world consolidation and domination. Amusingly this process is spoken of as creating a World Village, which, is a falsification of language. With political and religious motivation, a group of billionaires, adept at international trade and criminal activities, together with a few well paid intellectuals, pimps to be sure, conspire to rule the world under a One World Order, which they will control. [2]

It is important also that one understand the workings of the human mind and the effects of sin. Concerning economics, especially is greed evident as individuals fantasize over their great wealth. Interestingly, our dollar is now worth perhaps five or ten cents, compared with 1950 dollars. Accordingly all goods and property should cost ten to twenty times in funny money what it cost when money had a certainly determined, as in the past value (see Chapter I). *Divide your fortune by ten or twenty to see where you stand.*

There is much talk about affordable housing; most of which is uninformed and laced with emotion. What is not merely chatter, is the dialogue of encouragement issued in pursuit of commission payments given for closing one or another deal. Coincidentally, when speaking of housing one is addressing the issue of a "nesting place", wherein the most intimate of instances might occur, involving parents, children, lovers and friends.

Unfortunately the entire subject is beholden to subtle influence, not truthfully understood by the common man or his wife.[3] There are many factors in this complex equation, including the Imposition of Bankers, Politicians and Professionals

---

2   **Knupffer, George,** *The Struggle for World Power. Revolution and Counter-Revolution,* Forth Edition. ISBN # 0-85172-703-4. "Millions of false words, volumes of self-deception, innumerable pages philosophical abstractions, all claim to explain why Bolshevism was born, why it came to power and what it tried to do when it was in the saddle....We are faced with a struggle for global authority, and we now observe its final stages. The fundamental fact, which we must bear in mind is,...that Communism is not of Russian origin....{Russia] is a Christian country converted a thousand years ago...Communism is a terrible Western disease, which has affected Russia because it was so new to it in its essentials....The fall of the innocent is often more dramatic than the slips of the hardened sinners." (Pg. 163) Bolshevism was simply the product of greed and conceit as brought forth in the various meeting of they who would rule the world with tyranny as a means. "They made no secret of their ideas. All methods were used; subversion, espionage, propaganda, war, trade, dumping, popular fronts, trade union penetration, etc. of their ideas." (pg. 163)

3   **Roberts, Archibald E. Lt.Col. USA,** Retired. *Who is transforming the Republic into a One-World Dictatorship?* From the Bulletins, Jan. 2004, # 506. The Committee To

that push a product, from which they earn a very generous living. There are also subtle and not so subtle emotional ingredients brought about by divorce, location, size of family, level of employment and a longing to fulfill "the American Dream," so called. The Internationalists intend to flood this country with millions of aliens, with whom we will share our dream and our prosperity. "Come to America" is a popular song heard by millions, sung by one that is both presumptuous and over paid. The American dream is actually something quite different for each individual. For the millions, being robbed and who will be robbed, it is or will become a nightmare!

One must consider the millions of *illegal aliens* in our midst,[4] who must find places to live. *They must resort to clever actions to accomplish their purpose, namely not be deported from the country.*[5] These same illegal aliens do occupy much of substandard housing in the inner cities, thus to provide income to a slum lord from a near worthless structure, tens of thousands of which have been overvalued so as to provide collateral for an ever increasing debt currency. In addition adamant aliens encourage the migration to the suburbs of many former natural citizens, who are more upwardly mobile or are better able financially to assume a greater debt load and who are better able to *move about legally* in a contrived and perverted economic system.

Restore the Constitution, a Colorado Non-profit Corporation. P. O. Box 986. Fort Collins, CO 80522. Tel. (970) 484-2575.

4   **We have been and are being invaded** by millions most of whom come in peace nevertheless we will be much altered as a nation by their presence, in ways difficult for most to imagine. *It is the hope of this author that our Catholic, meaning universal, Christian moral and social Imperative will remain as the strongest force in support of this nation.* One should consider that Catholic Christianity in Europe and the Americas leads the Western Culture and Civilization in general. Nevertheless we should consider that, Asians and others who benefit from what, for humanity, has been accomplished by a **Catholic/Christian** Imperative, will have plans of their own.

5   **Politicians** especially use this as a tool in their electioneering. When this is done ethnicity and a misunderstood notion of democracy play an important role. **Politicians pander** to their own kind, or to any group who can and will elect them to an additional term. Such **pandering** is decidedly related to a divide and conquers technique, which is working effectively to destroy the nation and the Western Christian Civilization. And, politicians have money, to give away to one cause or another, money, which has been extorted from a docile population or created, by a corrupt and illegal system. Additionally, mass media guarantees to confuse all issues and work most against what is righteous, decent and in a word "good". What is being asserted directly above is provable, when the truth is known, however distractions are numerous and "the people" are not truthfully informed, where such truth would obviate corruption!

It is not often admitted what is _imagined as a minimum wage._ Simply, _a minimum wage is what is paid to they who are least able to perform a task considered worth more than a token sum._ Nevertheless, these same people must find places to live and they do have personal and other requirements, which are often quite demanding of their limited resources; especially vulnerable are, mothers with children, whom have been deserted by their fathers. _This, tragedy is the consequence of the sins of either adultery of fornication._ However, considering the political and social dialogue, Mortal Sin is not named and is left out of the equation. Psychologists and sociologists prefer to sweep this issue under the carpet. Those guilty speak of love children and may assume they should be supported by people with legitimate children, who pay outrageous taxes to support a corrupt system.

Everyone knows _simple-minded people do dumb things;_ such is reality! And, eager lechers, team up with anxious young women to engage in life's most necessary _performance_, knowing any _fetus_ can be aborted, or they will receive governmental assistance to raise the child at another man's expense. They think of the other man as being stupid nevertheless they imagine he does owe them such courtesy. So, how do such as we have named and do consider find affordable housing?

Amusingly the simple-minded, those which benefit from the monumental blunders that we have come to know and the politician, whose business is to create such blunders, imagine raising the minimum wage will cure all things, even illegitimacy. To increase the minimum wage as inflation is robbing everyone of the purchasing power of the dollar is to provide fuel for a fire that is already raging. _They who argue there is no inflation are clever and scheming Liars!_ The Liars hide behind a notion that prices are relative. Indeed they are. Nevertheless it does take ten or twenty dollars to buy what in the past did cost fifty or seventy-five cents. Thus a place to live increases, as do all other things. The tide is rising! And, though certainly intelligent and very clever, the head of the Federal Reserve, whoever he is or has been, is the biggest Liar of all! Liars are paid well as government functionaries or as Traitors, who betray their country. It must be understood that they who control our money are engaged in an unconstitutional and illegally imposed form of sophisticated theft affecting the entire Civilization.[6]

Inflation is the euphemism, used to disguise what is, in reality, Grand Theft. Just a little bit is stolen from ever dollar each and every day, like filing the Coin of the Realm. The dollar is supposed to be a _monetary Standard, against which all_

---

6   Adelmann, Bob, Economist and Broker. Reprint from THE NEW AMERICAN, 345 Concord Av. Belmont, MA 02178. _The Federal Reserve System, Creature of a Triumphant International Banking Establishment._ From the Bulletins, Feb. 2004, # 507 & Feb. 1989 # 324. The Committee To Restore the Constitution, Colorado Nonprofit Corporation. P. O. Box 986. Fort Collins, CO 80522. Tel. (970) 484-2575.

other things could be fairly and accurately judged. However it has proven to be more profitable, for those who manipulate money and what is imagined as money, when the standard is flexible, or vacillates, thus to provide cheaper money to pay for past expenditures.[7] Part of this manipulation is accomplished using hom*es and other structures as a means to create additional funny money.* This is termed creative financing, is clever however not wise, if one has concern for the common man and his children. Some do benefit immensely from inflation whereas most are victimized. Affordable housing is just one factor among many.

In the past twenty years, the cost of housing has skyrocketed, so as to place families and individuals in ever-greater debt. Low interest rates have recently provided the impetus for the doubling of what was already an excessive Liability. Regarding debt, the future is bleak. Admittedly, there has been much progress regarding the acquisition of more stuff, especially made with cheap labor, purchased with monies taken as a presumed *reward from escalating liabilities on property, especially homes. This entire circumstance is generally misunderstood in the light of economic reality?*

To consider another point; given the current outflow of money to other nations, one is well advised who will buy what is made in America, our native land, even if it might cost a bit more. One might bridge the shortfall by making fewer unnecessary purchases of what is not needed. Thrift shops and Good Will stores are glutted with unwanted and unneeded items that are resold for a fraction of the original cost. This alone tells us that we have much more than we need. For many, shopping is a form of neurosis, a means to relieve anxiety. Huge bundles of stuff are sent back to poorer countries, those that supplied the stuff in the first place. One must believe in and support his people and nation or soon both will disappear. By shopping smart one will find housing more affordable.

Inflation is driven by the Sin of greed although few might understand the implications. Greed, Vanity and Deceit, to mention some, will dance, to the same tune. And, imagining that one has become rich does encourage all forms of vice, especially gambling and bawdy entertainment. Eager participation is seemingly rewarded, by one's encountering a good feeling. If individuals would stop throw-

---

7   Governments are notorious spenders, so as to please those who are both wise and foolish. Payment is given as farm subsidies, credits, foreign aid (especially Israel), plunge protection and disaster relief in many forms. Certainly some of this spending is reasonable however, much is totally unnecessary, beside which it provides that many of our leaders to become involved in corruption. Millions of people are and will become dependent upon some government handout, thus will not do for themselves what should be done.

ing money at silly and bawdy forms of amusement, they would have more to spend on what is necessary, a place to live.

As inflation continues they who hold what is importantly tangible, especially Real Estate, other stable tangibles as well, do benefit in that they keep up, so to speak. Precious metals and Commodities are cyclical and work in concert, following the main line. Some defense is possible, however one must be a specialist (generally speaking) to benefit from the fluctuations, or very lucky. The not well informed will probably lose.

Unfortunately, a token sum, meaning a minimum wage, is not sufficient to provide a decent existence in the environment of a large city,[8] excepting that individuals so impaired occupy those parts of any city, which are least desirable or simply destined for demolition.[9] No individual wants to work for a token sum, _imagining, presuming, hoping or believing_ he is worth more.[10] This presents a complex social,

---

8   **Those, who are vicious, anti-social or overly aggressive, beside being simply stupid, uncaring, irresponsible and lacking foresight,** often turn to crime and become a menace for they who are decent and good. Young punks intimidate each other and the community as a whole, when such community has no workable answers to mostly misunderstood questions. Every Social Body requires a form of Discipline and a positively worthwhile Tradition from which youth can learn and benefit. The acceptance of Graffiti and scribbling on buildings, as an Art form, will not solve the problem, albeit, such scribbling is interesting as a symptom, which obviates social disintegration and ignorance. University trained and indoctrinated Sociologists would not agree, nor do they encourage mention of what is really irresponsible behavior, recklessness or sin! To consider sin, especially, is to be imagined as coming from a distant past!

9   **The cost of Labor, driven by a minimum wage,** continues to rise. Thus it becomes impossible for most, which might be interested, to invest what is necessary in time required to repair what is in need of such repair. As time is valued more highly, all costs are increased proportionately. Inflation and cheap money (our money is very cheap) provide a temporary fix however, in time, shoddy and inept repairs will compound the problem. Consider the story of the Three Little Pigs. This is America in a Nutshell. Decent effort is rewarded with a minimum wage whereas cleverness in cooperation with the government is, for a few, lucrative beyond imagination. This is named Urban Development, which has ruined hundreds of decent and compatible neighborhoods (Jones), so to place more and more people in a small space at huge profits to they who cause the problems. And, they who occupy the slums are least adept in performing the necessary improvements at the minimum wage, that wage which indemnifies their economic worth.

10   **Be all that you can be, in the Army!** Learn to kill an imagined enemy, some other man's child, rape his daughter as a prize for the victor and ruin his cities, even as your

moral, emotional and economic problem.[11] Thus, it is important, that each individual address the problem from where he stands. *No politician knows what to do, that will satisfy all in need.* No government program will help,[12] except superficially and coincidentally. Government programs are designed to benefit those that invent and administer the programs.

There are many that believe that raising the minimum wage will solve the problem of housing. To repeat, politicians pretend that this is a solution to our problems as do union bosses and other malcontents determined to bring communist, socialism to the world. All such opportunists are hypocrites and pretenders that does not, can not or simply refuses to understand what they are doing. One could imagine, those that refuse to understand do so because of some personal motive. Or, they may be coerced, intimidated, threatened or bribed to play dumb. They do not have perfect knowledge and do not see or even try to see the whole picture. Actually raising a minimum wage to a higher level will not benefit the poor for more than a few weeks, at most.

Who remembers a ten-cent loaf of bread? At that time the minimum wage was thirty-five cents an hour.[13] The Politician blathering about a minimum wage is engaging in political subterfuge, to capture the votes of millions who do not understand the meaning of words or of the minimum wage. That same blathering Politician knows that if he tells the truth he would, most likely, not be re-elected! *Succinctly, to raise the minimum wage guarantees what will follow, prices increase, all*

---

own are rotting from the core! It has happened and will continue to happen. Perhaps there are better things to do than kill those whom you do not and cannot know!

11 **Working Mothers** not on hand to care for their own children must depend on others, for a price in money. Children are confused by their mother's absence and are subject to other influences, which may exploit their innocence and youthfulness. Problems are rampant. Sex education has compounded problems, which might have been avoided without such overt imposition.

12 **Jones, E. Michael, Ph.D.** *Philadelphia Delenda Est:The Republican Convention and the Reality Tour.* Culture Wars Magazine. Sept. 2000, Vol. 19, No. 9. Pp. 28-41.

13 **A loaf of bread** costing ten cents with a minimum wage of thirty-five cents is no different from the present loaf costing two dollars against a minimum wage of seven dollars. And, many presently work for less than the minimum wage, especially illegal aliens. We have been running fast to stay in the same place. Nevertheless, illegal aliens are only about 5 percent of the population. Interestingly there are millions employed in the restaurant business serving those who might better be fed in their own homes by women that are determined to maintain the family and the culture. Real men would provide subsistence for their own legitimate children and loving wives. Men should abandon adultery and stop fornicating with strangers for a moment of ejaculation that, considering the nature of being, is a waste of man's substance.

expenses involving labor will increase proportionately and jobs will be moved to coun-
tries with lower standards of living. To survive, we will necessarily have to lower our
standard of living. The first thing will be to reduce the quality of the goods being
produced so they can be sold for less. This is exactly what has and is happening right now. Coincidentally cheap foreign labor encouraged by *free trade, the*
Opiate of One World Government, has proved disastrous for millions of skilled
and semi-skilled workers. There may be some beneficiaries, however they are not
found in those neighborhoods requiring assistance. Economically, *given any pre-*
cise point in Time, all in this world is relative. What is "tangibly available" and
what it will cost, in terms of money, depends on how it was produced,[14] where
and when it was produced,[15] and at what cost it is produced.[16]

---

14 **More expensive labor** requires, indeed demands, higher cost to the consumer.
Interestingly, older cities evidence the consequence of hand labor and appear somewhat artful, incorporating the evidence of individual movement, frozen in the form
of art, which decorates a structure. Newer cities evidence the presence of modular
production and appear clean however less artful, displaying the result of efficiency
and regimentation. Herein is seated a number of philosophical, moral and esthetic
questions, which involve time and the nature of human being, one way or another.
The subject is too broad for this presentation.

15 **Transportation** is an important factor in the cost of any item. Abraham Lincoln suggested it is wise to purchase what your need from a nearby neighbor, whenever possible. Then, when you hope to sell something, your neighbor will have the money to
make the purchase.

16 **Labor has been the single most important cost in production.** The percentage
may be declining because of the high cost of robotics and mechanized production.
However, it is important to keep the cost of labor as low as possible. This presents a
contradiction and an unimaginably complex dilemma. To imagine that raising the
minimum wage will do much to correct this situation is fool hardy. There are exceptions, however, it would be prudent and wise to produce and distribute any commodity in the location where it will be consumed, whenever possible. And, it might
be wise to consider how one might increase the need for our own labor rather than
eliminate such need, or export labor to other countries. In part, government-pro-
moted Inflation will provide necessary funds, which have been given to other nations
in the process of free trade. In so doing, the government is assuring that all paper
money is becoming worth less! Free trade is a questionable practice, at best, a disaster
where the poor are concerned. Poor people in other nations are paid near-nothing
thus are robbed of their time, even as the poor in our nation, with marginal skills and
little opportunity to develop what is possible, have no outlet for the skills and abilities that they do have. The result is that the rich become richer, whereas the poor are
increasing in numbers. This is happening at a time, when the world is suffering from

Those individuals, families and groups, which occupy the Slums, do not have the resources, the tools, the materials or the *trained intelligence* necessary to correct a bad situation. When they (some) do acquire the resources or when they (some) are able to benefit from a superior level of education and training, such individuals and families move away from blighted and unsafe accommodations. Those who become wealthy, move to wealthy neighborhoods, they do not build their mansions in the neighborhoods where they grew up, which might improve the circumstances from which they evolved, Very likely such neighborhoods are destined for some government program that will likely fail.[17] Life is as it is and one can only pursue their chosen path.

Slums provide affordable housing (rent subsidies are provided by government, of course) however, personal habits being what they are, many of those who live in a slum make matters worse, for themselves and for others as well. Most of the problems are seated in personal behaviors, which can be anti-social, defiant, destructive or the result of sin such as slothfulness, anger and personal vices. Vulgar ostentation is obvious in the glaring signs and cheap gaudy dress. Although abortion is legal,[18] illegitimacy is rampant.[19] We witness defiance and immaturity amongst irresponsible young men, who imagine vulgar forms of sex and illegitimacy are a joke. Many young men exhibit a vainly immature attitude toward a woman and her children, which is disgraceful and confirms that such manliness lacks responsibility, decency, intelligence and compassion. *What is required is that aggressive young men begin to understand and function with a greater sense of humility.* However, ignorance engenders a contemptuous form of vainly inspired and aggressive indignation. This is especially true in really rough areas inhabited by ignorant and aggressive adolescents and wannabe youngsters. Large governmentally subsidized apartment complexes have become almost as war zones, wherein morons without means and no intention of doing gainful work [ever] assume a stupidly arrogant form of command. They, in their minds, control the turf, even as the government makes restitution for their folly. Glaringly contrasting examples of supercilious indigence and Christian decency and moderation, are obviated within the shabby neighborhoods by a few single family homes with a garden and flowers

---

volumes of overproduction of almost all items. We face a real "chicken come first, egg come first" situation!

17 **Mumford, Lewis,** *The City in History,* Harcourt, Brace and World, Inc. N. Y. 1961. LC# 61-7689

18 **Collison, Joseph,** Writer and Director, Office of Pro Life Activities, Norwich, CN. *Abortion in America: Legal and Unsafe.* The New Oxford Review Magazine, June 2000. Pp. 33-35.

19 **Jones, E. Michael, Ph.D.** *Nowhere Men.* Fidelity Magazine. Sept. 1995, Vol. 14, No. 9. Pp. 38-40.

tended by the elderly owners, disciplined, generous and faithful who have remained in the place called home. *Even then, gangs of young morons victimize the Elderly.*[20] *Many of the young, have been the issue of sinful fornication, thereafter the victims of child abuse and desertion and a youthful life of street imposition. Such youth do not have or, very likely, may never have the will to learn how to live in harmony with another human being.* This is a social, moral and educational dilemma of monumental scale, having complex origins. Public Education, though perhaps (in some instances) driven by good intention cannot or will not do what is necessary.[21] Simply, it is not possible to provide adequate and affordable housing for they who ruin what others have built in former times.[22] We require that *the young must be taught how to care for property* and why this is important.[23] The young should be taught useful and productive skills associated with a Manuel Trade that does interest them. Furthermore, they must be taught how to respect the rights and the property of others.

We spend tens of billions of dollars on prisons, fences, walls, alarms and barricades to contain and discourage an anti-social and ignorant segment of a diverse and distracted population. Such money might certainly be better utilized. As the

---

20 **Courts, where law is contrived** are not able to address most questions honestly; being there is a separation of Church and State, so we are told. Nevertheless, a Catholic Christian inspired morality is a primary Tenant within our confused system, albeit the System does work in perverted ways. If Morality is a bad word, then simply consider Tradition; does one wish to follow the Tradition of a savage, a charlatan or a wise and holy Man. Shall one follow the Leaders of the French Revolution, Stalin, Mao or Jesus the Christ?

21 **Public Education** is handmaiden to the Politician. Therefore, much of what is deemed educational is in reality a form of indoctrination with political purpose. It is not always easy to define what are motivations and the objectives desired by those in power.

22 **Objectives and intention** vary with one's ability to conform to what is required to succeed. This is an intellectual as well as a personal, moral, social and economic problem. Personal habits have knowable consequence and it is said that we learn from experience. How one may react to what has been experienced is difficult to imagine. Do-gooders fail to recognize reality as they attempt to "steer" individuals and groups in the right direction. This is especially true, when one dismisses the truth of an issue or attempts to redefine reality.

23 **Property rights** are second only to the right to life. Without a right to [own] property, that being a proprietary right, one is unable to function as a free and independent person. The ignorant Revolutionary cannot imagine this, therefore condemns what is not understood. Even Karl Marx, presumed a scholar, certainly an intelligent man, nevertheless perverted in his thinking, was completely in error in his imagination of what was reality.

dilemma is compounded, we have fewer and fewer of the poor being able to acquire what is reasonable for their existence, without the assistance of the government, which is largely responsible for the problems. We support prisons and feed criminals, provide the finest accommodations for those who, when released will kill, rob, murder and maim whomsoever they may encounter, that might oppose their stupid nature. We worry about the rights of anti-social perverts and criminals, whilst good men, women and children are sleeping on the pavement. Bureaucracy is most complex in respect to the ineptitude of the system. The system is run for those who benefit from the inherent complexities of a contrived politicized legality. As the dilemma is compounded, we have fewer and fewer of the poor being able to honestly acquire what is reasonable for their existence.[24] *Big government wants dependents thus to justify an expanding bureaucracy,* which has a way of compounding error in even the simplest of procedures. What might take a few minutes for a wise man to accomplish could, very well, take a government years to consider, after which consideration the government would come to an unworkable compromise. This is [THE] fatal flaw in all democratic governments.

There are certain technical requirements, which must be met in every circumstance. Modern technology is awesome; therefore we have no reason to doubt that what is possible, can be done. However, the first requirement is that space must be allowed for decent accommodation.[25] The use of space, especially in a crowded city, calls into play the sin of greed. *Most of our cities are products of greed* as is certainly apparent.[26] If government should do anything, government should stop spending billions on fighting senseless wars. *Is it noble to annihilate an imagined enemy, living on the other side of the Planet?* More should be done to insure that

---

24 **Abortion is encouraged,** which often (perhaps most often) opens the womb of a young woman. *To kill the first-born has a cabalistic or ritualistic connotation.* Even as we are unable to whip or hang one who has committed the most heinous crime, we are able to murder millions of infants. The "Social System" feels no remorse. No Bureaucracy can feel remorse! Nevertheless, the mother must live, for the rest of her life, with a mortal sin bearing upon her Soul. Ironically, affordable housing seems a rather mundane issue as compared with murder however; no one seems to notice.

25 **Space is infinite,** although the earth is somewhat limited. Nevertheless, most all humanity lives on perhaps 2 or 3 percent, of the land. Even so, millions are crowded within a squalid environment. This has something to do with the psychology of a mob. Few are able to make the connections necessary for understanding, beholden as they are to trend and fashion.

26 **Inflation** appeals to greed, a Cardinal Sin. Individuals believe they are becoming wealthy, when in fact they are being pauperized. Values (seemingly) increase in terms of Money, as Money tends to become worth less [worthless]. What is extraordinary is that few understand the nature of what is this most significant economic reality.

cities become less crowded and more desirable, better places to live, for those who live and work in them; especially for the poor who have what many consider menial and marginal occupations. We do not suggest wider freeways, rather we suggest opening up more areas to parks and greenery as populations move back to smaller cities and the more desirable places to live. Admittedly, this is happening in some places, whereabouts common sense is somewhat in evidence. The problem is that many, they who can afford to do so, commute many miles to a home, in an atmosphere of serene beauty. Commuting many miles creates a need for wider and more costly roadways. Most people might prefer to live where there are spacious grounds and greenery, flowers and sunshine (like all the rich people have). A well-maintained building, one or two hundred years old, would (probably) be a better place to live, than a new (600 square foot) fifteenth floor apartment, in the middle of a dirty city, next to the freeway.

That vain Planners and Architects are causing people to be piled high in confined spaces, where they can have almost nothing of their own and have no title to the earth upon which they tread. This should be reconsidered. The process of compaction should be halted and a return to a more decently inspired small town should be reconsidered. _To hell with those who would confine humanity within a cubit of space owned and controlled by a corrupt form of governmentally inspired corporate usurpation_. Life is not a new dishwasher or a granite counter in the kitchen.

Such congestion as now exists guarantees that noise and pollution are always present. Like the frog in the pot, millions have become and are becoming acclimated to the heat, noise and congestion of the city. It can be imagined that the noise and movement in any metropolitan location will have negative consequence, physical and psychological, over the long term on those who must tolerate what they imagine is normal.

What is affordable housing is relative and is tied to expectation. When one requires more than is reasonable, of that which is mostly unnecessary, then one is disappointed if and when goals are not met.[27] There are many things for sale and the advertisements are enticing. One can see 42-inch television screens, purchased on a credit card, in apartments where the rent is unpaid. Such as this defies common sense. Consider also, personal chaos, bad manners, slovenly behavior and the outrageous dress that is apparent on Television. The excesses of the celebrities are beyond the means of the poor however, factor in their expectations, albeit subliminally.

Indians and Eskimos had affordable housing; ice was free, however they also had an indigenous existence close to nature. Nature is not exactly like most people imagine. Nature is primordial, unchanging, and relentless and is certain to outlast

---

27   Reconsider, being most satisfied with having the least the smallest portion.

what is of human origin, frail in substance and of vain and futile expectation. No intelligent person imagines our Civilization will last forever. Which one has? We do know that buildings made of real stone and properly formulated mortar will last for hundreds of years, perhaps thousands, if cared for. We learned, from three little pigs! We also know many are ready to fall in fifty to seventy five years. We are reminded that we change for reasons not clearly apparent. Nevertheless, one wonder why the very rich would buy a Castle from the twelfth century?

Where individuals are able to escape the developer, speculator, petty politician and self-aggrandizing bureaucrat, they are able to provide for themselves what it is that they might need.[28] Our modern Civilization has a way of dominating what it is that man might accomplish for himself. Mass media insures that few will have any ideas of their own and *the possibility of creative thinking, for the average person, is non existent.* Engineers and scientists, intelligent and clever as they may be, have brought man to the brink of disaster (Spengler). We admit that some accomplishments are profound and of the highest order. Nevertheless, it is time we separate fantasy from reality, mythology from history and what is real from what is only imagined. Our institutions of entertainment and distractions must be tamed so as to allow reality to bloom and to flourish without the imposition of some middle-aged movie director or the youthful pseudo Scientist. Especially must we avoid the imposition of the planner, beholden to political favor, those who will determine what is to be done, according to their own level of learned ignorance and vain incompetence?

We will gain most from the study of the World's past mistakes,
With the hope that they will not be repeated.
We must adhere to the Catholic, Universally Christian Tradition
Cooperation seated in humility has given much goodness to humanity.

---

28 **An Underground Economy does exist,** which accounts for an unknown degree of prosperity for millions. Such economy is imagined (by some) to be about thirty to forty percent of the total. Many, who appear prosperous, work outside the system however; their success is falsely attributed to the workings of our monumentally imposed Bureaucracy. The underground economy is; in fact, they only free economy in this nation, some other nations as well. Intelligent people do barter and trade one item for another, thus to avoid a middleman and the tax collector. Interestingly, because of the complexity of the system, encouraged by Internationalism, sales tax is often just about equal to what any given item would cost to produce. Many avoid such taxation by doing much work for themselves thus they do not pay for the overhead imposed by bureaucratic fiat. Certainly, if more than one person is able to utilize an item or service the cost is proportionally lower. There are many possibilities, when a population is more intelligently disposed and given the freedom to do what they might wish to do. Big brother might well take a vacation!

Epilogue

No amount of study or learning will lead one to the **absolutely correct** understanding of **universal truth** or to comprehending the *meaning of reality,* without paying special attention to what, *truthfully speaking,* underlies motives and actions of one group or another. Thus we consider the attitude and disposition of the individual, the group, the nation and the present Culture and Civilization. Primarily, our concern might be for the Soul of Western man, which has been *incessantly and relentlessly compromised* by a monumentally negative and profoundly opposite and aggressively antagonistic alien Disposition. In addition we pray for the conversion of others to a more fairly determined and comprehensive understanding of what is infinite and timeless, that being what is Universal Goodness. Truth is what is.

We assert, in this supposition and will continue the assertion that, individually, men are corruptible. Corruption bears upon the manner of attitude, thus perverts knowing and doing. Also each individual inherits the Sins of the father, which [can be] understood as Original Sin. The consequence of Sin is all around, unfolding day by day. Admittedly, much good is accomplished as well, each and every day, *indeed most accomplishments may be considered as being in some manner for the good.* If this were not true, men would have destroyed themselves long ago. Indeed a few have done and are killing each other at this very moment! (2006) Keep in mind that, "The evil that men do lives after them, whilst the good is interred in their bones."(Shakespeare) Wise men understand that an infant is *absolutely innocent,* therefore *common sense dictates* that any infant must be blameless. God, whether or not one believes that he exists, is hopeful, pure Spirit and infinite, He that values the pure soul and being of an infant above all else, such being a manner of *biological and sociological continuation* each time a new child is born. Biologically, a new generation of cells is *destined to become discreetly human,* at inception. The Law seems somewhat confused regarding this understanding,

225

nevertheless reality is as it is. Catholic Christians, some other religions as well, believe that every human being has an eternal soul. There are different understandings as to what exactly is a Soul. Nevertheless, there is consensus, to a degree, regarding man's relationship to what is supernatural.

In terms of the present, millions of children are suffering because of the sins (of the father) being committed at this very moment, which *in fact* determine the *exact nature* of the future for every living being. Because of ignorance, lust, greed and all manner of sin and vice, millions more will suffer and die prematurely in the future. Notwithstanding, every infant remains blameless and is destined to an immortal existence, providing certain requirements are met. This foregoing Statement is at the heart of Catholicism, the One Universal Holy and Apostolic Faith, without which there is no Salvation.[1] Suffering has peculiar and unforeseen consequence, not the least of which is alienation from others. Millions have been alienated from the one true Faith, by others vain in their assumptions and deceitful in their methods that did spread lies, and rumors, falsehoods and blasphemy and who work in secretly malicious ways. And, individually, we have been convinced by the subtle imposition of such ways, as we learn from the complexities within experience.

It may be imagined that attitude and disposition are learned behaviors, which evidence peculiar characteristics. Peculiar characteristics are evident and obviate as they define the nature of one individual or another. Combined, we understand attributes to be a question of Tradition. Some Traditions are seated in goodness others are seated in evil. What is good for one must be good for all, conversely, what is evil has negative consequence for one and all. The Catholic Christian Church understands and has indemnified this Universal Truth, during the course of twenty centuries. Many who have believed this and that understood the meaning of Universal Truth have paid with their lives as exemplified by the excruciating deaths of many Martyrs and Saints. Importantly, though not all would agree, Sainthood is a state of ultimate human grace, attained only by those who are believers in the One Holy, Catholic and Apostolic Faith. The English have had a way of determining what they imagine is a Lord, by means of Knighthood. They are very pompous in their *"gilded"* manner of determining, such as are to be awarded with a noble honor. It is quite amusing that many recent awards should be given to those that are in truth vulgar and ostentatious reprobates.

Even when we consider the earth upon which we tread and upon which we depend for substance, the Political Systems, in place, function toward ultimate control. The manner of control has political, social, economic and spiritual ele-

---

1   **The Apostolic Digest.** Our Lady of Victory Publications. P. O. Box 80636, San Marino CA. Pp. 280-281

ments and includes how the earth is cared for.[2] *Finance Capital has combined with bogus Science, controlled by a fascist, Corporate imposition in collusion with a Secret Government, which aids [by legal means] a monopoly imposition, depriving millions of the kind and quality of food stuffs which should be eaten.* As a substitute, we have processed-foods, known to be killing us, which cause obesity, and many other serious afflictions. And, the cures formulated by the giant Pharmaceutical houses are even more destructive than the foodstuffs being produced. This understanding is being addressed in some quarters, however the millions of individuals living in vast metropolitan areas are mostly victims of a malicious madness driven by greed.

In respect to what is mentioned immediately above, Corporations do not help, rather, they make a bad situation worse, then worse and finally, it can certainly be imagined that we will have the greatest disaster ever known to befall mankind. We are in the middle of that right now. There are many indications that much is in need of restructuring. Because we now suffer from corporate-mania (driven by greed and vanity), we shall see, in a not too distant future, the greatest loss of human life that the world has ever known. Perhaps this will be understood as Armageddon. Or, this may be understood as the accumulated evil that men have done, which has lived after them; evils coming to fruition simultaneously, long after the evildoers have died. And the good, will have been interred in the bones of good men and women, children as well. The lists of dead, because of senseless conflict, already can be counted in hundreds of millions soon it will be billions.

Corporate technology, meddlesome governments and appealingly deceitful, sensually implicit advertising, combine with slovenly behavior and a lack of virtue. The dilemma so presented is with us right now and is already responsible for hundreds of millions of killings by abortion; each death is the death of an innocent child. Giant corporations in the business of armaments production and sales are responsible, by means of senseless war, for the death of hundreds of millions of all ages, mostly innocent.

Giant corporations, by means of clever advertising and the use of the vending machine, are encouraging young people all over the world to *consume debilitating food, to view destructive imagery and to fornicate indiscriminately.* Hollywood sets the tenor, in many respects concerning present manners, habits and custom. The giant pharmaceutical corporations and the modern hospital will provide the antidotes, in the form of pills, creams and operations, for a price, of course. Consume, view and screw, however, be discreet. Start today, don't wait, you might miss

---

2 **Fahey, Dennis, Rev., C. S. Sp.,** *Money Manipulation and the Social Order.* Christian Book Club of America. P. O. Box 900566, Palmdale, CA 93590. First Published 1944. Appendix II, Pp 89-97.

something. Tits and Ass sell! Eroticism has been "schmeared" all over the place. The "in your face" attitude and the "advertised screwing" of ignorant, savage-type celebrities is no sign of progress, no matter how far you push, malign and confuse the definition of progress. The level of illegitimacy and child desertion is no sign of progress either. Political correctness *imposes* that we not mention the word "Bastard," instead we are admonished to bespeak of a "love child" as *insinuated* in Rap Lyrics, coming from the imaginations of young fools and other seriously deformed immature minds.

The _silly and the stupid_ Television productions *impose* that fornication and adultery is a matter of fact in any normal heterosexual relationship. Comedians make millions with their silly grins in attendance and acquiescence to smut, vulgarity and ignorance, all for fun of course, just kidding. When questioning the decadent morals being promoted on television, one immediately becomes the enemy of free choice, free speech, consenting adult laws, liberalism, pornography and the publishers of smut, which denigrates virtue. Sex sells, so sell sex! The salesman's mentality is certainly evident in many instances, other than selling tires. Nevertheless, _we kick the tires before we buy a car, don't we?_ So, why not test the depth of the crotch or the length of the stick? This is simply _an issue concerning shopping around,_ isn't it? All such eager shoppers should consider some questions. Then consider the Golden Rule in respect to those that you love. Is this your mother, your sister, your daughter, or your wife? Consider also, is the reprobate your father, your husband, your brother or you son?

We mention some of these facts at this juncture, together with the compounding of interest on money because evil and sin compound in the same way, exponentially. And the tremendous sums generated because of the prurient interest of 'we the people', apparently to form a more perfect [union], as in conjugal, are equated with the compounding of interest on money and debt-as money. One can easily imagine that screwing is not love. Love is a product of virtue in reference to the correct understanding of biological necessity. Screwing is animalistic, engaged in for instant gratification of those who lack self-restraint, honor and confidence and are generally irresponsible.

Homosexuality, considered by millions as an abomination, is *imposed as a cool alternative* to heterosexual behavior. Homosexuality is **compounding**, as is debt. And, switch hitters are really cool, especially in the mind of the deviate and the fool, working in tandem with the Corporate Execs that promote something for all tastes and pleasures. And don't forget the Coke and French-fries, a must before or after the action! Did we use colored or glow in the dark condoms? We must practice safe sex, you know, safe for the promiscuous lecher and the whore. Ms. "Wisenheimer" is certain to approve, as she checks out the dildos! We do recognize that much of what we hear and see is simply boastful vanity or is pumped up by the media, nevertheless there is much that is rotten on "Fantasy Island". Millions have distanced themselves. When defining the nature of sin, one is admonished who do you think you are? Or, who made you God? Or, don't you have any fun? Or, give me a break? Or, what's your problem? In contrast with what is holy, decent and profoundly good, many have chosen what is evil, destructive, perverse and unwholesome.

Youngsters have been led to believe, by an intrusive corporate presence, that sin and nonsense are necessary for an active and healthy adolescence. Young people previously held hands or cuddled and they grew old and died just as now, without any help from a corporate director. Corporate directors and very important persons (like, you know, they think they are) should ask themselves how often they want their daughter to be used (by this is meant f-----) by a lecherous drunk, or by some wise-mouthed little moron, so many of whom now roam our streets. Or, how often shall their son be enticed by an ignorantly aggressive, curious teen-age slut or given to the lustful pleasure of a simple-minded, disease-ridden whore? Interesting questions, no doubt. Tough answers, for sure. As long as mass media, generally speaking, continues to depreciate every virtue, whilst encouraging every vice and every sin known to man, circumstances will become even more perverse than they are right now; if one can imagine.

Most of what is written above centers on the Green, the color of money.
Indeed, Money is the Jolly Green Giant!
And
Murder, would you believe is as War and Abortion?
Madness, is as inflation, the consequence of greed and malfeasance?
The love of money corrupts and has corrupted the entire Western Civilization

Without question the International Financiers, the Monopoly Corporation and the Politician beholden to lust and greed have a tight grip on the Western Culture and a Civilization, struggling to exist. Politically, economically, socially and spiritually what exists for millions goes far beyond an even fertile imagination.[3]

The End

---

3   Mullins, Eustice, *The World Order, Our Secret Rulers,* (Ezra Pound Institute, Publisher, Staunton, A 24401, Secon Edition, 1992)

The Gingerbread Man

Bibliography

Anderson, E. L., Ph. D. *The Upright Spike I & II.* © 1978, Government Educational Foundation, P. O. Box 1622, Washington, D. C., 20013.g

Allen, Gary, *None Dare Call It Treason,*

Apostolic Digest. Our Lady of Victory Publications. P. O. Box 80636, San Marino CA. Pp. 280-281

Aquinas, Thomas, Saint, *Summa Theologica* 1, 14, 13, ad. 1, Translated by, Anton C. Pegis (New York, Random House, 1944), Vol. One,

Architectural Digest, October 2002. *One Central Park Tower*

Barabanov, Evgeny, *From Under the Rubble,* (Little Brown & Co., Boston, Toronto, 1975),

Barzun, Jacques, *The House of Intellect,* Harper and Row, NY 1959

Barzun, Jacques, *From Dawn to Decadence, 1500 to the Present.* Harper Collins Publishers Inc., 10 East 53rd Street. New York, NY 10022. ISBN 0-06-017586-9.

Bearden, T. E., Col. *Aids, Biological Warfare,* Tesla Book Co., P. O. Box 1649, Greenville, TX 75401. ISBN # 0-914119-04-4.

Blumfield, Samuel, *Is Public Education Necessary*

Bondi, Herman, *The Universe at Large,* Anchor books, 1960

Butler, *The Lives of the Saints*

Carlson, Elof Alex, *Human Genetics,* (D. C. Heath and Company, U. S. A., 1984, Ch. 6, Mendel's Laws and Genetic Disorders).

Carpenter, Lynn, Editor, *The Fleet Street Letter,* Vol. 67, Issue 7, Special Forecast Issue 2004. P. O. Box 925, Frederick, MD 21705-9913.

Collison, Joseph, Writer and Director, Office of Pro Life Activities, Norwich, CN. _Abortion in America: Legal and Unsafe._ The New Oxford Review Magazine, June 2000. Pp. 33-35.

Cusa, Nicholus, _On the Quadrature of the Circle._ Fidelio, Magazine, Vol. X, #2, Summer 2001. Publisher, Schiller Inst., Inc., P. O. Box 20244, Wash., D C., 20041-0244. Ed. Wm F. Wirtz, Jr.

Davidson, James, _Vantage Point, Newsletter._ July 2003 Issue.

Diamond, Michael, Bro. _Creation and Miracles._ Most Holy Family Monastery, 4425 Schneider Road. Fillmore, NY 14735.

Disraeli, Benjamin, later Lord Beaconsfield, Prime Minister of England, 1868; 1874–1880

Dillon, George E., Mgr. D.D. _Grand Orient, Freemasonry Unmasked._ Fahey, Denis, Rev., C. S. Sp., _The Kingship of Christ and Organized Naturalism._ October 1993, reprinted with the permission of Angelus Press, Kansas City, Missouri.

Engle, Randy, _Sex Education, the Final Plague._ Publisher, Human Life International, 7845-E Airpark Road, Gaithersburg, Maryland, November 1989. ISBN # 1-55922-025-2.

Eugene IV, Pope _The Council of Florence,_

Fahey, Dennis, C.S.Sp. Rev. _The Kingship of Christ and Organized Naturalism._ Christian Book Club of America, P.O Box 900566, first published June 1943. Reprint October 1993, Palmdale, CA 93590.

Fahey, Dennis, C. S. Sp. _The Mystical Body of Christ in the Modern World_, Third Ed.,

Fahey, Dennis, Rev., C. S. Sp. _Money Manipulation and the Social Order._ The Christian Book Club of America. P. O. Box 900566 Palmdale, CA 93590.

Fahey, Dennis, Rev., C. S. Sp. _The Rulers of Russia._ Cum Permissu Superiorum Religiosorum. First Edition, 1938. Twentieth Edition, 1975. Printed in USA.

Flynn, John T. _The Roosevelt Myth,_ (The Devin-Adair Company, New York, Copyright, July 1948, eighteenth Ed., July, 1953).

Freeman, Richard & Tucker, Arthur, _Wal-mart Is Not a Business, It's an Economic Disease._ From, Executive Intelligence Review. Nov. 14, 2003, Vol. 30 No. 44.

Freeman, Richard, *Reverse the 35 Year Devastation of America's Industry and Labor Force,* Executive Intelligence Review, March 21. 2003, Vol. 30 #11.

Gerber, Richard, M.D. *Vibrational Medicine, The # 1 Handbook of Subtle-Energy Therapies.* Third Edition. ©2001, Richard Gerber. ISBN 1-879181-58-4. Bear and Company, Rochester, Vermont, 05767.

Gregory XVI, Pope

Grand Prix, Don, Col. USA Ret.

Gromyko, Nina, Ph. D., *Pedagological Exercises in a Russian Classroom.* Fidelio Magazine, Journal of Poetry, Science and Statecraft. Summer 2003. Published by the Schiller Institute, Inc., P. O. Box 20244, Washington D. C. 20041-0244.

Hackett, Ken, Executive Director, Catholic Relief Services. *Letter of appeal, dared October 2002.*

Hadrian I, Pope, *Second Council of Nicaea, 787:*

Hoppe, Donald J. *How to Invest in Gold Stocks and avoid the Pitfalls.* ©1972 Arlington House, New Rochelle, NY. LC # 72-77641. ISBN 0-87000 178-7.

Jaki, Stanley D.D. *The Road of Science and the Ways of God.* The University of Chicago Press, 1978

Jones, Michael, Ph. D., *Fidelity Magazine* (Issue, #, date)

Jones, Michael, Ph.D. *Degenerate Moderns*

Jones, E. Michael, Ph.D. *Monsters from the Id, Part III., The Monster travels from Germany to America,* (Spence Pub., Co., Dallas, Texas 75207),

Jones, E. Michael Ph.D. *Libido Dominandi, Sexual Liberation and Political Control.* St. Augustine's Press, South Bend, Indiana. © 2000 E. Michael Jones. ISBN # 1-890318-37-x.

Jones, E. Michael, Ph.D. *Philadelphia Delenda Est: The Republican Convention and the Reality Tour.* Culture Wars Magazine. Sept. 2000, Vol. 19, No. 9. Pp. 28-41.

Jones, E. Michael, Ph.D. *Nowhere Men.* Fidelity Magazine. Sept. 1995, Vol. 14, No. 9. Pp. 38-40.

Knupffer, George, *The Struggle for World Power, Revolution and Counter Revolution.* 4th ed./, 1986. ISBN # 0-85172-703-4.

Knuth, E. C. *The Empire of the City, The Jekyll/Hyde Nature of the British Government,* 1983 Edition, The Noontide Press, P. O. Box 1248, Torrance, California 90505

Kuehnelt-Leddihn, Erik Maria, Ritter von, *Leftism, From de Sade and Marx to Hitler and Marcuse.* Arlington House 1974. ISBN #0-87000-143-4

LaRouche, Lyndon H. *What is God, That Man Is In His Image?* (Fidelio Magazine, March 18,1995

LaRouche, Lyndon, *Dope Inc.,* Executive Intelligence Review, 1992, Wash. DC

LaRouche, Lyndon, *The Essential Fraud of Leo Strauss,* Executive Intelligence Review, Mar. 21, 03, Vol. 30 No. 11

Larson, Martin Ph. D. *The Federal Reserve & Our Manipulated Dollar.* The Devin-Adair Co., Old Greenwich, CONN, 1975.

Lonergan, Bernard J. F. *Method in Theology.* Pub., 1972, Herder and Herder. Winston Press, Inc., 430 Oak Grove, Minneapolis, MN 55403. ISBN: 0-8164-2204-4.

Lukacs, John, *Historical Coinsciousness and the Remembered Past.* Harper & Row, Publishers, New York, Evanston and London. © 1968 by John Lukacs. LC # 67-28809.

Lundberg, *The Rich and the Super Rich, Who rally owns America? How do they keep their wealth and power? Bantam Edition, June 1969.*

Manifold, Didirae, *Karl Marx, a Prophet of Our Times.* G. S. G. & Associates, Publishers. P. O. Box 6448, Eastview Station, Rancho Palos Verdes, CA 90734. ISBN# 0-945001-00-2.

McMasters, R. E. *The Reaper, Newsletter*

Mechizedek, Drunvaldo, *The Ancient Secret of the Flower of Life, Vol.II.* Light Technologies Publishing, P. O. Box 3540, Flagstaff, AZ 86336. ISBN # 1-1891824-21-X.

Mendelsoh, Robert, M.D. *How to Raise Healthy Children in Spite of Your Doctor.* Contemporary Books, Inc. 180 N. Michigan Avenue, Chicago, IL 60601. Copyright ©1984. ISBN 0-8092-5808-0.

Michili, Vincent, D.D. *The Antichrist*

Morgan, Dan. *Merchants of Grain, The Power and Profits of the five Giant Companies at the Center of the World's Food Supply.* The Viking Press, 625 Madison Avenue, NY, 10022. July 1979, 2nd. Printing. ISBN# 0-670-47150-X.

Mullins Eustice, *The World Order, Our Secret Rulers*. (Pub. Ezra Pound Institute, Staunton, VA. 24401, Second Edition, 1992).

Mullins, Eustice, *Murder by Injection, The Story of the Medical Conspiracy Against America* The National Council for Medical Research. P. O. Box 1105, Stanuton, Virginia 24401, © Eustice Mullins, 1988. 2nd. Printing 1992, Library of Congress # 88-060694.

North, Gary, *Unholy Spirits, Occultism and New Age Humanism.* Dominion Press, 7112 Burns St., Fort Worth, TX 76118. ©1986, Gary North. ISBN # 0-930-462-02-5.

Oparin, A. I., *The Origin of Life.* Second Edition, 1953. Dover Publications, Inc. N. Y. Originally publicshed by the MacMillan Co. 180 Varick Street, New York. © 1938. L. C. # 53-10161.

Orwell, George, *Animal Farm*, Harcourt Brace, 1982 San Diego © 1945

Orwell, George, Thorndike, Me.: G. K. Hall, 2001

Pierce, William L., Ph.D. Editor, National Vanguard Books, Cat. #14, December 1992. Reprint in the *Committee to Restore the Constitution*, P. O. Box 986. Ft. Collins, CO 80522. Bulletin #376, May 1993

Pius IX, Pope, Dec. 8, 1864, *The Encyclical Quanta Cura* and *The Syllabus of Errors,* Reprinted by The Remnant, 2539 Morrison Ave., St. Paul, MN 55117

Pius X, Pope, The Syllabus condemning the Errors of the Modernists (LAMENTABILI SANE) issued in 1907. Reprinted by the Remnant, 2539 Morrison Avenue, St. Paul, MN 55117.

Pius XI, Pope, Encyclical Letter, *Mortalium Animos*, Gregorian Press, Most Holy Family Monastery, Berlin, NJ

Pius XI, Pope, Encyclical Letter, *On Fostering True Religious Unity,* (Gregorian Press, Most Holy Family Monastery,

Pius XI, Pope, Encyclical Letter, *Ubi Arcano Die, On the Peace of Christ.*

Pius XII, Pope, Encyclical Letter, *Humani Generis*, Daughters of St. Paul Press, N. C. W. C. Translation.

Podhoretz, Norman *Breaking Ranks, a Political Memoir,* NY, Harper and Row, 1979.

Privitera, James, MD. and Stang, Alan, MA., *Silent Clots, Life's Biggest Killers.* The Catacombs Press, 105 N. Grandview, Covina CA 91723. ISBN # 0-9656313-0-3.

Pursley, Leo A. D.D. *The Apostolic Digest,* Our Lady of Victory Publications, Ed., Kieth E. Gillette, P. O. Box 80363, San Marino, California 91008,

Quigley, Carroll, Ph.D. *Tragedy and Hope.* Chapter V.

Rafferty, Max, *Suffer Little Children,* (The Devan Adair Co., NY).

Ratzinger, Joseph Cardinal, (Now Pope Benedict VI). *Theologische Prinzipienlehre.* 1982 Erich Wewel Verlag, Munich. Translation by: McCarthy, SDN., Principals of Catholic Theology, 1987 Ignatius Press, San Francisco, CA.

Reed, Douglas, *The Controversy of Zion.* Veritas Pub. Co, P. O. Box 20, Bullsbrook, WA, 6084 Australia.

Sombart, Der modern, Kapitalismus. II,

Reisman, Judith, Ph.D. *Kinsey, Crimes and Cosequences.* The Institute for Medical Education, P. O>. Box 15284, Sacramento, CA 95851-0284.

Roberts, Archibald E. Lt. Col. AUS, ret. *Committee to Restore the Constitution, Inc.*, Bulletin Number 489, Aug. 2002).

Rueff, Jacques, *The Monetary Sin of the West.* Translated by Roger Glemet. Macmillan Inc., NY {1972]

Rutler, George W. DD. *The Fatherhood of God.* (Homiletic and Pastoral Review, June 1993)

Schlossberg, Herbert, *Idols for Destruction.* Thomas Nelson Pub., Fourth Printing, 1983. ISBN # 0-8407-5828-2 & 0-8407-5832-4

Schmidt, Austin G., S. J., and Perkins, Joseph A., A. M., *Faith and Reason.* (Loyola University Press, Chicago, IL., 1937).

Schulze, Richard, MD. *Understanding Your Immune System,* Get Well, Nov. 2002. Natural Healing Publications.

Schulze, Richard, MD. *The Ultimate Get Well Newsletter Collection,* (Natural Healing Pub. Jan. 2002),

Sears, Alan E. President and General Council, Alliance Defense Fund, Scottsdale, AZ., *(Memorandum to Concerned Christians.)*.

Spannaus, Edward, *Shock and Awe': Terror Bombing, From Wells and Russell to Cheney.* Executive Intelligence Review, Oct. 31, 2003.

Spengler, Oswald, *The Decline of the West, Vol. II. Perspectives of World History.* Authorized Translation with notes by Charles Francis Atkinson. Alfred A. Knopf, Publisher, NY.

Struve, Otto, *The Universe,* The Massachusetts Institute of Technology. ©1962. LC 3 62-16928.

Sutton, Anthony, Ph.D. *The Secret Cult of the Order.* Research Publications, Inc., Phoenix, AZ. 1984 © ISBN # 0-914981-09-9.

Sutton, Antony C. Ph.D. *Wall Street and FDR.* Arlington House, Pub., [1975], New Rochelle, N. Y.

Sutton, Antony C. Ph.D. *How the Order Controls Education,* Research Publications, Inc., P. O. Box 39850, Phoenix, Arizona, 1983. ISBN 0-914981-00-5

Sutton, Antony, *An Introduction to The Order, Vol I.* Research Pub., P. O. Box 39850, Phoenix, AZ. ©1983, Antony Sutton. ISBN # 0-914981-01-3

Sutton, Antony, *How the Order Creates War and Revolutins.V9ol. III.* Research Pub., P. O. Box 39850, Phoenix, AZ©1983, Antony Sutton. ISBN # 0-914981-02-1.

Sutton, Antony, *The Secret Cult of the Order.* Vol. IV. Research Pub., P. O. Box 39850, Phoenix, AZ©1984, Antony Sutton. ISBN # 0-914981-09-9

Thielicke, Helmut, *Nehilism:Its Orogons and Nature with a Christian Answer.* Trans. John W. Doberstein, Schocken Books, NY., 1969 [1961],

Tugwell, Rexford G. *The Emerging Constitution.* Reprint; Bulletin, The Committee To Restore The Constitution, June 1991 # 352 & Aug. 2003 # 501. Colorado Non-profit Corporation. P. O. Box 986. Fort Collins, CO 80522. Tel. (970) 484-2575.

Tolstoy, Leo, Count Von, *War and Peace.*

Varghese, Abraham, Ed., *Intellectuals Speak Out About God,* (Regnery Gateway, Chicago, Ill., 1984),

Verange, Ulick, LLD. *Imperium.* The Noontide Press, ©1962, Sausalito, CA. LC # 62-53156.

Vitz, Paul C., Professor, *The Intellectuals Speak Out About God,* Edited by Roy Abraham Varghese, © 1984, Pub. by Regnery Gateway, Inc., 360 W. Superior St. Chicago IL, 60610. ISBN 3 0-89526-827-2.

Von Kuenhelt-Leddihn, Erik, *Leftism, From de Sade and Marx to Hitler and Marchse,* Arlington House-Publishers, New Rochelle, New York, Copyright © 1974, ISBN 0-87000-143-4,

von Mises, Ludwig, *Human Action, a Treatise on Economics.* Third Revised Edition. Henry Regnery Company, Chicago. © 1949 by Yale University Press. *Revised Edition* © 1943 by Yale University. Library of Congress # 62-17874.

Wardner, Names, Ph.D. _Communist Infiltration of the Catholic Church._ Video produced by: Most Holy Family Monastery, 4425 Schneider Road, Fillmore, NY 14735.

Webster, Nesta, _The French Revolution, a Study in Democracy._ First Published 1919, Republished 1969.Second Edition, The Christian Book Club of America, Hawthorne, CA 90250

Webster, Nesta, _World Revolution, The Plot Against Civilization,_ Veritas Publishing Company, 7th. Ed., 1994, Cranbrook. Western Australia 6321,

Wickliffe, Vennard B. Sr. _The Federal Reserve Hoax, The Age of Deception._ Meador Publishing Co., 324 Newbury Street, Boston 15, MA. Seventh Ed. Pp. 14-70.

Wilton, Robert, _The Last of the Romanovs, How Tsar Nicholas II and Russia's Imperial Family were Murdered._ Copyright © 1993, the Institute for Historical Review. First British Edition, pub. 1920 in London by T. Butterworth. First U. S. Edition published 1920, in New York by George H. Dorn. French Edition, pub. Paris 1921. Russian language edition, pub. Berlin 1923. ISBN # 0-939484-1.

Wormser, Rene A. _Foundations, Their Power and Influence_, (Covenant House Books, 1993, P. O. Box # 4690, Sevierville, TN 37864, ISBN 0-925591-28-9).

Yockey, Francis Parker, LLD. _Imperium._ The Noontide Press, ©1962, Sausalito, CA. LC # 62-53156

978-0-595-41500-7
0-595-41500-8

www.ingramcontent.com/pod-product-compliance
Lightning Source LLC
Chambersburg PA
CBHW030259290526
45785CB00001B/148